THE BLOODIED FIELD

CROKE PARK. SUNDAY 21 NOVEMBER 1920

MICHAEL FOLEY

THE O'BRIEN PRESS
DUBLIN

This edition first published 2015 by
The O'Brien Press Ltd,
12 Terenure Road East, Rathgar, Dublin 6, Ireland
Tel: +353 1 492 3333; Fax: +353 1 492 2777
E-mail: books@obrien.ie
Website: www.obrien.ie
First published 2014.

ISBN: 978-1-84717-767-4

Acknowledgements for photographs: the author and publisher thank the following for permission to use pictures in this book: map of Croke Park: the UK National Archives, Kew, and *History Ireland*; Dunleary Commercials and Patrick Moran: May Moran; Sir Nevil Macready: the National Portrait Gallery, London; Michael Collins, Luke O'Toole, Harry Boland at Croke Park: Croke Park GAA Museum; Joe Traynor: Michael Nelson; Thomas Hogan: Noel Collins, Kilmallock & District Historical Society; Auxiliaries at Beggar's Bush: courtesy of Kilmainham Gaol Museum – 19PO 1A32-14; Dublin firemen: courtesy Las Fallon; Croke Park on the day after Bloody Sunday: the National Library of Ireland; the relatives of those killed at Jervis Street Hospital: the National Library of Ireland; the survivors and relations at Croke Park in 1960s: Lensmen/Irish Photo Archive. For any unsourced pictures, we request the holder of such copyright to contact the publisher.

8 7 6 5 4 3 2 1
19 18 17 16 15

Printed and bound by Norhaven Paperback A/S, Denmark.
The paper in this book is produced using pulp from managed forests.

Dedication

To Karen and Thomas

Author's Note

This account of the events leading up to the incidents at Croke Park on Bloody Sunday, the subsequent deaths, inquiries and political fallout is based heavily on the evidence supplied to the courts of military inquiry at the Jervis Street and Mater hospitals in the weeks immediately after Bloody Sunday, the autopsy reports therein and first-hand testimonies from relatives of the dead recorded in November–December 1920. These documents were kept from public view until 2003, but offer a dramatically graphic account of the events at Croke Park.

I have also utilised first-hand accounts supplied to the Irish Bureau of Military History between 1947 and 1957 by 1,773 veterans of the revolutionary period in Ireland from 1913–1921, accounts from players including Frank Burke and Paddy McDonnell of Dublin and Tipperary's Bill Ryan and Tommy Ryan, and contemporary newspaper accounts spanning the UK and Ireland.

The chapter dealing with the findings of the courts of military inquiry also leans heavily on the outstanding work of Professor David Leeson, whose piece 'Death in the Afternoon: The Croke Park Massacre, 21 November 1920', published the *Canadian Journal of History*, Volume 38, is a landmark work in the modern investigations into the events at Croke Park.

I have tried to avoid all fiction, save for reconstruction of some conversations based on recollections of those involved, cross-referenced with other contemporary and historical accounts. Where recollections have differed sharply, and they often did, I have tried to apply Occam's razor – that the simplest explanation with the fewest assumptions is most likely the truth – but endeavoured at all times to respect every side of a tense, complex conflict.

I would like to thank in particular the relatives of the Bloody Sunday dead who shared their knowledge and time: Michael Hogan, Grangemockler, County Tipperary; Michael Nelson (Joe Traynor), Dublin; Frank Robinson (William Robinson), Dublin; and Alec Ryan (Tom Ryan), Glenbrien, County Wexford. Thanks also to Mick Egan, nephew of Tipperary player Jim Egan, and to Tony Synnott, son of Stephen Synnott, Dublin.

Thanks to Noel Collins, Kilmallock, County Limerick, for his assistance on the life of Tom Hogan, to Alice Speidel-Hall for her help in researching Speidel's Butchers, Dublin, workplace of Jane Boyle, and the Irish Jewish Museum, Dublin, for their assistance in reconstructing the streets of her youth around Portobello and Lennox Street.

Special thanks to Christopher Hill, Brian Taylor and Peter and Judith Simon, Australia, for their extraordinary help and generosity in researching the life of George Vernon Dudley. To Jim Herlihy, whose work in recording the history of the RIC and other Irish police forces will prove an invaluable historical resource for decades to come, to Mick Dolan and Robert Reid, South Tipperary Military History Society, Michael Moroney, Fethard, and John Hassett, Third Tipperary Brigade Old IRA Commemoration Committee.

Thanks also to Mark Reynolds at the GAA Museum, John Costello, Dublin GAA County Board, Willie Nolan, and the staffs at the National Library of Ireland, Dublin, Pearse Street Library, Dublin, the National Archives, Kew, London, and the British Library of Newspapers, London.

A special word of gratitude to Peter Keogh for an insightful trip to

Luke O'Toole's homeplace in Wicklow, Ann-Marie Smyth at Glasnevin Cemetery and Jim Langton of the Michael Collins 22 Society who assisted in sourcing pictures and made a trip to Glasnevin a far less stressful ordeal than it promised to be and immeasurably more fruitful.

A special word of gratitude to all at O'Brien Press, to Nicola Reddy and to Íde ní Laoghaire, in particular, whose patience and attention to detail helped bring a long, difficult project to fruition. Thanks also to Lorcan Collins, Las Fallon and Niall Bergin for terrific work on the picture section.

Thanks, finally, to work colleagues, family and friends for listening to interminable stories from another century and in particular to my wife, Karen, for her unceasing love and support.

Contents

PART III CROKE PARK AND BLOODY SUNDAY,

21 NOVEMBER 1920

PART IV THE BLOODY SUNDAY INQUIRIES

AND THE SEARCH FOR TRUTH, 1920–1921

Names and Acronyms

Auxiliary Division of the RIC (Auxiliaries/ADRIC): an additional police force recruited among ex-service officers, designed to become the officer corps of the RIC. Established in July 1920

Black and Tans: an additional force recruited to reinforce RIC numbers from March 1920

Cumann na mBan: Irish republican women's organisation, established in April 1914

Dáil: unofficial Irish parliament formed by absentee MPs (from Westminster) on 19 January 1919

Dublin Metropolitan Police (DMP): police force for Dublin city and suburbs

Gaelic Athletic Association (GAA): sports organisation founded in 1884 governing Gaelic football, hurling, athletics and rounders

Gaelic League: organisation founded in 1893 as part of the Gaelic revival to promote the Irish language

Irish Parliamentary Party: Irish nationalist party in the House of Commons, Westminster

Irish Republican Army (IRA): a new term for the Irish Volunteers in use from January 1919

Irish Republican Brotherhood (IRB): a secret, oath-bound fraternity formed in 1858, devoted to promoting Irish republicanism

Irish Volunteers: armed nationalist movement formed in 1913

Royal Irish Constabulary (RIC): partly armed police force, established in Ireland in 1822

Sinn Féin: Irish republican party, founded 1905. The largest party in the 1919 Dáil

Ulster Volunteers: armed pro-union movement formed in 1913

PLACE NAMES

Gloucester Street: now Sean McDermott Street, Dublin

Hill 60: original name for Hill 16, the famous bank of terracing in Croke Park

Kingsbridge Station: now Heuston Station, Dublin

Maryborough: now Portlaoise, County Laois

Queenstown: now Cobh, County Cork

Rhodesia: now Zimbabwe

Sackville Street: now O'Connell Street, Dublin

Cast of Principal Characters

THE POLITICIANS AND MILITARY

Winston Churchill – British Minister of Munitions, Secretary of State for War

Sir John French – Lord Lieutenant of Ireland

David Lloyd George – British Prime Minister

Sir Hamar Greenwood – Chief Secretary for Ireland

General Sir Nevil Macready – Commander in Chief of the Armed Forces in Ireland

Major EL Mills – Commanding Officer, Auxiliary force at Croke Park

Éamon de Valera – leader of Sinn Féin

Field Marshal Sir Henry Wilson – British Army Chief of Staff

THE IRA

Dan Breen – Quartermaster, Third Tipperary Brigade

Patrick Butler – Commanding Officer, C Company, 8th Battalion, Third Tipperary Brigade

Dan Hogan – Vice-Commandant, Monaghan Brigade, Monaghan footballer, brother of Michael Hogan

Sean Hogan – Volunteer, Third Tipperary Brigade

Seamus Robinson – Commandant, Third Tipperary Brigade

Sean Treacy – Vice-Commandant, Third Tipperary Brigade

Harry Colley – Adjutant, Dublin Brigade

Michael Collins – Director of Intelligence, President of the Irish Republican Brotherhood, Dáil Minister for Finance

Richard Mulcahy – Chief of Staff, Dáil Minister for Defence

Sean Russell – Director of Munitions

Vinny Byrne – Squad member

Joe Dolan – Squad member

Tom Keogh – Squad member

Joe Leonard – Squad member

Dan McDonnell – Squad member

Paddy O'Daly – Leader of the Squad

Phil Shanahan – IRA Volunteer, Dublin publican

THE GAA

Luke O'Toole – Secretary General

Jack Shouldice – Leinster Council secretary

Frank 'Scout' Butler – Tipperary goalkeeper

Michael (Mick) Hogan – Tipperary defender, IRA member

Ned O'Shea – Tipperary captain and defender

Jerry Shelly – Tipperary defender

Bill Ryan – Tipperary defender

Tommy Ryan – Tipperary centrefielder, IRA member

Gus McCarthy – Tipperary forward

Johnny McDonnell – Dublin goalkeeper, IRA member

Paddy McDonnell – Dublin defender

Stephen Synnott – Dublin defender

Frank Burke – Dublin forward

THE SPECTATORS AT CROKE PARK

Jane Boyle

Monsignor Maurice Browne

Daniel Byron

Daniel Carroll

Michael Feery

Thomas (Tom) Hogan

Mick Kerrigan

James Matthews

Patrick O'Dowd

Jerome O'Leary

William (Perry) Robinson

Tom Ryan

John William (Billy) Scott

James Teehan

THE POLICE

Brigadier-General FP Crozier – Commander in Chief of the Auxiliaries

Major George Vernon Dudley – Commanding Officer, Black and Tan force at Croke Park

Roland Knight – Temporary Cadet, Auxiliary Division

Sir Henry Hugh Tudor – Police Advisor to Dublin Castle

Brigadier-General Sir Ormonde Winter – Chief of British Army Intelligence, Deputy Chief of Police

GRANGEMOCKLER

John Browne – friend of Michael Hogan

Kate Browne – wife of Maurice, mother of John and Monsignor Maurice

Master Maurice Browne – schoolteacher

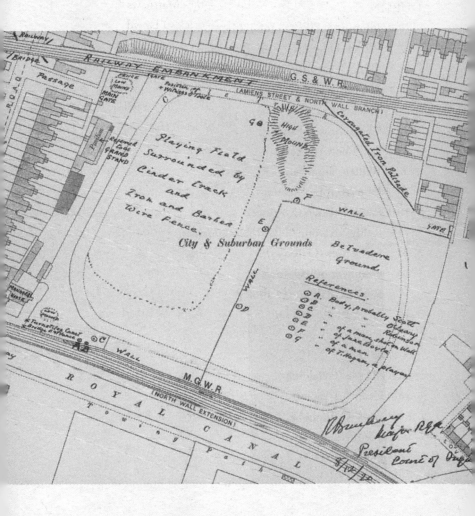

Map of Croke Park and surrounding areas used during the Mater Hospital Inquiry into the killings at Croke Park, 21 November 1920.

THE TEAMS

DUBLIN

1   Johnny McDonnell (O'Tooles)
2   Patrick Hughes (Keatings)
3   Patrick Carey (O'Tooles)
4   William Robbins (O'Tooles)
5   Josie Synnott (O'Tooles)
6   Christy Joyce (Parnells)
7   Jack Reilly (O'Tooles)
8   William Donovan (Kickhams)
9   John Murphy (Keatings)
10 Frank O'Brien (Keatings)
11 Paddy McDonnell (O'Tooles): *captain*
12 Jack Carey (O'Tooles)
13 John Synnott (O'Tooles)
14 Stephen Synnott (O'Tooles)
15 Frank Burke (UCD)

Substitutes

Gerry Doyle (Geraldines)
Tom Carey (O'Tooles)
Joe Norris (O'Tooles)
Joe Joyce (Parnells)
Tom Fitzgerald (O'Tooles)

TIPPERARY

1. Frank 'Scout' Butler (Fethard)
2. Mick Hogan (Grangemockler)
3. Ned O'Shea (Fethard): *captain*
4. Jerry Shelly (Grangemockler)
5. Bill Ryan (Loughmore-Castleiney)
6. Jim Egan (Mullinahone)
7. Tommy Powell (Clonmel)
8. Tommy Ryan (Castlegrace)
9. Jim Ryan (Loughmore-Castleiney)
10. Bill Barrett (Mullinahone)
11. Jimmy McNamara (Cahir)
12. Jimmy Doran (Mullinahone)
13. Gus McCarthy (Fethard)
14. Jack Kickham (Mullinahone)
15. Jackie Brett (Mullinahone)

Substitutes

Dick Lanigan (Grangemockler)
Tommy O'Connor (Castlegrace)
Mick Nolan (Mullinahone)

Prologue

SUNDAY, 21 NOVEMBER 1920

The day began under a crisp autumn sun in the heart of a sleeping city. Johnny McDonnell, Willie Maher and Michael Lawless met after eight o'clock in front of O'Tooles GAA club on Seville Place near Sackville Street and hurried to the docks. They crossed the River Liffey by boat and walked to Dunlop House, a giant redbrick building at the corner of Westland Row and Merrion Row. Sean Daly was already there. Herbie Conroy was with him, holding a sledgehammer underneath his coat. Then came Tom Ennis, the senior IRA man among them. McDonnell and the others also knew Ennis from O'Tooles. Years before the IRA made different men of them, football and O'Tooles was the bond that first brought them together.

Some Sundays they went to see Johnny play in goals for Dublin. The rest of the country knew Johnny from the newspaper pictures as 'the man in the hat', famed for keeping his peaked cap on during games to shield his eyes from the sun. His brother, Paddy, was an even bigger star. They were all neighbours and friends, teammates and family before they became comrades. Before they went any further, Ennis reminded them why they were here. Today they were members of E Company, Second Battalion of the Dublin IRA. They headed for

Upper Mount Street to kill a pair of spies.

The city was quiet. Newspaper boys on the street corners prepared their bundles as McDonnell and the others walked past. It was nearly nine o'clock. After a month of careful reconnaissance and planning, groups of IRA men across the city were on the move. As the IRA's Director of Intelligence and the organisation's most compelling driving force, this was Michael Collins's great project: a swift, brutal strike at the heart of the British intelligence service in Dublin.

Between July 1919 and May 1920 alone, his Squad had killed four Dublin Metropolitan Police (DMP) constables, six detectives and an Assistant Commissioner. The British authorities had reacted with ferocity. They hunted and cornered IRA men and sympathisers. Their intelligence moles had burrowed so deep into the IRA they were within touching distance of Collins. His own intelligence people had compiled a list of thirty-five suspected British agents and spies to be eliminated. This operation wasn't just a dramatic statement of war. They were fighting for survival.

The bells of St Stephen's Church near Mount Street would soon toll. Vinny Byrne led McDonnell, Ennis and the others towards 38 Upper Mount Street. Byrne was nineteen and already a veteran of the Easter Rising. Having Tom Ennis there made him uneasy. Ennis was older than Byrne and carried a more senior rank in the IRA, but for the business at hand, Byrne had been chosen to lead.

Other things made Byrne edgy. His first-aid man made him nervous – he was older than everyone else and didn't carry a gun. Byrne asked if he had brought enough bandages.

'I have nothing,' he replied.

'Did you not hear the instructions I gave last night?' asked Byrne.

'I did,' said the first-aid man, 'but I couldn't find a thing at home.'

They diverted to a safe house on Denzille Lane seeking a first-aid kit. Jackie Dunne was home, but had nothing. Instead, he handed Byrne a revolver. Byrne pressed it into the hand of the first-aid man.

'Here,' he said. 'That might be of some use to you.'

They hurried to Mount Street. The church bells had already rung when they knocked on the door. A maid answered. Byrne asked where Lieutenants Peter Ames and George Bennett were sleeping. Collins's information insisted both were spies. Further research suggested they could be the hub of the entire British intelligence operation in Dublin.

Bennett was twenty-eight years old and had worked in intelligence in Holland during the Great War. He had befriended Ames at Kidd's Back, a bar near Grafton Street. Ames had been born in America and survived gassing during the war before an attack of trench foot invalided him out of active service. His engagement to Miss Millicent Ewing was announced in the *New York Times* that morning. Both men had moved to Mount Street the previous day.

'Lieutenant Bennett sleeps in there,' the maid said, pointing at the front parlour. 'The other officer sleeps in the back room.'

Ennis went to the back room and gently turned the handle. The door was locked. 'You can get in by the back parlour,' whispered the maid. 'The folding doors are open.'

They opened the doors. Ames went for a gun under his pillow. 'Hands up!' shouted one of the men. While Ames and Bennett were brought into the back bedroom, Johnny McDonnell stayed in the hallway with Sean Daly and a few others. Michael Lawless was outside on the street keeping watch, walking slowly towards the church before turning and wheeling back towards the open front door. He heard shots echoing from Lower Mount Street. Shortly afterwards he heard the heavy footsteps of a man running towards him. He glanced over his shoulder. The man was wearing a khaki-coloured uniform.

Lawless kept on walking and passed the house, then turned around suddenly, pointing his gun at the soldier.

'Don't shoot!' the soldier shouted.

A man appeared at a window across the road. 'What's going on down there?' he shouted. Lawless spotted a gun in his hand.

'Get in from that window!' Lawless shouted, grabbing the soldier and crouching behind him for cover. He fired a shot at the window.

'Get up the steps and ring the bell,' he told the soldier.

Sean Daly opened the door. Lawless pushed the soldier through the hall and into another room. Vinny Byrne was in the back bedroom. Ames and Bennett stood on the bed, their backs turned. Hands against the wall. Byrne trained his gun on them.

'The Lord have mercy on your souls,' Byrne whispered. Then he shot them both.

The noise rattled through the house like thunder. The maid broke down in tears. Byrne told the captured soldier to stay in the room for fifteen minutes while they made their escape. As they tried to leave, revolver fire from the window across the street peppered the front door and steps. They returned fire and bought enough time to get across Mount Street. Vinny Byrne's first-aid man held up his gun.

'Vinny,' he said, 'what will I do with this?'

'Give it to me,' replied Byrne, 'and you make yourself scarce and away from us.'

Everyone else made for the river. A boat was waiting with no one to row it. One man finally agreed to take them across. In a few minutes McDonnell, Lawless and Maher were walking briskly back to Seville Place. Back home. Lawless and Maher disappeared into the city. McDonnell went home and took refuge that afternoon in a familiar place: the football field.

At one o'clock Monsignor Maurice Browne's car pulled up at Portobello Bridge, Rathmines. The weekend was already full of news and activity. The Tipperary footballers were playing Dublin in Croke Park. A handful of neighbours at home in Grangemockler were on the team. Mick Kerrigan had visited Browne from Grangemockler that week, and travelled with him from his parish in Maynooth. Before he left home Kerrigan was told to bring his shorts and boots to Croke Park. Depending on numbers, Tipperary might need him.

A police constable came to the car window. 'Proceed into the city at your own peril,' he said. The IRA were killing British spies and servicemen in their beds. Browne and Kerrigan parked the car, crossed the bridge and boarded a tram. All the talk on board was of the dead agents. By mid-morning the billboards had already blared the news across the city: fourteen British agents murdered by the IRA, many in their beds. Trucks of policemen and military hared through the streets. The families of servicemen, police and civil service people tied to British rule for their livelihoods poured into Dublin Castle for protection. When the steel gates were closed they crowded the street outside, pleading for refuge from the gunmen.

The police had taken over the Mansion House, the seat of the Irish Dáil, an unofficial parliament established in January 1919 and populated by seventy-three Sinn Féin MPs who refused to take their seats in Westminster. If the Dáil was the face Irish republicans presented to the world, the IRA were its teeth, waging guerrilla war in the cities and across the countryside against the police, army and every instrument of British power.

No person or position was safe. That Sunday morning the Lord Mayor of Dublin turned up at the Castle, looking for police protection. Some had heard that an officer inside the Castle had committed suicide on hearing about the killings. People on the tram wondered out loud: some said Dublin would be burned; others expected prominent Sinn Féin men to be taken out and shot. Whatever happened, the city would suffer.

Browne and Kerrigan got off as the tram reached Sackville Street and strolled up the hill towards Parnell Street, turning right for Barry's Hotel. When they arrived the Tipperary team was togged out in their jerseys, white with a green hoop. With everyone present and fit, Mick Kerrigan was relieved of his duty to play. Monsignor Browne spotted Mick Hogan, his old neighbour, in the milling crowd.

Mick Hogan flickered with excitement and news. Where to begin: maybe the train trip to Dublin the previous day, wrestling with British soldiers in the carriage before bullying them out of the train? Or Sean Hogan, the famous Tipperary IRA man, sitting at his kitchen table in Grangemockler the previous morning planning an attack on an RIC barracks near home and giving Mick despatches to take to Dublin, tucked in his shoe to avoid detection. Or his night in Dublin around the famed Monto with his teammate Tommy Ryan, having a drink in Phil Shanahan's bar surrounded by whores and rebels and spies.

Hogan was twenty-three. On Friday he had become Company Commander of the Grangemockler Volunteers. He knew of the killings that morning and spoke of different things with Browne and Kerrigan. But his mind was in Croke Park, thinking only of Dublin forward Frank Burke.

Of all the famous names in Dublin the newspapers spoke about, none glittered and leapt from the pages like Burke's. He won matches by himself. His name alone terrorised the opposition. After Browne and Kerrigan left for Croke Park, Hogan looked for Bill Ryan. Ryan had been picked to play at right-half-back, standing in front of Hogan, who was at right-corner-back. Ryan had won Munster championships and played in an All-Ireland final. He was on the Tipperary team longer than Hogan. Marking Frank Burke might come easier to him.

'Would you swap with me, Bill?' Hogan asked.

'I can't,' he replied.

Ryan's boots had been flung out the window of the train the previous day by a soldier. He had spent the rest of Saturday hunting out a new pair and walked the corridors of the hotel all night trying to soften them out, but they still didn't fit right. They felt too loose on his feet. When it came to Frank Burke, Hogan would have to fend for himself.

It was getting late. The team left Barry's Hotel for Croke Park, mingling among the crowd like bright splashes of white in a great mass of brown and grey. A few miles away police and army trucks rattled out of barracks across the city. A boy sat in the crook of a tree at the corner of the ground above the heads of everyone, enjoying the finest view in the place. Another boy sat on the wall behind the goal. Croke Park was full. An aeroplane circled overhead and fired a flare. It was a rare thing for the crowd to see.

The teams were on the field. Johnny McDonnell was in goals for Dublin. At the other end Mick Hogan stood beside Frank Burke, waiting for the first ball. A truck crested the canal bridge outside. Over a dozen trucks filled with Black and Tans and Auxiliaries stopped behind it.

The men inside the trucks smelt stale from sweat and liquor. Their minds were clouded by anger and fear. They expected trouble in Croke Park. Some hoped for it. This was war without rules, waged against an invisible enemy on quiet country roads and dimly lit streets, nurtured in farmhouses and the hearts of once mild, modest men. Their orders were to search the crowd. The men checked their guns, leapt from the trucks and ran towards the gates. If Croke Park became a battlefield, conscience wouldn't make cowards of them.

PART I

POLITICS AND
WAR 1918–1920

CHAPTER 1

The Boy with the Penny Package

TIPPERARY, 1860–1919

The first Hogans settle in Grangemockler. Patrick Hogan raises a family of footballers and rebels. Mick Hogan inherits a farm as the sky darkens over the country.

GRANGEMOCKLER, TIPPERARY, JANUARY 1919

The dark mornings in Aughvaneen were bitten with cold. Mick Hogan's days were reset to the winter clock. The cows were in and the fields were empty. He sliced the heads off turnips to feed the animals. He dug potatoes. He skimmed the top grass and soil from a stretch of ground and dug a shallow trench to store mangold beets as animal fodder. When winter really took hold he collected the beets from beneath the soil and chopped them up.

Some days he hacked back briars and brambles from the ditches. He cleared leaves and mud from the small drains that bordered his fields so the spring rainwater would flow better when it came. When the sun came out Mick did some ploughing, gently guiding the horse and plough in straight lines, stepping over the heftiest chunks of earth, leaving them to nature. A winter's frost would break them down to nothing.

Winter farming demanded patience. It made him accept the limitations of what could be done and wait for the weather to turn again in favour of the land. Ploughing was slow and hard when frost turned the ground to concrete until the beginning of spring. It was a strange thing about this place: when it got cold in nearby places, it snowed in Aughvaneen. When the weather felt milder everywhere else, there was a chill in the air around Hogan's farm. The coach drivers travelling between Dublin and Cork swore the road between Ninemilehouse and Grangemockler was the coldest stretch of them all. Reason enough to stop in the village for a hot toddy.

Home was a neat cottage with a kitchen and parlour, two bedrooms and a loft beneath a thatched roof, set against a clean, cobbled yard. It was barely twenty years after the Famine when Mick's grandfather Dan Hogan came across a few fields from Hardbog to take on the farm a mile from Grangemockler. Their front door faced away from the road and the village. Little humps of countryside enveloped the cottage on all sides. A string of houses stretched out along the roadside protected it further from view. Tyrrell's place was first. The Healys were next door. Power's farm began at the end of Hogan's yard. The farm fanned out around the house for seventy acres, stretching to the invisible border between Tipperary and Kilkenny. Some of the land was wet and boggy. Most of it fed their cows and provided a good living.

When Dan died in 1886 his son Patrick continued the work on the farm. He married Margaret in 1894. Dan jnr was born the following year. Michael came in 1896. Kattie was born in 1901, followed by Tom in 1903. Margaret and Paddy came next and Mary was born in 1909. Two other daughters died. They mourned the children, placed them in

God's hands and concentrated on the living.

The farm held its own through every season. One day a man in town was taking pictures. Patrick Hogan stood for a portrait. His eyes were dark and stern, almost entirely hidden beneath the shade cast by the rim of his bowler hat. His moustache was thick and black and perfectly trimmed. He wore a fine morning suit with a perfectly starched collar and a white shirt. He hung the picture on the wall of the parlour at home, a monument to the good health of his farm and his family, and the prosperity that allowed him to engage the services of this photographer.

His children went to the small village school in Grangemockler where the pupils packed tightly into a couple of rooms. The infant class would gather around a fireplace or sit on the floor, slate boards on their laps, chalk in their hands. An older boy would guide each child's hand in turn as they copied letters from a chart. When the slate was full they would spit on it, wipe the slate clean, and begin again.

There were benches for half the pupils. The rest gathered in circles and semicircles chalked on the floor. In the middle of the circle the teacher would pivot around to face each child as they recited and read. For the semicircles, he erected a blackboard on an easel in front of them near the end wall.

At the top of the room Maurice Browne, the schoolmaster, sat on a high stool, his bearded chin supported by his left hand, elbow on the desk. Although the school was always noisy and bright, Master Browne was strict. Boys were punished for mitching or missing homework, being late for roll call, telling lies, throwing stones, or anything else that fell into his definition of mischief.

On Mick Hogan's first day at school, his mother, Margaret, took him down to the village. Master Browne appointed his own son, Maurice jnr, to be Hogan's minder for the day. 'Mick looked lonely and bewildered,' wrote Browne in his memoir. 'Soon his eyes filled with tears. He cried out with trembling underlip: "Want to go home to see

Da." This refrain he kept up for some time like a robin redbreast, not varying his note.'

Maurice tried to amuse him with marbles and a ball-frame. Mick kept sobbing. He opened a book and showed him pictures: Baa Baa Black Sheep, the old blind harper with his poor dog Tray. None of them staunched his tears.

'Home to see Da,' Mick said.

Master Browne's wife, Kate, ran a shop in the village. An outing seemed the only solution. Maurice jnr took Mick to visit and soon he was sampling sweets from every tin. As a special treat, Kate gave him a penny package; one in every five hundred penny packages contained a ticket that entitled the winner to a watch. Maurice saw Mick with his lucky dip, and wished it for himself.

As the tears dried up and school became a familiar part of his routine, Mick grew to be a bright scholar. Maurice Browne remained a friend. Maurice's brother, John, was even closer to Mick, and for years after, Kate cared for Mick Hogan like a kindly aunt, keeping an eye on the boy with the penny package.

Mick's brothers Tom and Dan had shown an academic potential that required a different kind of schooling. Word reached the Hogans of a progressive young teacher in nearby Windgap, versed in the latest methods of teaching maths, reading and English. The school was over the border in Kilkenny, five miles away by road but no distance from Hogan's across the fields. Tom and Dan walked every day to Windgap and excelled at their studies. In time Tom would join the Christian Brothers. Dan earned a scholarship to fund his schooling and took exams to join the railway company. Perhaps they were wise to leave home: it wasn't the country or the climate for crops. The corn just a few miles across the Kilkenny border in Callan always looked a different, healthier colour. Even the names of the townlands around Grangemockler suggested the land was harsh and infertile. Ballinruan: homestead of the moory place. Glenaskagh: glen of the whitethorn bushes. Cruan: hard place. Moin Cruadh: Hardbog. This was ground for grazing, not growing; small farms, not sprawling family ranches.

Off in the distance to the west, Slievenamon hill loomed over the village. When a storm assailed the mountain it always exerted the last of its temper on Grangemockler. In winter it hung like a white backdrop on the horizon; in summer the sun glinting against the heather draped the mountain in a blue-grey veil. Boys and girls talked every summer about climbing it. People judged the weather from the mood of the mountain. Con Feehan was the village weatherman. When Con was asked for his thoughts on the prospects of rain or sun, he would delay his answer until after he'd walked to where he could get a clear view of Slievenamon.

The countryside was everyone's playground. The older boys in school went mitching along the River Lingaun, hiding in a small hut by the bank and catching trout by hand from the river or trapping them beneath the hollow rocks on the riverbed. They roasted the fish in a fireplace made from flat stones, and washed it down with the bottles of milk they brought to school every day.

When the boys got caught they faced Master Browne. One day he sent Mikey Tobin out to fetch him some sally twigs, his cruellest instruments of punishment. They were a brutal product of nature, scything through the air like a whip. The boys held out their hands and braced themselves. The twigs whistled through the air and smacked against their palms, but snapped harmlessly on impact. The Master tried another sally. It also broke. Before delivering them, Mikey Tobin had notched the branches with his penknife. Master Browne stifled a smile. There would be no punishment that day, but no more handy jobs for the favoured Mikey Tobin.

The rhythms of life were gentle and subtle through the seasons. Fr Phil Dooley was parish priest of the village. He was a tall, strong man, with a bright sense of humour and a contagious laugh. He wore thick-lensed glasses. Bushy mutton chops framed his face.

When he walked for a while he rested on a stout stick, blowing out his cheeks as he strolled along. He always had a bag of sweets for children and spent many hours visiting the sick. People often told the story of Fr Phil and one dying man. After many hours at his bedside, Phil made to leave. 'Goodbye now, Michael,' he said. 'I've brought you to the gates of Heaven.' 'Ah, Father Phil,' the man replied, 'don't leave me at the gate.'

When it came to gathering hay, setting vegetables and slaughtering animals, people came together in haggards, farmyards and kitchens to help one another. Dan Meagher was the man who salted pigs. People knew him better as a footballer. As he worked, he often stopped to talk tactics and players. No one ever objected.

Nothing made Grangemockler buzz like football. Whether it was Tipperary or Grangemockler playing, the weeks before any big game were dominated by talk of the match. Every evening after the cows were driven home, milked and fed, boys and men would gather in the football field for practice. Every Sunday was dedicated to training and a match. The scene after mid-morning Mass was always the same: men quietly saying their prayers and eyeing the door, rushing home for potatoes, cabbage and pig's head, then football.

Grangemockler were known as the 'ass and cart' team for the way their supporters guided their carts in convoy to big matches in Carrick-on-Suir and nearby Clonmel. An old song captured the sight.

> One glorious fine morning on the thirteenth of May,
> To the sweet town of Carrick they started away.
> With horses and asses and good old Shank's mare,
> They went for to witness a great contest there.

Years before Mick Hogan's time, players would set out for Clonmel and Carrick on foot and pick up a lift. In time wagonettes would charge players and supporters two shillings each for the round trip. Footballers occupied a special status in every house. One day Tom Cooney was walking back to Grangemockler after playing a game when the wonderful smell of bacon and turnips came floating over the ditch. He followed the smell across a field to a farmhouse and knocked on the door.

No one answered. He pushed the door open. A table was set out. He sat down by the fire, waiting for the people of the house to return so he could ask if he might join them for dinner. Steam seeped out from the pot of potatoes hanging over the fire. Time passed. No one came. Eventually the hunger overwhelmed him. As he finished his plate of food, a woman appeared at the front door. She was furious. The food was being readied for those who had been to Clonmel for the football. What would she tell them now? When Tom told her he played for Grangemockler, everything changed. She took his plate and filled it with more bacon, potatoes and turnip, and a jug of buttermilk to help everything down.

Every boy was reared on the legend of Tom Kiely from nearby Ballyneale. In 1904 Kiely had travelled to St Louis, Missouri, to compete in the Olympic decathlon. Britain had offered him a place on their team but he insisted on competing as an Irish athlete. He raised the money to travel by selling many of the prizes he had won in competition over the years. When he arrived, the Americans also wanted him for their team. Again, he declined. All ten events were staged on the same day and Kiely won gold. He was thirty-five years old, and returned home a hero.

Kiely also played football for Grangemockler. Although he had a great leap, Kiely rarely caught the ball but fisted it further than some could kick it. When Kiely returned from the Olympics, football was thriving in Grangemockler. Although hurling dominated most of Tipperary, Gaelic football was everything in the southern pocket of the county around Clonmel and Carrick-on-Suir. Grangemockler won five successive championships between 1903 and 1907. Of the twenty-one Tipperary county championships between 1900 and 1920, only Nenagh in north Tipperary and Loughmore-Castleiney near Thurles in the middle of the county had taken the title away from a club in the south.

Grangemockler and the neighbouring parishes of Fethard and Mullinahone shared thirteen championships out of twenty-one between 1900 and 1920. The hardest matches always came with their nearest neighbours. Those rivalries bred great players. Dan Hogan was among them but when work with the railway company despatched him two hundred miles north to Monaghan as a clerk, he settled in Clones and lined out for Monaghan.

Dan was tall and athletic, scraping the clouds like Tom Kiely when he rose to catch a ball and booming kicks downfield like a cannon. He became friends with Eoin O'Duffy soon after settling in Clones; O'Duffy was an engineer and surveyor in Monaghan County Council, active in the GAA and moving through the ranks of the IRA. They visited Grangemockler together during the summer holidays. As secretary of the Ulster GAA Council, O'Duffy wound GAA affairs into Irish Volunteer business, binding sport and politics tightly together.

Some days O'Duffy's and Hogan's intentions were deadly serious; sometimes they got up to mischief. Hogan was appointed to referee the 1918 Ulster final between Armagh and Cavan at Cootehill, but when the teams arrived, they found British soldiers occupying the pitch. O'Duffy and Hogan left Cootehill on bicycles with a party of RIC men on their tail. It was a hot day and the RIC laboured on heavier machines. With no match to play and plenty of spit in his guts, O'Duffy took off across the countryside, through byways and along narrow lanes almost swallowed by hedgerows. For fifteen miles the RIC pursued them, sweltering in their heavy uniforms, hauling their bicycles over worsening terrain. In the end, the RIC lost them.

It was all a worry to Margaret Hogan, but that was her son. In autumn

1918 Dan and O'Duffy were arrested for illegal assembly after a football game and imprisoned in Belfast. One night after Christmas 1918, having been granted temporary parole, Hogan returned to the jail at 10pm for re-admission, but the authorities refused. Hogan checked into a nearby hotel instead. The following morning he returned to jail with a receipt for his lodgings the previous night. The prison paid the bill.

That was Dan: methodical, controlled, disciplined. Around the time Dan was in jail, his father had taken ill with stomach trouble. Patrick died on 28 October 1918, aged just fifty-seven, leaving a grieving family with hard choices to make. Tom was in Dublin with the Christian Brothers. Dan was in Clones. The girls were still young. The youngest boy, Patrick, was only eleven. Margaret was still only fifty-three but severely weakened by her husband's death. Mick was twenty-two, two years younger than his father had been when he took the farm over. Now it was his.

So Mick Hogan snagged turnips and cleared drains and found what distraction he could at home. A general election in 1918 had transformed the complexion of politics in Ireland. The country was changing. Rebels interned in jails and camps across Britain after the 1916 Easter Rising were released and returned home as heroes. Sinn Féin had existed as a political party since 1905, but were lifted dramatically by the same rising tide of support and won seventy-three seats in Ireland out of 105.

The ripples were felt in every house in the land. Sinn Féin clubs grew up everywhere around the country. Mick Hogan's old friend John Browne organised the Grangemockler branch at the beginning of 1919.

Hogan was happy to join. The Irish Volunteer movement, initially organised before World War One – in response to the Ulster Volunteers who swore to resist Home Rule with their last drops of blood – had been decimated by the Rising but began to reorganise again. In Grangemockler, the Volunteer unit still numbered about twenty-five. Mick Hogan and John Browne joined the others marching through the village a couple of times a week, hurleys against their shoulders like guns.

The overlap between the GAA, politics and the Volunteers was already visible. Playing Gaelic football and hurling had been a vivid expression of cultural independence since the GAA was formed in 1884. The Sinn Féin club gave that voice a political form. Drilling with the Volunteers was another symbol of defiance and difference.

Soon the Volunteer movement would ask more of them. The hurleys on their shoulders would be replaced by actual guns. A few miles across the fields, away from easy Sundays of football and the familiar tolling of a church bell to gather people to pray, men and boys were preparing for war.

CHAPTER 2

The Outlaws

Two shots by a lonely quarry start a war. Four Tipperary men go into hiding and escape to Dublin. The gaudy lights of Monto, drinking dens and kip houses. Michael Collins seeks a different kind of rebel for a new war.

SOLOHEADBEG, COUNTY TIPPERARY, 21 JANUARY 1919

They sat shivering for days in a tin hut near Greenane and the warm civilian comforts of Tipperary town. Waiting. Seamus Robinson was their commander. Sean Treacy and Dan Breen had made this cold, orphaned place their second home since October 1918. They were joined now by five more Volunteers: Sean Hogan, Michael Ryan, Paddy McCormack, Tadhg Crowe and Paddy O'Dwyer.

Their target was a consignment of gelignite due for transportation from Tipperary town to a small quarry at Soloheadbeg a few miles away. They had gathered ammunition for revolvers and Treacy's rifle. Paddy O'Dwyer cycled to Tipperary every morning to see if the gelignite was on the move. Other Volunteers from the area helped out, sharing news and local knowledge. One day when Treacy cut bushes from a nearby moat to make a fire, one man warned it was bad luck to cut bushes from a moat for fear of angering the fairies. 'The fairies won't say anything to us for trying to keep warm,' said Treacy.

For a week they waited. Some slept on the burst mattresses in two derelict bedrooms. Others curled up on the ground close to the fire. They spent evenings talking about what might happen when the waiting ended. They assumed the police accompanying the gelignite would surrender. They talked about the best way to hold the escorts as prisoners while the gelignite was unloaded. Robinson laid down an order: if there were two RIC men, they were to be held up; if there were six, they were to be met by a volley of fire. 'I'm certain none of us contemplated that the venture would end in bloodshed and a loss of life,' said Tadhg Crowe years later.

Treacy and Breen listened to Robinson every night without interrupting, but they thought differently. They wanted to rush the cart and take the RIC men on in a fight. For months they had stolen rifles from idling army and RIC men, but this wasn't simply about gelignite. To get their enemy's attention they believed the RIC men had to die.

Early on 21 January Paddy O'Dwyer cycled back from Tipperary with news. The gelignite was coming. This time they sat around the fire making real plans. Six of them would take positions near the gate into the quarry. Robinson and O'Dwyer would stay thirty yards away to the left, ready to stop the cart if it tried to get away or didn't halt.

They set out for the quarry. As they neared Soloheadbeg, Breen talked about attacking the RIC men. The reality of their intentions was dawning on Robinson. He might be in charge, but when it came to battle Treacy and Breen could control the rules of engagement regardless of what anyone else wanted.

They took their positions. The cart trundled towards them, driven by two council men, its wheels creaking and squealing against the road. Two RIC men walked behind. Breen pulled a handkerchief over his mouth and nose, pulled out his revolver, and jumped over the hedge.

'Hands up!' he shouted.

Robinson and O'Dwyer jumped out, grabbing the reins from the council men. Both RIC officers raised their rifles. Treacy and Crowe fired. The horse reared up. The RIC men fell dead. Breen spoke to the council men and calmed them down. The others hid guns, handcuffs and ammunition carried by the dead RIC men in the ditch a few hundred yards up the road. Treacy, Breen and Hogan mounted the cart. Breen took the reins and the horses bolted. Robinson threw his eyes to heaven. With such delicate cargo, Hogan had told Breen to take it easy. Instead, they rode away like three rustlers in the Wild West. Their plan had worked. They had started a war.

On the same morning, the Dáil had convened in Dublin's Mansion House for the first time. Of the seventy-three Sinn Féin MPs, forty-three were in prison or on the run. The proceedings were conducted entirely in Irish. Cathal Brugha was elected Chief Speaker (Ceann Comhairle). With Éamon de Valera in jail, Brugha was also elected President. Among the raft of ministerial appointments, Michael Collins was elected Minister for Home Affairs. In this coterie of high political thinkers, Collins was among the links to the Volunteers, but no one knew about Soloheadbeg yet. If the Dáil represented the political dream of an independent Ireland that day, Soloheadbeg was the unfolding reality in the countryside.

Two days after Soloheadbeg the south Tipperary region was declared a Special Military Area. Fairs, meetings, markets and processions were outlawed. The army and police swarmed Tipperary, and Breen, Treacy and the others disappeared into the countryside. Life on the run was an endless round of strange beds and keeping close to the hedgerows. Some locals talked about them like gunslingers after Soloheadbeg. Many more saw them as murderers. They were denounced in newspapers and in their own villages and towns, by their own people and from the pulpits.

'We must show our abhorrence of this inhuman act,' parish priest Monsignor Arthur Ryan told his congregation in Tipperary town. 'We must denounce it and the cowardly miscreants who are guilty of it – and all who try to excuse or justify it. It used to be said "where Tipperary leads, Ireland follows". God help poor Ireland if she follows this lead of blood.'

To some people, they were freedom fighters rooted in the traditions of militant Irish nationalism. To others they were a nuisance, bringing more police and soldiers to Tipperary and upsetting the normal rhythms of business and life. As far as the public knew, folk heroes didn't come with families either. They rarely dwelt on how Dan Breen's mother was left almost in penury and tormented by soldiers and police as her son spent years on the run.

After his father had died, Sean Treacy was sent to live with his aunt, Mary Anne Ellis. She expected Treacy to work and sustain the small family farm. When she saw the company he kept, she got angry. For decades afterwards, she called Breen 'The Murderer'.

People whispered the news if they spotted them out on the roads or cutting across the fields. They sometimes saw them at dances. The odd few might help them away to safe houses if the police got too close. 'Wanted' ads were plastered onto walls across south Tipperary seeking the killers. One poster in the village of Rosegreen was torn down and replaced by another.

*Take notice that anyone caught giving information as to the shoot-
ing of the peelers at Soloheadbeg will meet with the same fate.*
Signed, Veritas.

As the story of Soloheadbeg travelled further, it got bent and twisted
in the telling. Ask Breen, and he would tell you that he and Treacy
had always intended to kill those men. They wanted the ambush to
leave a deep, lasting mark on the RIC and the people. They had been
frustrated by the inactivity around Tipperary in 1916 when the Rising
was crushed in Dublin. They had always said when their time came, it
would be different.

Breen recognised Seamus Robinson as a decorated hero of the Rising,
but also a patsy leader of Breen and Treacy's choosing. The ideas and
intentions behind Soloheadbeg were fixed in their minds long before
Robinson arrived. Breen would talk about the night they called to Robinson on a farm where he was milking cows to ask about being their
commander, and how he hadn't stopped to talk properly to them but
said he'd do whatever was required of him.

Ask Seamus Robinson, and the idea for intercepting these RIC men
and their convoy of explosives near Soloheadbeg had started in Sean
Treacy's head before Christmas 1918. One night he and his girlfriend
had called to Robinson. After tea, Robinson and Treacy headed outside
to a haggard for a chat. Treacy outlined the scenario: there would only
be two RIC guards with the gelignite. Robinson threw him a look.
'Only two?' asked Robinson. 'Well, maybe six,' Treacy replied.

The operation still required the nod from the Volunteers' General HQ
in Dublin before it could happen, but Treacy and Robinson were restless.
What if they said no? Not telling them, said Robinson, would remove
that option. He saw the tip of Treacy's tongue flick across to the corner
of his mouth in response. In time, he'd recognise it as a little tick that
told everyone Treacy was happy. He'd never make a good card player.

Soloheadbeg caused as much disquiet at Volunteer HQ in Dublin as it did with the British authorities, but it also energised the Third Tipperary Brigade. Stretching across a swathe of south Tipperary, they quickly increased the intensity of their training and the ferocity of their attacks. They took target practice at Tobin's quarry in Shrough, near Galbally hidden in the forests and hills of Ballyhoura. Their brigade headquarters were in a nearby sawmill. They studied signalling and musketry, made simple bombs and repaired weapons in a small munitions factory at Mooresfort.

Cartridge cases were filled with buckshot and lead chippings. Guns were hidden inside a statue in Galbally church. In Clonmel, Frank Drohan stored ammunition inside empty paint cans that sat on open display in the family coachmaking business. Sean Treacy hollowed out stairposts and rafters in his own home to hide arms.

Stealing such an amount of gelignite represented a significant munitions haul and a publicity stunt, but it had also happened without official approval. Seamus Robinson was summoned to Dublin by Michael Collins. There were things Robinson always noticed about Collins. He never looked Robinson in the eye. Collins didn't seem to like him. They didn't meet in Collins's office but in the street. Collins opened his notebook.

'Well, everything is fixed up,' Collins said. 'Be ready to go in a day or two.'

'Where to?' asked Robinson.

'To the States,' Collins replied in exasperation. 'Isn't it the usual thing to do after things like this?'

'But we don't want to go to the States or anywhere else,' said Robinson.

Collins's eyes flicked back and forth across the street. 'Well, a great many people seem to think it's the only thing to do.'

When they had talked about Soloheadbeg, Treacy and Breen never imagined skipping the country. To them, killing an occupying force was a legitimate act and the most visible, chilling signal they could send that it was time for Britain to leave. Robinson gritted his teeth, lowering his voice to a whisper. 'To kill a couple of policemen for the country's sake and leave it at that by running away would approximate too closely to murder.'

Collins smirked. 'Then what do you propose?'

'Fight it out, of course,' replied Robinson.

Collins snapped his notebook shut and smiled. 'Well, that's all right with me,' he said and strode briskly away, disappearing into the thicket of people.

Robinson, Treacy, Breen and Hogan stayed on the run. Dublin kept an eye on them. They were a strange crew of disparate characters. Breen had been born in Donohill, close to Tipperary town, and raised in a family of eight by his mother after his father died of blood poisoning. Robinson was born in Belfast and descended from old Fenians and a grand master of the Orange Order; he was raised in Scotland with family roots in France. While Robinson came to south Tipperary with a clipped Belfast accent and a liking for puns that made people groan with exasperation, Breen had been shaped by everything about Tipperary, from the books his mother bought him about Wolfe Tone and Robert Emmet to his own cousin dying on a roadside in Donohill having been evicted.

Treacy grew up near the Breens and joined the Irish Republican Brotherhood in 1911, aged sixteen. He formed a Volunteer group in 1913 and cycled to different districts in Tipperary when the Easter Rising began, trying to drum up a fight. Where Breen was fiery and compulsive, Treacy was quiet and intelligent with a dry sense of humour. He wasn't squeamish about killing or battle, and neither was Breen, but Treacy's way was more clinical.

Sean Hogan was eighteen and still going to dances, disappearing into

the night with women and waking in strange, unfamiliar houses, unflus-
tered by the danger that surrounded him. Hogan, Breen and Treacy
moved around the county together. Robinson tried to return to work as
a farmhand but joined them within a month. In the Dáil's opening ses-
sion the Irish Volunteers had been recognised as its legitimate army and
renamed the Irish Republican Army (IRA). To drive home the message
of Soloheadbeg, Robinson printed posters for display across the county,
and sent the text to Dublin for approval.

> *Whereas a foreign and tyrannical Government is preventing Irish-*
> *men exercising the civil right of buying and selling their own markets*
> *in their own country, and whereas almost every Irishman who has*
> *suffered the death penalty for Ireland was sentenced to death solely*
> *on the strength of the evidence and reports of the policemen who,*
> *therefore, are dangerous spies, and whereas thousands of Irishmen*
> *have been deported and sentenced solely on the evidence of these same*
> *hirelings, assassins and traitorous spies the police, and whereas the*
> *life, limb and living of no citizen of Ireland is safe while those paid*
> *spies are allowed to infest the country, and whereas it has come to our*
> *knowledge that some men and boys have been arrested and drugged,*
> *and whereas there are a few Irishmen who have sunk to such depths*
> *of degradation that they are prepared to give information about their*
> *neighbours and fellow countrymen to the police, and whereas all*
> *these evils will continue as long as the people will permit: We hereby*
> *proclaim the South Riding of Tipperary a military area with the fol-*
> *lowing regulations:*
>
> *a.   A policeman found within said area on or after the _ day*
> *of February 1919 will be deemed to have forfeited his life. The*
> *more notorious police being dealt with, as far as possible, first.*
>
> *b.   On or after the _ day of February 1919, every person in*

the pay of England (magistrates, jurors, etc) who helps England to rule this country or who assists in any way the upholders of foreign Government in this South Riding of Tipperary will be deemed to have forfeited his life.

c.   Civilians who give information to the police or soldiery, especially such information as is of a serious character, if convicted will be executed, i.e shot or hanged.

d.   Police, doctors, prison officials who assist at or who countenance or who are responsible for, or who are in any way connected with the drugging of an Irish citizen for the purpose of obtaining information, will be deemed to have forfeited his life and may be hanged or drowned or shot on sight as a common outlaw. Offending parties will be executed should it take years to track them down.

e.   Every citizen must assist when required in enabling us to perform our duty.

By Order

The response from IRA headquarters came within twenty-four hours. 'That proclamation must not be published!' The posters still appeared all over Tipperary. The British military and the RIC found it amusing. As far as Treacy, Robinson, Hogan and Breen reckoned, this was a statement no one in Dublin, or those behind walled barracks across Tipperary, should trifle with.

On 11 May 1919, all four fugitives attended a dance in Ballagh organised to raise funds for the purchase of a revolver. Sean Hogan reached the end of the night with a girl and plans to head for another dance.

One of Treacy's favourite lines came to Robinson's mind: 'Ireland can never be free,' he said, 'until she can produce a Robert Emmet who doesn't give a damn about women.'

Hogan headed off with a warning to take care as the rest headed to Kinane's, their safe house for the night. The following morning Robinson and the others were woken by Mick Kinane with news. 'Do you fellows not know one of your fellows was arrested?' he said. 'Is it young Hogan?' asked Breen. They didn't need an answer.

Hogan had escorted his girl home, and police had surrounded the house and arrested him as he tried to escape. He would be transported by train from Thurles to Cork. If Hogan were taken to Dublin or Tipperary town, the IRA stood a good chance of staging a rescue. Taking him to Cork, where Robinson and the others had few contacts, seriously reduced their chances.

Two stations were suggested as possible points for an assault: Emly, near Cashel, and Knocklong in County Limerick. They settled on Knocklong. The train was due in at eight that evening. Treacy was on the platform. A group of IRA men from Galbally had stepped aboard at Emly and spotted Hogan. Breen and Robinson waited near the entrance gate to follow Treacy on his signal.

They waited. The tension grew. The train eventually came chugging towards the platform. They knew Hogan would be heavily guarded. Once they entered the carriage, they ran the risk of facing a barrage of fire. But there was no other way.

The train slowed and stopped. Treacy's nerves sparked like live wires. Two Galbally Volunteers jumped off the train and pointed at Hogan's carriage. Treacy jumped on board, followed by Eamonn O'Brien, another Volunteer. Four RIC men were sitting around Hogan.

'Hands up!' shouted Treacy. 'Come on, Sean. Out!'

Constable Michael Enright jammed his gun into Hogan's neck. Treacy and O'Brien opened fire and killed Enright. Hogan crashed his handcuffs into the face of Constable Jeremiah Ring, who was sitting opposite him. The two other RIC officers, Sergeant Peter Wallace and Constable John Reilly, charged Treacy and O'Brien. The other Galbally Volunteers flooded the train and knocked Reilly out. Treacy continued to struggle with Wallace. 'Surrender,' Treacy muttered.

As he tried to wrench his gun away, Wallace managed to turn it towards Treacy's head. Two shots rang out. One, from O'Brien's gun, killed Wallace. The other, from Wallace, sent a bullet through Treacy's neck. One of the Volunteers turned to Hogan. 'Get the hell out!' he said.

Hogan made for the door. Out on the platform Breen was lumbering towards the carriage. Having recovered, Constable Reilly peppered the platform with shotgun blasts. One bullet went through Breen's arm. Another perforated his lung. Breen fell. Hogan was out of the carriage and running.

Robinson made for a nearby safe house, the chain on his bicycle coming loose with every few turns of the wheel. When he arrived there he learned that Hogan, Breen and the rest had headed for another nearby safe house. When they had been through the area a few weeks before, Robinson had remarked to Treacy on the unusual shape of the mountain that overshadowed the Foley's small house at its foot. If ever they got separated or found trouble, they would make for there. That's where they waited for him now.

When Robinson arrived, the rest of the story took shape. Breen had already received the last rites from a local priest. Treacy had run from Knocklong, his neck wound so bad he held his head up with his hands.

After escaping the carriage Hogan had eventually scrambled to a butcher's shop and persuaded the owner to split the chains on his hands with a cleaver. A doctor removed the bullet from Treacy's neck before operating on Breen. Although Treacy was stable, the doctor insisted Breen couldn't be moved, but Foley's was too well known to police for them to stay. They set out on a jolting horse and cart for west Limerick, the others holding Breen steady in the back to cushion him against the bumps and hollows. Treacy made no fuss, occasionally turning away to cough while holding his throat.

The newspaper accounts of the Knocklong rescue read like an excerpt from an adventure book. 'Sensational Occurrence in Limerick,' reported the *Ulster Herald*. 'Prisoner Gets Away' said the *Freeman's Journal*. 'Policeman Killed In Limerick; Sergeant Also Shot; Prisoner Rescued from Escort in Train,' screamed the *Irish Independent*.

'In the struggle one constable was shot dead,' read the *Freeman's Journal* report, 'and another so seriously wounded there was little hope of recovery …. when the train reached Cork, an hour after its scheduled time, the carriage in which the incident took place was taken in charge by the police authorities. Many bullet marks and blood splashes bore evidence of a deadly and terrible struggle.'

Two policemen were dead. Constable Ring turned up a few days later near Knocklong wearing only his shirt and trousers, carrying his boots in his hand. His rosary beads were draped around his neck. His nerves were shredded.

To some, the killings at Knocklong were murders. On a visit to Knocklong, Archbishop John Harty of Cashel and Emly spoke of another crime against God and Ireland. 'I have to offer you my deep sympathy in the unmerited slur cast upon the good name of your parish by the horrible crime committed here within the past few days,' he said. 'It was an imported crime, with which the people of Knocklong had no connection, and while I sympathise with the parishioners I congratulate them on their having absolutely nothing to do with anything that would in any way stain the grand Irish and Catholic spirit.'

To others it changed everything about Hogan, Treacy, Breen and Robinson. The public saw Knocklong as a straight and fair shoot-out, not like Soloheadbeg. It was a thrilling episode that translated well into legend and song. Hogan was young, handsome and a dashing character known from the dances around south Tipperary. For all the trouble the four had caused, the IRA had stumbled on an unlikely group of heroes.

After the Knocklong escape Breen, Treacy, Hogan and Robinson travelled to Birr in County Offaly where they stayed with the Bulfin family. Nearly ten days after the incident, Treacy was strong enough to cycle about seventy-five miles from Birr to Maynooth, County Kildare. Michael Collins had sent a message to him with a name to contact. Patrick Colgan was a prominent IRA man in Kildare. Couriers carrying despatches from IRA units in the west and south passed through his shop every week. Colgan approached Treacy as he dismounted his bicycle.

'Who do you wish to see?' he asked.

'I'm here to see Patrick Colgan,' Treacy replied.

'Who shall I say is looking for him?' said Colgan.

'I'm a friend of his,' Treacy said.

'Well, I'm Patrick Colgan,' Colgan replied.

Treacy pulled a notebook from his jacket and opened a page bearing Colgan's name. 'Do you recognise the writing?' he asked Colgan.

'I do,' he said. 'That's Mick Collins's hand.'

While the Bulfins were happy to have them, explained Treacy, it was time they moved to Dublin and arrangements were being made. In the meantime, they needed a safe place to wait in Kildare. Colgan found a safe house in Maynooth. They stayed a week. Treacy passed his time reading a manual on handling small arms.

They reached Dublin in early June. Colgan made two separate trips a few weeks later carrying a large suitcase filled with guns and grenades. The first day he made for Phil Shanahan's pub on Foley Street, a nerve centre of IRA activity in the middle of the city. He bought a bottle of lemonade from the barman.

'Is Mr Shanahan in?' he asked.

'Do you know Mr Shanahan?' replied the barman.

Colgan heard some movement behind him. He remembered noticing a man talking to a woman by the door, drinking a pint. He froze for a moment. Had he walked into a trap?

It was Shanahan. With the suitcase delivered and its contents hidden in the cellar, Colgan asked about his former guests. 'Gone to Clontarf baths for a swim,' replied Shanahan. Colgan couldn't fathom whether the Tipperary men were the bravest he had met, or the most foolish.

The night of his second trip, Colgan attended a play in the Abbey Theatre. When the house lights went up at the end of the first act he recognised the man sitting on his right. It was Breen. That settled it. 'I gave the Knocklong fellows up,' Colgan said, 'as being a set of loonies who knew no fear.'

Dublin suited them. They were given board in a network of safe houses and money for everything from the theatre and food to buying guns and ammunition. If they needed clothes, those were provided too. Breen boasted of bestriding Dublin by day and keeping his head down when the new curfew came in at night. He travelled down the country by train, car or bicycle. If he cycled, he could make it to Tipperary from Dublin in ten hours. Cork was a fifteen-hour journey. If he walked, he could make Cork from Dublin in five days across the fields. Breen often went to Croke Park to watch football and hurling. Tipperary hurlers and footballers were doing well. That gave him plenty to crow about.

'Croke Park was a great place to stay,' said Breen years later. 'It was in Croke Park that all the IRB men met. Most of the heads of the GAA were IRB men. It was generally recognised that Croke Park was a safe meeting place. We walked the streets of Dublin free as anybody. In Dublin we always went fully armed and determined to fight. But we avoided acting foolishly.'

Treacy and Breen often stayed with the Fleming family in Drumcondra who had Tipperary connections, and they passed the nights listening to Treacy and Breen tell stories about their scrapes and tumbles. They teased Dinny Lacey, another IRA man from Tipperary who often stayed with them, about how he – such a devoutly religious man – could rub men out without a thought.

'I admired and envied their carefree attitude,' said Joe Lawless, a member of Collins's Squad. 'Treacy, in particular, had an impish sense of humour which showed sometimes in mock-serious conversation or in relating a recent event in which he pretended to attribute a humorous intent to the enemy forces involved.'

To Breen, Treacy was his leader. If Treacy fell in with a battalion back in Tipperary for any operation, he was automatically assumed to be in charge. 'He was prepared to go through hell and high water at Sean's bidding,' said Lawless.

The Monto, and Shanahan's pub, was the centre of their universe in every way, with its bars and brothels offering ready access to women, drink, guns and adventure, all hemmed into a small patch between Montgomery Street, Talbot Street, Amiens Street, Gardiner Street and Gloucester Street. It was a playground for adventurers, crooks and acute observers of the human condition.

Phil Shanahan was an infectious character in his mid-forties from Hollyford who smoked a pipe and had hurled for Tipperary, fought in Jacob's factory during the Rising and won a seat in Dublin for Sinn Féin in the 1918 general election. During the campaign he often reminded his supporters he was a soldier, not a politician. He still swept to victory.

One night in May 1920 Treacy and Breen attacked the RIC barracks in Hollyford, Tipperary, with a large group of Volunteers, but despite setting the barracks alight they failed to take it. Back in Dublin, Phil Shanahan showed the newspaper story to his friends in the bar. 'I'll never have anything again to do with these Tipperary fellows,' he said. 'They're after burning the only decent house in my native town.'

His bar was a safe house and meeting place. Guns and ammunition were routinely stored in the cellar and elsewhere. His customers ranged from artists, writers and poets to dockers, prostitutes, criminals and self-anointed freedom fighters. Peadar Kearney, composer of 'Amhrán na bhFiann', later adopted as the national anthem, was a regular. Moggie Comerford was an old friend from Knutsford prison with an endless thirst. Playwright Sean O'Casey was also a familiar face in Shanahan's. In time, O'Casey would write characters all bearing different aspects and reflections of Moggie Comerford in *The Plough and the Stars* and *Juno and the Paycock*.

Where O'Casey and James Joyce harvested the area for characters, others revelled in its bars and gambling dens and kip houses filled with prostitutes. During the day the girls leaned out the windows lowering cans filled with money for the boys below to run to the shop for cigarettes, matches and food, or a drink from the pub. At night the brothels filled with people from across Dublin and the world. When ships docked in Dublin port, the Monto became a babel of accents and languages. Chinese men mingled with Norwegians and French sailors. Hackney cabs would pull up outside the kip houses, allowing well-heeled gentlemen make a discreet entrance.

In Shanahan's IRA men mingled unnoticed with detectives, soldiers and policemen. Prostitutes often pinched guns and ammunition and harvested information from their clients for the IRA. Customers traded guns as well as cash. When they landed in Dublin, Phil Shanahan gave a revolver each to Breen, Robinson and Treacy from a small consignment brought back from Chicago.

At the time Breen, Treacy and the others arrived in Dublin, the conflict there was getting tougher, but also more subtle. In April 1919, the Dáil agreed a policy of ostracisation against police officers across the country. Having taken over as the IRA's Director of Intelligence in January 1919, Michael Collins set up an office in Crow Street, a few hundred yards from Dublin Castle, the heartbeat of British rule in Ireland. Liam Tobin was in charge of Intelligence HQ, which processed information gathered by intelligence officers connected to every IRA company. Newspapers were combed for references to RIC and DMP personnel. News of police transfers, weddings, social engagements, parties and any stories that outlined police movements were clipped out, pasted to a piece of card and filed.

The latest editions of *Who's Who* were studied for police backgrounds and connections to any clubs and organisations. Mail was intercepted. Intelligence officers in each IRA company and brigade focused on different sources of information. Some found sources in hotels, restaurants and at sports events. Others infiltrated the civil service. House servants and maids provided intimate detail about their masters. The IRA found their information everywhere and from anyone.

On 19 September 1919 Michael Collins gathered a group for a meeting at 46 Parnell Square. Richard Mulcahy, the IRA's Chief of Staff and the Dáil's Minister for National Defence, was accompanied by Dick McKee, head of the IRA's Dublin Brigade. The rest were IRA men picked from across the city: Paddy O'Daly, Joe Leonard, Sean Doyle, Ben Barrett, Tom Keogh, Vinny Byrne and Mick McDonnell. Collins made them an offer: O'Daly would lead a four-man team, completed by Leonard, Doyle and Barrett, devoted entirely to targeting British spies and informers. They would leave their jobs and take a wage from the

IRA. They would tell no one, within the IRA or outside, of their work or their duties. They would answer to Collins alone. They wouldn't undertake independent operations. Every hit would be planned and sanctioned by Collins. The others would be retained for different duties connected to the Squad. They began work almost immediately, scouting suspects from a long list and picking off their targets. G Division of the DMP was a plainclothes detective department, numbering between forty and fifty active men. The Squad started with them. As the number of assassinations increased, 'Wanted' posters began appearing in the city, some offering up to £10,000 for information.

There was a place for the Tipperary men in all this, but not everyone wanted them around. Later that autumn Seamus Robinson attended a meeting with Richard Mulcahy, who had never hidden his concerns about the Tipperary men. Mulcahy didn't appreciate their indifference to the chain of command when neglecting to gain official approval for the Soloheadbeg ambush and wanted them shipped to America. Collins disagreed. They were the right men for some of the work he had in mind.

The IRA wished to organise an Active Service Unit in tandem with the Squad and was looking for men for a variety of different jobs, dangerous enough that the men might have to be disowned if captured or killed, said Mulcahy. Treacy, Hogan and Breen were initially indignant at the idea. Why disown their own soldiers after a battle in a time of war? But Robinson saw Mulcahy's logic. Although the IRA was technically the army of the Irish Republic and of the political house of the Dáil, that relationship was brittle. The IRA weren't fighting a conventional war. In their own way, Breen and Treacy had dictated those terms at Soloheadbeg.

The Tipperary men agreed to join the new unit, but continued to flit between Tipperary and Dublin. On 19 December 1919 all of them fought beside members of the Squad when they attempted to ambush

Sir John French, the Lord Lieutenant of Ireland, near the Viceregal Lodge in the Phoenix Park. The IRA had aborted so many attacks and failed to get near French so many times, they had almost lost count. This time they pulled a cart across the road and waited in a nearby pub, talking handball with the owner, listening for the whistle of the train.

Collins had approved the plan, but it was a messy operation. The cart wasn't pulled properly across the road to slow down the convoy. One IRA man, Martin Savage, was killed in the fight. Sean Hogan accidentally pulled the pin on a small bomb and dropped it between himself and Paddy O'Daly. Both of them dived to the ground. The explosion only covered them in clay.

Dan Breen had been shot through the leg and was bleeding badly. As French's convoy careened off towards the safety of the Lodge, Savage's body was propped up outside a nearby pub and Breen hoisted onto the back of O'Daly's bicycle. They cycled back towards the city, O'Daly and Breen hidden in the cluster of IRA men. They brought Breen to a safe house in Phibsborough. Treacy, Hogan and Robinson insisted on staying with him. This was the bond they shared. For all the high ideals and politics of the Dáil, and the scheming on Crow Street, this was their fight. Monsignor Ryan's greatest fear had been made real. Where Tipperary led, Ireland had followed.

CHAPTER 3

The Reluctant General

A story of hatred and resentment by a student of Dickens. A new kind of terror in the countryside. A chilling new addition to the police force.

DUBLIN, JANUARY–JULY 1920

Some days Nevil Macready wondered what had brought him to this pass. What sleight of hand dealt him this misfortune, to be hemmed in by the walls of a castle he didn't care for in a city he hated, trying to keep order over a country he despised?

Ireland made him weary. There was nothing honourable about this country or this campaign. It was neither war nor criminality. He was Commander-in-Chief of the military in Ireland, but the politicians treated him as neither soldier nor policeman.

He sat in his office reading demoralising despatches on burnt-out creameries and cottages, RIC men shot to death in the streets by murderers in civilian clothes and snipers hiding in the countryside, propagating a war that didn't deserve such a title. He'd never found much amusement in the Irish sense of humour but always thought any man who set foot on their soil needed a good sense of humour to deal with them.

Ireland represented all the frustrations that accompanied him through his military service. Yes, Macready had occupied positions of great power in the previous three decades, but he had also been coralled and compelled into taking roles he had no interest in. Somewhere between the heaven of his ambition and the hell of war, Ireland was his purgatory.

Macready was thirty years old and a junior captain when he was first despatched to Dublin in 1892 from his base in India with the 1st Battalion of the Gordons. Dublin bored him. In the absence of anything more suitable he used the Phoenix Park to train his men with South Africa and its Zulus and Boers in mind, imagining the neatly ordered footpaths as impassable rivers and the large clumps of rhododendron that decorated the park as rocky hills that required surmounting.

When Lord Garnet Wolseley, the Commander-in-Chief of the military in Ireland, took his rides out from his residence at Kilmainham's Royal Hospital, he often trotted over to Macready and his men, asking about their manoeuvres, examining their training. His presence made Macready nervous and frightened the wits from his men. On top of being imprisoned by duty in Dublin, being monitored almost daily by a field marshal did nothing for Macready's morale.

The good things about Dublin? Not much. Macready had married Sophia Atkin in 1886 – her family was from Cork – and when in Dublin he enjoyed how the dome atop the Custom House glinted in the sun, and he admired the imperial grandeur of the colonnades that supported the Four Courts, holding up the virtues of justice, law and decency. But there was always something irritating about the Irish.

One spring, as an ailing Home Rule bill was labouring through the Commons, unrest flared in the countryside between landlords and their tenants. The St Patrick's Day Ball in Dublin Castle was the annual occasion for the city's business classes to take their place in high society, but this time they refused their invitations.

Macready was placed in charge of the guard at the castle. The crowd that turned up in place of the great business magnates of the city were plain to his eyes. Dowdy. The women were not to his taste. He noted that any lady who did capture his attention was invariably the wife of a British officer.

He watched his soldiers smirk at one Irish lady in the crowd, nervously adjusting her gloves as she ascended the stairs apparently unaware she had forgotten to fix her dress, having turned it up from the hem and pinned it at the waist while riding in her cab. Now she tottered up the steps towards Macready, exposing both the inner lining of her dress and a white petticoat.

For a moment it occurred to Macready to let her pass without a word, but he couldn't. 'Madam, your dress,' he whispered. She stopped and placed her hand on his shoulder to steady herself. He held her up until she made herself presentable.

A shoulder to lean on was what Ireland always needed. The Irish, he thought, were like children: uncouth and in need of controlling, undisciplined and intolerant of restraint. The IRA's refusal to engage now in a fair fight confirmed that the Irish lacked any real moral centre. The Irish didn't just need government. They needed the threat of a garrison.

He was back in Ireland in 1914. When talk of Home Rule had fomented riots in Belfast and the Ulster Volunteers prepared to resist any detachment of Ireland from the empire, Macready was sent to Belfast to take charge of the British troops in the city and prepare for the possibility of civil war. By then the Ulster Volunteers were armed. Macready's own chauffeur in Belfast had helped gather guns. When

Macready asked him about the prospect of Home Rule, it was clear the driver truly believed government in Dublin would have the Pope living in Dublin. Macready recommended his chauffeur save up for a tour of Italy, 'then decide if the Pope would leave it for a God-forsaken place like Dublin'.

Back then, Prime Minister Herbert Asquith had asked Macready how Ireland should be managed. Macready's advice was simple: 'Govern or get out.' What he now saw in Ireland in 1920 was a result of government's failure to do either. All the institutions of the state were in crisis. Ulster had been let drift. Even the RIC, once revered among all the police forces of the empire, was a weak shadow of its old self.

'This once magnificent body of men had undoubtedly deteriorated into what was almost a state of supine lethargy,' Macready wrote, 'and had lost even the semblance of energy or initiative when a crisis demanded vigorous and resolute action. The immediate reason was not far to seek. If an officer of whatever rank took upon himself to enforce the law, especially during the faction fights which are the popular pastime of the Irish, his action would as often as not be disavowed by the authorities at Dublin, on complaint being made to them by the Irish politicians by whose favour the Government held office.'

He saw the IRA as a difficult enemy but not as an army that made him fear the empire might recede from Irish shores. He sometimes recalled a story from the fight for Dublin Castle during the Easter Rising: at one point the rebels gained the outer yard of the Castle; at that moment only a thin line of British soldiers stood between the rebels and the whole place, with its documents and secrets, its symbolism and its flag. What had held the rebels back? To Macready, the answer was simple: their lack of soldiering. Their cowardice when faced by the bullet. He looked at Sinn Féin and the IRA in the same way now, hiding behind rocks and hills and hedgerows, posing as soldiers and harmless citizens, then unveiling their guns to wreak death and terror.

It had been an idle day in March 1920 when the telephone call came from Downing Street. Macready was lunching at The Garrick Club in London. The Prime Minister wanted to see him. Somehow Macready knew why. He had been shocked by the news of another assassination attempt the previous December on his old friend Lord French. The entry in Macready's diary that day was prophetic: 'Will Lloyd George want me to go there?'

David Lloyd George greeted Macready in the hall and led him to the dining room. He looked around the table, populated by politicians finishing a sumptuous lunch, and noted their plates stained with streaks of sauce, their wine glasses bearing a tiny pool of claret at the bottom. All the faces were familiar to him. Andrew Bonar Law was leader of the Commons and the Conservative Party, a veteran of the struggle to resist Irish Home Rule over the previous decade. Walter Long was First Lord of the Admiralty and former leader of the Irish Unionist Party, now chairman of the Cabinet's committee on Ireland.

Lord French was also there. If they knew Macready would rail against the idea of returning to Ireland, French was their ace card. Macready had been a loyal servant during World War One, serving as Adjutant-General of the British Expeditionary Force in France where French was Commander-in-Chief, and from 1916 as Adjutant General to the Forces, one of the most senior posts in the army. If French counselled him towards Ireland, they all knew Macready would listen.

Lloyd George skipped pudding and got straight to the point. He wanted Macready in Ireland. The military force there needed a good hand. The police were struggling to enforce even civil law. Lieutenant General Sir Frederick Shaw was Commander-in-Chief of the military, but following Sinn Féin's election triumph and the creation of the Dáil, Soloheadbeg and the gradual slide into naked violence across the country, Shaw wanted to impose full martial law. With a Home Rule Bill to process for Ireland, the government weren't ready to concede that much.

Macready's heart sank to his boots. At the end of the war in 1918 he had attended a similar meeting at Downing Street when Lloyd George asked him to become Commissioner of the Metropolitan Police at Scotland Yard. Macready was dismayed then. This felt worse and even more impossible to escape. Two different stints in Ireland gave Macready experience on the ground and his work in Scotland Yard made him the ideal person to coordinate the movements of the military and police. Indeed, Lloyd George said, if Macready thought it prudent, he could take charge of the RIC too. Macready frowned. 'The RIC needs the attention of one man,' he said.

As for the army, at least he would be back among soldiers. He looked to Lord French whose desire for Macready's presence in Ireland was the key. 'But for that, nothing would have induced me to return to a country to which I was never attracted,' Macready wrote, 'or to take up a task which I instinctively felt would be affected by every variation of the political weathercock, and in which it was doubtful any satisfactory result could be attained.'

His doubts were amplified that afternoon when he visited Winston Churchill at the War Office. Churchill, he noted, was unimpressed at Macready's appointment. Maybe he was annoyed at being excluded from the meeting. Then Macready found out that Churchill had someone else in mind for the job – Sir William Robertson. Old Wully had been Chief of the Imperial General Staff during the war and was a good friend of Macready's. If he had known that Churchill had Wully in mind, he would have spoken to French again and found a way to step aside.

But, as he sat now a few months later surveying the paper mounds on his desk in Dublin, detailing the mayhem and futile attempts to stamp out the banditry outside the Castle walls, as he scanned the newspapers with their flagrant headlines and provocative depiction of his men as demons against a plucky foe, he thought perhaps there was a certain pride in sparing his old friend this indignity. That was the only nobility he could find in his duty.

Macready had studied the terrain before he left for Dublin. He read a copy of future Sinn Féin leader Arthur Griffith's book, *The Resurrection of Hungary – A Parallel for Ireland*, to try to access Sinn Féin's soul. Griffith had written about abstentionism and the failure of engaging with parliamentary democracy in London. Years of Irish MPs had only resulted in stalemate. Griffith wished to return to the eighteenth-century arrangement between Britain and Ireland of two governments and a shared king.

Macready read on. The book had been written in 1904, a year before Sinn Féin was founded. There was no talk of revolt and murder here. For years afterwards Macready wondered if any of the politicians wringing their hands in despair in London and catching a fit of nerves at every outrage in the Irish countryside had ever taken the time to read it. What trouble it might have saved them all.

In London the jokes at The Garrick Club had already begun. 'Hello,' said one old friend, 'glad to see you're still alive.' One day he received a letter from Jack Cowans, his Quartermaster-General in the Metropolitan Police. 'What is this I see?' he wrote. 'Going to Ireland? Now *do* take care. The devils don't play cricket just now, and it's worse than strikes.'

Shortly before Macready left London, he accepted an invitation to lunch at the Palace with King George V and Queen Mary. They spoke about Ireland and ended a pleasant afternoon hoping better times would soon visit that troubled country. Macready politely hoped for the same, but he knew differently. The country didn't trust him. And he didn't trust the country.

Macready left for Dublin in April 1920 and sought meetings in Ireland with two key Irish Party MPs: Joe Devlin of Belfast and Captain William Redmond of Waterford, son of former Irish Party leader John. Neither deemed it politically prudent to meet him. Macready spread his net wider. He spoke to Dominican friars and lawyers, other churchmen and peers of the realm. He spoke in confidence to widows of some 1916 rebels. One woman in the street, who claimed lineage back to Cromwell, volunteered one solution: 'Shoot them all, General. Shoot them all.' An effective policy if it could have been carried to its logical conclusion, he thought.

In April 1920 the British army in Ireland numbered twenty thousand; they were under-strength and weakened by the war. Many junior officers were only partly trained. The infantry units were mainly tasked with guard duties, escorting prisoners and supporting beleaguered RIC stations and personnel in situations none of them were trained for.

'Mere children,' said Brigadier-General CB Thomson, military advisor to the British Labour Party Commission that toured Ireland in late 1920, 'reared on a diet of cake and chocolate. Don't blame these boys. Don't blame their officers but put the blame where it is due. Put it upon the policy which has turned Ireland into a place where violence reigns supreme; where a man's house or his church are not secure from violence.'

The numbers among the RIC were also dwindling. At the beginning of 1919, the RIC had 9,676 policemen across the country. Between then and June 1922 when the force was disbanded, 765 would be killed. Sixteen more would commit suicide.

The Soloheadbeg murder of two RIC men might have spooked the IRA's powerbrokers in Dublin, but it jumpstarted the rest of the movement. In January 1920, the RIC began committing more policemen to south Tipperary than anywhere else in the country. By November, the number had risen from 203 to 369, equating to one policeman for every 243 civilians. In 19 months, 12 barracks were attacked and 28 patrols ambushed. Twelve policemen were shot and 39 other sniping incidents were recorded. Over two thousand soldiers were committed to south Tipperary. While 51 Volunteers were killed in action, the Crown forces lost 114. In time each RIC barracks would have a gun in every room in case a policeman was cornered in an attack.

It had never been like this for the RIC. Since its establishment in 1822, the RIC had lived almost a century without too much fuss or tension. They looked after their own. RIC families tended to socialise together. When World War One began, over 700 RIC men joined the Irish Guards. The survivors came home to a different country, and a different life. Life as a policeman had traditionally passed like an heirloom from father to son. They now lived like outcasts in some parts of the country in a poorly paid job, living in fear for their lives as the IRA grew more ambitious and more audacious.

On 15 February 1920, Dan Hogan crouched in the darkness with his commandant Eoin O'Duffy and twenty other IRA men in a small village midway between Carrickmacross and Castleblayney close to the Monaghan-Cavan border, watching Ballytrain RIC barracks. The roads around the station were blocked by trees, the debris from a disused house and an iron gate. Telegraph and telephone wires had been cut. Bombs were made using gelignite stolen from Monaghan County Council.

Inside the barracks, the RIC men heard the sound of breaking glass. The IRA had taken positions in a shop nearby. A dog started barking furiously. Suddenly, a barrage of shots peppered the barracks from across the road. Another group of IRA men released a herd of cattle from a byre next door to the barracks and fired from there.

The RIC men returned fire and lobbed hand grenades across the road. More hand grenades came bouncing back into the barracks. The fighting lasted for three hours before the shooting stopped. A scratchy voice echoed from a megaphone across the road into the barracks. 'Surrender,' it said.

The RIC replied with even more firing. With the gelignite secured at the gable end of the barracks, the raiders played their most devastating card. Three long whistle blasts rang out. Everyone took cover. The bombs shattered the gable end of the barracks, sending an iron bedstead through the ceiling and furniture smashing through the house. A mass of sandbags exploded out onto the street. This time, the RIC men were ready to surrender. 'Throw out your arms quick,' shouted O'Duffy, 'or we'll fire the place.' The IRA men stormed in and raided the ammunition stores. Four RIC men lay injured. One constable told them there was £60 in a safe box, but asked them not to touch it. O'Duffy shrugged. 'We don't want your money,' he replied. 'It's too much money we have.' They only came, he told the policemen, for guns. One constable with serious leg injuries was helped onto a table. Another was placed carefully in a chair. O'Duffy found some bandages and told one of the policemen to fetch a doctor from Carrickmacross. He implored them to consider changing sides, but didn't stay to labour the argument. The most seriously injured constable was given a linen packet containing lint and religious emblems. With that, the IRA men disappeared and one RIC man set off on the lonely nine-mile walk to Carrickmacross.

The news spread across the country. It was the first time an RIC barracks had been taken by the IRA, and the attack amplified the worsening odds facing the average policeman. Providing extra police had already been proposed in September 1919 by the former Commander-in-Chief, Lieutenant General Sir Frederick Shaw. Britain's streets were filled with ex-servicemen struggling to find work and adapt to civilian life. Advertisements began appearing in *The Weekly Summary*, the official RIC newspaper, offering an escape route. Becoming a policeman in Ireland now promised good pay, uniform and allowances, free subsistence money when away from the station and a month's paid annual leave with a free railway pass from Ireland to home and back. Promotion was a serious possibility. There would be compensation for any wounds received and the highest pension payable to any police force in the United Kingdom. 'If you have the physique,' read the advert, 'if you have a good character, and especially, if you are an ex-service man, you can join the RIC today.'

The first new recruits appeared on the streets in Dublin in March 1920, a few weeks after the Ballytrain attack. They struggled to fit in from the beginning. They were army men trying to deal with civilians. Their training wasn't recalibrated to accommodate that change. Ireland initially seemed easy pickings, like walking the beat in a sleepy village somewhere in middle England. They assumed the IRA was a rabble, easy to disperse with some hard talking and the sight of a gun. All the years huddled together in the trenches as the earth shook above and below them insisted there was nothing left to frighten them. What they didn't realise was that nothing in the trenches could prepare them for Ireland. Even their khaki-coloured uniforms, sometimes combined with blue tunics, made them stand out from the regular RIC in their dark green uniform. A newspaper reporter in Limerick who saw a group of new recruits at the train station in Limerick Junction wrote how their clothes reminded him of the Black and Tans, the old Kerry Beagles that once ran with the Scarteen Hunt. The name stuck.

While the Tans were trained for the choreographed horror of trench warfare, the IRA's guerrilla attacks required a more nuanced approach. This enemy was invisible, hidden in the villages and towns and communities. The Black and Tans lit fires to smoke them out. IRA attacks were routinely followed by equivalent attacks and arrests in the same area. If an RIC barracks was attacked, a creamery or shop could get burned down. IRA suspects were lifted from the streets. Their families were harassed.

It was an ugly conflict on both sides. Any contact in the community with the RIC was brutally punished by the IRA. One man who acted as a taxi for the police had his car burned. Another was fined £10 for selling barbed wire to them. Women who stepped out with RIC men had their heads shaved. One police report described how an armed party took two girls from their home, marched them to an IRA court martial and accused them of 'walking with the Peelers'. They were sentenced to death, but had their punishment commuted to having their hair shaved off. Another report detailed a letter received by a policeman's widow that her house would be burned and she would be shot if she took another sergeant's wife as a lodger. Barracks servants and others who worked for the RIC were threatened with ejection from the area, or worse. One woman who took over as a barracks servant from another who had left owing to the boycott of the police, was lifted from her home one night and taken to a field; her hair was cut off and she was beaten by her captors. One night in August 1920, four IRA men entered a house and seized another woman. They held her by her hands and feet and covered her mouth. Then, they put three pig rings in her buttocks using pincers. Her crime was supplying the police with milk.

Threatening letters were sent to landlords with an English background. The owners of lodgings housing policemen and soldiers were targeted. Jurors were intimidated. Telegraph lines and telephone wires were cut. Mail was robbed. Republican courts were set up and an independent police force was established from within the IRA brigades in the summer of 1920. Without prisons to detain offenders, suspects were often simply banished from their parish or county. Others were detained in abandoned buildings in remote places.

When the IRA hit them, the Black and Tans tried to strike back even harder. In response to women's heads being shaved for associating with police, Black and Tans shaved the heads of local Sinn Féin leaders. Many of the new recruits drank hard. Their RIC superiors could fine and dismiss men if they breached the force's disciplinary code, but the shortage in police numbers made dismissals a rare occurrence. Fines didn't impact either on policemen being paid ten shillings a day with no designs on staying in Ireland longer than their one or two-year contract.

The Tans' revenge was often recklessly violent and aimed at the heart of the community. Creameries were a popular choice. These co-operatives, created and run by local people, were both a place of business in rural areas, reckoned in 1920 to be worth over a million pounds annually to the economy, and an important social hub. When the IRA shot policemen or raided barracks, the police wreaked their revenge by targeting everyone. They wanted the public to see how the IRA's actions could deprive them of their safety, their possessions and their lives.

On 24 August 1920, Shanagolden village in west Limerick was shattered by a grim episode of atrocity and reprisal that was repeated frequently across the country. After a group of Black and Tans set fire to the cheese shed beside the local creamery, one Black and Tan and another policeman were kidnapped by the IRA. Both men were forced to march through the village without their shoes.

That night, two Black and Tan trucks returned to Shanagolden. A house was burned out. At the top of the street an elderly man named Jack Hines was shot dead crossing the road on his way home for dinner. Some Tans entered the creamery and sprinkled petrol, leaving a five-gallon drum inside. Soon after they left, the creamery burst into flames. When it came to court, the co-operative was awarded £12,000 in damages. Over £4,000 worth of cheese, due for export to Britain, had been destroyed. Before its destruction, the creamery had served 200 farmers who supplied nearly 6,500 gallons of milk a day.

The story of Shanagolden was repeated throughout the country. On the night of 20 September, after an RIC policeman was shot, Black and Tans descended like a fog on the town of Balbriggan, County Dublin. A hosiery works employing 109 people and over 120 outside workers was burnt out. Shops, houses and pubs along the main street were set alight. Alcohol was looted from the pubs before they went up in flames. The locals escaped to the fields.

If a constable was kidnapped or disappeared, notices appeared in newspapers threatening dire reprisals. In 1920, a poster appeared on the walls around Tipperary town.

It occurred some time ago that some of our gallant RIC officers of Tipperary were cowardly murdered behind the hedges, not far from Tipperary, by Tipperary murderers. If the ambushes do not cease forthwith, Tipperary and district will be an ocean of blood, and you may take this as final warning.

If those cowardly murderers want a good fight they can come out from behind those hedges where they wait day and night to shoot down those innocent men.

It was in Tipperary town the murder started in 1919, when two innocent men were shot dead like dogs, and they did not even give them time to say a prayer or prepare to meet their God above. But remember that is not forgotten.

Any person pulling this notice down does so under penalty of death and destruction, and fire will follow.

Any person with his hands in his pockets will be shot at first sight.

A skull and crossbones was scratched out underneath. Many of the first Black and Tan recruits were Victoria Cross medal holders but left after a few months in Ireland, demoralised and repulsed by what was unfolding in front of them. For those left behind, there was no glory in Ireland either.

Homes, farms and shops across the country were routinely burned in response to IRA attacks. As military convoys cruised through towns, soldiers pointed their guns onto the street, cocked and ready. The intimidation in Tralee grew so bad and the damage to local offices so irreparable, the town council was forced to hold its meetings secretly in a small ravine near the town. A printing works was destroyed. Young men were cornered in the street and forced to denounce the Pope or spit on a picture of Éamon de Valera. Shops with Irish names printed over the door had the letters obliterated.

Husbands were threatened with violence against their wives. A journalist in Tralee returned home one evening to find his wife had been visited by an RIC officer and a Black and Tan who had threatened to shoot her husband. Lorries drove around with the Black and Tan flag fluttering, often with a tricolour or Sinn Féin flag tied to the back of the truck, trailing along the road. At night, above the growl of a lorry engine, people would often hear the same song outside their windows.

We are as happy, as happy as can be,
We are the boys of the RIC.

In June 1920 Lieutenant Colonel Bryce Ferguson Smyth, RIC Divisional Commander for Munster, made a speech in Listowel that reflected how the Black and Tans' sense of duty and discipline had become warped and distorted by Ireland.

Sinn Féin have had all the sport up to the present, and we are going to have the sport now,' he said. 'The police are not in sufficient strength to do anything to hold their barracks. This is not enough for as long as we remain on the defensive, so long will Sinn Féin have the whip hand. We must take the offensive and beat Sinn Féin at its own tactics ... If a police barracks is burned or if the barracks already occupied is not suitable, then the best house in the locality is to be commandeered, the occupants thrown into the gutter. Let them die there – the more the merrier.

Should the order ['Hands Up'] not be immediately obeyed, shoot

and shoot with effect. If the persons approaching (a patrol) carry
their hands in their pockets, or are in any way suspicious-looking,
shoot them down. You may make mistakes occasionally and innocent
persons may be shot, but that cannot be helped, and you are bound
to get the right parties some time. The more you shoot, the better I
will like you, and I assure you no policeman will get into trouble for
shooting any man.

A number of RIC officers resigned their commissions after the speech. Some joined the IRA. Less than a month later Smyth sat in his club in Cork city, sipping whiskey. Six men burst into the room. One of them stepped forward.

'Colonel, were not your orders to shoot on sight?' he said. 'Well, you're in sight now, so prepare.'

Six bullets pierced his head, heart and chest. He leapt at the gunmen and staggered to the hallway, where he fell dead. Another despatch for Macready's desk. Another step into anarchy.

CHAPTER 4

The Heritage of Hate

A new police force brings another kind of terror. Spies and hitmen track each other in the streets. A month of martyrs casts a long, inescapable shadow.

On 11 May 1920 DavidLloyd George, Sir Hamar Greenwood, Chief Secretary for Ireland, Nevil Macready, Winston Churchill and Field Marshal Sir Henry Wilson, Chief of the Imperial General Staff and an influential Irish unionist, convened to talk about the IRA. To combat a guerrilla war, Macready said, he needed the freedom to develop a more mobile army better suited to fight them.

Everyone else demanded something more provocative. Wilson suggested compiling a list of Sinn Féiners in every district and posting it on church doors across the area. 'Whenever a policeman is shot,' he said, 'pick five by the lot and shoot them … somehow or other terror must be met by greater terror.'

Churchill amplified the same theme. 'It is monstrous we have more than two hundred murders and no one hung. After a person is caught he should pay the penalty within a week. Look at the tribunals which the Russian [Bolshevik] government has devised. You should get three or four judges whose scope should be universal and they should move quickly over the country and do summary justice.'

Lloyd George seemed reluctant. 'You agreed six or seven months ago that there should be hangings,' said Churchill. Lloyd George now favoured increasing local rates and taxes to force the Irish to pay for the damage done to their own property. 'There's nothing the farmers so dislike as the rates,' he said. 'If they could be got to support the law, then you could deal with the terror.'

Churchill tried a different angle. He proposed recruiting 'a special force', one designed to 'make life intolerable in a particular area'. A letter from Churchill also landed on Macready's desk proposing the raising of a force drawn from thousands of ex-officers in Britain and attaching it to the RIC. Macready was reluctant. General Henry Hugh Tudor, chief adviser to the Police Services in Ireland, pushed the proposal again. It was a temporary force, he said, easy to train and quicker to install than reinforcing the RIC with more recruits like the Black and Tans.

With Tudor behind him, Churchill persisted. He reckoned over eight thousand men might be enough. Members of the new Auxiliary Division would earn a pound a day for a six-month contract that could be extended to one year; that was twice the wages of an RIC constable or a Black and Tan. That rate increased to a guinea a day in October 1920, and made them the highest-paid police force in the world.

An initial recruiting drive yielded five hundred men. In July 1920 the first Temporary Auxiliary Cadets received their dark blue uniform and glengarry cap bearing a harp insignia. They wore plus fours and a bandolier across their chests, a gun at their hip and a holster tied to their leg. They completed a six-week training course in the Curragh and each Auxiliary was given a rifle and forty rounds of ammunition, a revolver with fifty rounds and a bayonet.

In time 2,214 Auxiliaries would serve in Ireland along with nearly ten thousand Tans. Like the early Tan recruits, many of them had performed with distinction during the war. In October 1914 James Leach was in a party of twelve volunteers despatched to recapture a trench. A surprise bayonet attack killed eight German soldiers, injured two and yielded sixteen prisoners. George Onions was sent out with one man during battle to link up with a battalion that had become detached on the main force's right flank. As they made their way across the battlefield, a German force advanced on their position. Onions hunkered down and opened fire. Some of the Germans wavered and threw their hands up. By the end, Onions and his colleague had taken two hundred prisoners. James Johnson spent six hours repelling fire as his unit retreated and was the last to leave his position, carrying a wounded man. He went back three times to rescue more wounded men under heavy machine-gun fire. Leach, Onions and Johnson all received the Victoria Cross and ended up as Auxiliaries.

The Auxiliaries travelled the country in armoured cars and Crossley Tenders, a troop-transporting vehicle reinforced with one-and-a-half-inch steel plates along the sides, sometimes with chicken wire across the top of the vehicle to prevent bombs and grenades being hurled into the back. Brigadier General Frank Percy Crozier was appointed Commander of the Auxiliary Division of the RIC, and immediately faced a problem. The first recruits at the Curragh camp had racked up a bill of over £300 at a local pub. There was friction with the local RIC. To Crozier's eyes, the camp was in disarray. There was no provision for pay. Catering facilities were non-existent. There seemed an absence of any rule, regulation or routine. 'It all played into the hands of disorder,' said Crozier, 'before a shot was fired.' Crozier ordered the new Auxiliaries moved immediately to the Beggars Bush Depot in Dublin. He had a more sympathetic understanding of Ireland than Macready, but shared Macready's devotion to duty and a nagging suspicion about the men under his command.

Frank Crozier had spent tracts of his childhood in Dublin and his summer holidays in Limerick, walking a mile through the poorest streets of the city to church service every Sunday, ignoring the local children as they teased him for wearing a top hat. His family were military men, land agents, magistrates and landowners. His parents had met in Birr when his father was a soldier there. His grandfather, Percy, had been the local magistrate in Portumna, County Galway, and bore the dangers of his status easily and with good humour. When he told the story of returning early from petty sessions to find a coffin on the side of the road beside a roughly dug grave bearing his name, rank and position beneath a skull and crossbones, it was always softened by a macabre smile.

Sam Hussey was Crozier's granduncle. He was a prosperous land agent in Munster during the Land Wars of the late nineteenth century and spent his life being shot at or repairing the damage to his home near Tralee after another bomb attack from the Land Leaguers. Three policemen were constantly stationed at his home. A pack of dogs was unleashed on any suspicious visitors.

Crozier grew up in Dublin at Oatlands, near Castleknock. His family enjoyed the colonial life: dancing at the Castle, attending the races at Punchestown and shooting and fishing in Kildare and beyond. An Irish nurse cared for Frank at home. These were 'the bad eighties', a time of Fenians, dynamiters and moonlighters. Some nights his nurse would tell him about the Phoenix Park murders in 1882 of Lord Frederick Cavendish, the Chief Secretary for Ireland, and Thomas Burke, the Permanent Undersecretary. She showed him pictures of the killers in the lamplight, weaving their stories into his dreams. When Crozier and his nurse took the family carriage through the Park she would tell how his aunt's driver, O'Leary, had driven her brougham past the scene just before the murders occurred and how her head groom drove past with a luggage float soon after the killings.

When Crozier was older he told stories in England to try and illustrate some of the differences between the Irish and the English. He often retold the story of Biddy, who sold flowers from a basket in Limerick city and sometimes had kittens for sale. One morning the local Protestant rector passed by Biddy who offered him 'a good Protestant kitten'. He declined. Soon afterwards the local parish priest passed by. Biddy offered him 'a kitten of the true faith'. The priest also refused. Later in the day, the priest met the vicar. Biddy's kittens came up in conversation. The priest went back to confront her. 'You told his Protestant reverence the kitten was a Protestant,' he said. 'Ah,' said Biddy. 'It's had its eyes opened since then.'

He knew the Irish also had longer memories than any Englishman. John Stanhope, a friend of Crozier's, lived in Ireland till he was twenty-one. One day, on a visit to a well-heeled local farmer, Stanhope was shown a collection of large stones in a barn.

'These are the stones on which your English soldiers shot my kneeling countrymen not so long ago,' said the farmer.

'Nonsense,' said Stanhope. 'They don't do that sort of thing these days.'

'Yes, they did,' replied the farmer. 'In 1798.'

It all shaped Crozier for service in Ireland. So did war. He had fought in the Boer War and ascended the Spion Kop, the mighty hill that claimed 243 lives in one day. The brutality didn't faze him. He accepted war as a hellish existence and clung to the rule of duty to justify the coldness and cruelty it demanded. He deplored alcohol and watched some soldiers drink too much to try and escape their horrifying reality. His Auxiliaries were proving again that alcohol only imprisoned them in a different way.

He believed firmly in the union. When tensions in Ulster began to rise in 1913 he joined the British League for the Support of Ulster and the Union – and received a carbine in the post. At the same time as

Macready prepared the British army in Belfast to prevent civil war, Crozier was training a special unit of the Ulster Volunteers for any sudden military action. When the Great War broke out he fell back on old friends in Ulster to secure a position with the 9th Battalion of the Royal Irish Rifles, part of the 107th Brigade, 36th (Ulster) Division. These were the 'Shankill Road Boys'. He was their major.

It took three months to knock the politics and beer out of them, he told friends, and six more months to make them soldiers. They fought at Thiepval and through the Battle of the Somme. For all their flaws, the Shankill Road Boys followed Crozier into hell. Other officers saw them as an indisciplined rabble. Crozier admired them.

He was ferocious and reckless in battle. When the Battle of the Somme began on 1 July 1916, he flung himself into the fray, often ignoring orders. He constantly gathered raiding parties to attack German trenches. One lieutenant described the raids as showing off. Crozier, he said, was a 'callous and overbearing martinet'.

His superiors, though, liked his aggression. He was promoted to General Officer Commanding the 119th Brigade, 40th Divisions, going from the Shankill Road Boys to the Welsh Bantams. He surrounded himself with battalion commanders who shared his unstinting outlook on war. He refused one well-regarded officer a recommendation after a spell on the front line because he didn't hold the line with confidence or 'slaughter the enemy effectively'. He looked for men he could train into dogs of war. He knew people thought him mad. Some even called him a butcher, but his mind was hardened against loss. Nothing was more useless in war than a dead body. Losing a thousand men for a useful purpose, he said, was better than losing one for no reason at all.

He spent time in Lithuania after the war helping re-organise their shattered army and returned to England in March 1920. He had served with General Henry Tudor during the war in France. With Tudor now holding an influential post in Ireland, he enquired about work. Tudor remembered Crozier. The police needed fighters.

Crozier's post as head of the Auxiliaries militarised the police in Ireland in a way never imagined before. All their recruits were picked from the officer class, but the end of war had deprived them of work and status. Crozier sensed the conflict coming. These men were hardened soldiers. Before he had even left for Dublin, Crozier wrote to a cousin in Limerick.

'The difficulty is that Ireland likes a gentleman and is accustomed to be governed by gentlemen,' he replied. 'What are we in for?'

In May 1920, the situation was dire. While the RIC still held the towns, many rural barracks had been abandoned for the safety of the bigger urban stations. Atrocities against the RIC were widespread. While the IRA disappeared after every attack, the reprisals from the Tans against the public left out in the open were ferocious.

Imposing full martial law on Ireland had been discussed in early 1919 after Soloheadbeg, but the government was tortured by the idea that such draconian measures might be required to keep peace in the part of the empire closest to Westminster. Macready supported the idea in theory, but insisted he didn't have the men to enforce it properly. Neither did he trust that any politician in London had the conviction to see martial law through to its frequently brutal conclusions.

His concerns about the failure of his own government to grasp the political reality in Ireland were shared by others. 'Lloyd George is under the ridiculous belief that for every one of our people murdered, two Sinn Féiners were murdered, and he was gloating over this and hugging it to his heart as a remedy for the present disgraceful state of Ireland,'

Sir Henry Wilson wrote in his diary that July. 'I told Lloyd George that the authorities were gravely miscalculating the situation but he reverted to his amazing theory that someone was murdering two Sinn Féiners to every loyalist the Sinn Féiners were murdering. I told him that this was not so, but he seemed to be satisfied that a counter murder association was the best answer to Sinn Féin murders.'

Macready urged politicians and other influential people in Britain to visit Ireland and try to grasp a different reality. It wasn't a warzone, he said, but a different battleground to anything Britain had encountered before. In Ireland, a soldier was never off duty. After two small detachments were held up by civilians Macready issued an order that troops should consider themselves on active service when on duty, 'and to use their weapons with effect regardless of results'.

When off duty, officers were ordered to carry revolvers and travel in small groups. Macready always had an automatic pistol on his knee when in his motor car, and in the right-hand pocket of his coat when walking in the Phoenix Park or about town. 'An automatic pistol,' he wrote, 'became as constant and as friendly a companion as a watch.'

He dealt with orchestrated petty interruptions. When the dock labourers aligned to the ITGWU and railway staff refused to handle military stores, Macready reassigned soldiers to the docks and redeployed military motor transport to move their supplies. That lasted for six months. In July 1920, after military mail was robbed from the GPO, Macready threatened to stop all horse racing in the country if another letter was stolen. The theft ceased immediately.

In August, as a coal miners' strike in Britain threatened to turn violent, patrol duties in Ireland were reduced and troops kept close to barracks in case they were required to travel back to England. That gave the IRA even greater freedom to operate. As the Black and Tans continued to cause mayhem Macready requested a different uniform for them so they couldn't be mistaken for the army in their khaki-coloured clothes.

He never disguised his distaste for the Black and Tans, but reprisals were hard to avoid in the circumstances.

'The machinery of law having been broken down,' he told the *Freeman's Journal*, 'they feel there is no certain means of redress and punishment. It is only human they should act on their own initiative.'

Outside the daily drone of atrocities and reprisals, progress was being made in handling the IRA. The administration at Dublin Castle itself had been reorganised. After Macready requested more military and technical personnel, seven fresh battalions arrived from England plus a complete divisional staff by the end of July.

In August 1920 the government passed the Restoration of Order in Ireland Act, giving Macready power as head of the military to dispense justice. It still fell disconcertingly between the two stools of martial and civil law. Trial by jury was replaced by court martial only in places where the IRA were highly active. Courts martial also extended to capital offences.

Military courts of inquiry replaced public coroners' inquests. Arrests increased and more IRA men disappeared on the run. Having previously relied on large numbers of part-time rebels, the IRA was now strengthened by a new cohort of full-time guerrillas. Although civil courts also had their powers strengthened, no amount of legislation could ensure the co-operation of civilian witnesses as long as people lived in fear of offending both sides.

In September 1920, Macready wrote to Sir Hamar Greenwood, the Chief Secretary for Ireland. It was time, he said, for full martial law throughout the country, bringing the police and military 'under one authority, the police being in that case subordinate to the military, whereas today the military merely act in aid of civil power and are continually being placed in difficult or embarrassing positions'.

Failing that, he proposed the Government acknowledge that 'a status of insurrection exists in Ireland, that organised rebel forces are in active opposition to the government and that peace cannot be restored without military measures such as would be taken under martial law.' He proposed internment of suspects after any outrage, 'under conditions similar to those [of] prisoners of war in concentration camps, until such time as the condition of the country admitted of their release'.

Greenwood issued an order that, in the event of an outrage, a maximum of twelve IRA members should be summarily arrested. It was a weak, futile response. Dublin Castle was also locked down: identification cards with photographs were issued to those with business in the Castle; the square at its heart was illuminated by headlights every night as raiding parties came and went.

The one hundred men of the F Company of the Auxiliaries were billeted there. Their rooms were an extraordinary sight and bore testament to the different origins and backgrounds stitched together to form the force. There were airmen in full uniform, highlanders in kilts, naval officers and soldiers with different uniforms bearing insignias from across the world. Some of them did wear the RIC blue tunics with the letters TC – 'temporary cadet' – but only the glengarry cap seemed common to them all.

For all the IRA's terrorising of the RIC and the Black and Tans, these Auxiliaries rarely looked flustered. DMP Constable David Neligan, an informant for Michael Collins, told a story of how a group of Auxiliaries raided City Hall in broad daylight when they ran out of cash and left with thousands of pounds.

He often recalled one Auxiliary who wore a colonel's epaulettes and seemed to get frogmarched every night by his men to a lorry. 'He was so drunk he could not proceed under his own steam,' Neligan said, 'but at the same time insisted on going out to look for the "damn Shinners".'

The Auxiliaries were proving the IRA's stiffest foe. They patrolled the streets in open lorries. Most of the bombs hurled at them by the IRA were homemade. Few made any impact. 'I saw an open military lorry that had just been bombed,' said Neligan. 'Two grenades had exploded inside the vehicle. The occupants were not even scratched. From beginning to end, not one serious attack was launched on the Castle Auxiliaries.'

The Castle was also starting to get inside the IRA's mind. In May 1920 a Combined Intelligence Service under General Sir Ormonde Winter began collating and streamlining any incoming information. After a short course at a school in Hounslow, London, the first group of spies were on the ground in Ireland by early summer. They ranged from war heroes and regular soldiers to veterans of the intelligence services deployed in Europe during the war.

Between sixty and a hundred agents were sent to Ireland in the following nine months. At first they took their time acquainting themselves with Dublin. They mingled around the Cairo Café near Grafton Street and the local bars. Agents created new identities and blended into local communities, soaking up information on suspected IRA men.

Occasionally they struck with the same sudden ferocity as the IRA. In September 1920 John Lynch, a Sinn Féin councillor from Limerick, came to Dublin to pass on £23,000 in subscriptions to Michael Collins, and was shot dead in a Dublin hotel. The official inquiry said he was killed by British forces acting in self-defence. One of Dublin Castle's new spies, Henry Angliss, was among those suspected of killing him.

Policemen from across the country were brought to Dublin to spot suspects. Just as Collins had organised the IRA's intelligence and military wings, Dublin Castle now had its Auxiliaries, its Black and Tans and its own moles burrowed deep and out of sight.

On 12 October 1920 the noose started tightening around Sean Treacy and Dan Breen. News reached them of a possible raid on Fleming's,

their safe house in Drumcondra. They moved to Carolan's, beside St Patrick's teacher-training college, to escape detection, but a mixed group of army and intelligence men were already on their trail.

The attack came that night. Two officers were killed in the shoot-out. Professor John Carolan, who lectured at St Patrick's, was shot by the raiders and later died from his wounds. As Treacy provided covering fire, Breen dropped out of a first-floor window through the glass conservatory below. With no shoes on, his toes were broken and his feet and legs severely cut. Treacy leapt through the hole made by Breen. They split up and somehow made their escape.

Two days later Paddy O'Daly, the head of Collins's Squad, visited Treacy at Holland's, his new safe house on Silverdale Terrace. Treacy was lying on the sofa. Mrs Holland had just finished dressing his feet, injured by splinters and shards of glass. Treacy was anxious to meet with Dick McKee, head of the IRA's Dublin Brigade, to talk about Breen's safety as he recovered in the Mater Hospital. O'Daly promised to bring McKee to him, but Treacy was adamant.

Treacy first cycled to the North Wall and, unnoticed and unimpeded, watched the funerals of the men he had shot in Drumcondra. Afterwards he headed down to Boland's tailors shop in the city centre. On their first ever night in Dublin, Treacy and Seamus Robinson had arrived at Kathleen Boland's doorstep soaked from the rain and starving. Her brother, Harry, was one of Michael Collins's closest, most trusted men. They had travelled to Lincoln together the previous year to help Éamon de Valera escape from jail. Boland was also MP for South Roscommon and Sinn Féin's special envoy to America.

Now Treacy wanted to return Harry's bike. Kathleen was in the shop when he arrived.

'Do you not want it?' she asked.

'That bike could give me away as well as yourselves,' he replied. He ran his finger under the words scratched on the saddle with a pin: H Boland, 64 Middle Abbey Street.

Kathleen smiled. Although Breen and Treacy cut a cavalier dash around town, Treacy always tended the details. Things were pressing on his mind that morning. He was worried about Breen. His feet were sore. Treacy also missed the glasses he lost during the shoot-out. He crossed Sackville Street to the Republican Outfitters drapery store on Talbot Street. The shop was run by Peadar Clancy, second-in-command of the Dublin Brigade after Dick McKee, and was a highly visible hangout for republicans and IRA men.

When Treacy arrived, the shop was inordinately full of influential people. Paddy O'Daly was there with Joe Leonard and Tom Keogh, talking with Clancy about organising a guard for Breen in hospital. When Keogh, Leonard and O'Daly left for lunch in a favourite place of theirs on Bessboro Avenue, they tried to convince Treacy to come with them. It'd be the usual order: a full fry and teas all round. But Treacy wanted to wait for McKee. Clancy reckoned he should leave. There were too many people there, he said, too many chances someone had been followed. Treacy insisted on staying.

McKee eventually arrived. Clancy had already contacted Sean Brunswick, an IRA Volunteer, and instructed him to put a man on Breen's door at the Mater Hospital. Soon after 3.30pm, Brunswick called to the shop. McKee told him to get more armed guards to the hospital. Before he left, Brunswick remarked he had seen someone loitering suspiciously outside the shop. He hadn't reached the end of the street when he heard the whine of a Crossley Tender.

Two trucks and an armoured car stopped outside. Soldiers and Auxiliaries leapt down with fixed bayonets and created a cordon around Republican Outfitters. Those still inside the shop briefly considered the best way to leave. They didn't know what awaited them outside. Maybe arrest. Maybe death.

If staying in Ireland after the killings at Soloheadbeg was Treacy's most striking expression of self-determination, then he couldn't betray those principles now. Sean Brunswick stood on the corner. He watched McKee walk swiftly out the front door. Treacy followed him and quickly tried to mount a bicycle parked on the footpath, but the saddle was too high.

Gilbert Price, a twenty-five-year-old Auxiliary cadet sergeant from Lewisham near London was sitting in the truck, dressed in plain clothes. He had watched Treacy all day. When he saw Treacy emerge, he jumped down and walked towards him.

'That's Treacy,' he shouted.

Another officer, Frank Christian, pulled Treacy off the bike. Treacy drew his gun and fired. Christian was hit. Price charged at Treacy, held his pistol arm and forced him to the ground. They wrestled violently. More shots rang out. Treacy was forcing the barrel inwards towards Price. Having been hit by his first shot, Price was starting to weaken. The rest of the raiding party suddenly opened fire. Treacy dropped to the ground. Price slumped on top of him, dead.

A woman from the Globe restaurant nearby ran to Marlborough Street to fetch a priest. In the commotion Brunswick slipped through the crowd and crouched over Treacy. He was already dead. He rifled through Treacy's pockets, took some ammunition and pens, despatches and a field message book, and stuffed them into his jacket. All around him soldiers and Auxiliaries held the crowd back. 'Come on, you Irish bastards!' shouted one of them. 'We'll give you war!'

A handful of Auxiliaries raided Republican Outfitters. The street outside echoed with shrieks of shock. Patrick Carroll, a fifteen-year-old messenger boy for Gilbey's liquor store, was standing in the doorway when a stray bullet struck the door jamb and ricocheted through his head, sending him flying back through the shop. Another bullet injured a DMP constable. A bullet hit Joseph Corringham, a tobacconist with a shop near Liberty Hall, in the stomach. He crashed against a bicycle parked on the kerb and fell to the ground, dead. Bullets smashed through shop windows and ricocheted off the Masterpiece Cinema beside Republican Outfitters. The girl in the ticket kiosk outside crouched down in terror.

The following day's newspapers were dominated by stories and photos of the shootings on Talbot Street. Pictures of a man lying dead on the street went around the world, but no one knew his name. For a day, Sean Treacy was simply 'the man in the fawn coat'.

Two days after the shooting, Treacy's body was released from Ship Street barracks and taken to the Pro-Cathedral on Marlborough Street. By then, word had spread about his identity. The reaction among IRA men was predictable. In Treacy they had lost a rare leader. Many of his men in Tipperary compared his clarity of vision, determination and ruthless commitment to that of Michael Collins.

Dan Breen, still lying in the Mater, had lost a neighbour, a travelling companion, a mentor and his best friend. 'People were always telling Sean as he left their houses, "Be careful this time, Sean",' said Breen. 'His reply always was "The other fellas better be more careful." That meant that he would fight to the end – no matter what the odds.'

The following morning Treacy's coffin was placed on a train leaving Dublin for Limerick Junction. From there it was taken to Soloheadbeg church, completing the grim circle that began behind a hedge at the local quarry. The military maintained a significant presence but never interfered. A Republican flag was draped on the coffin. As it was removed from Limerick Junction station, a party of soldiers even presented arms.

They didn't intervene either the following day at the funeral in Kilfeacle village when three IRA men stepped forward and fired a volley over the grave. The only trouble came when armlets worn by the pallbearers were ripped off by a group of soldiers and a cluster of bicycles was taken. The commanding officer, Colonel Wilson, promised the bicycles would be returned to the owners if they came to the military barracks in Tipperary town with a photograph of themselves and a statement written on the back, signed by the District Inspector, stating they were 'known to the police to be a law-abiding citizen'.

The stories that took flight within the IRA proved how the intelligence services were getting closer to them. Some were convinced Treacy was tailed from Boland's shop by a policeman sent from Tipperary. Kathleen Boland wondered for years afterwards whether he might have escaped if he'd had Harry's bicycle, or if he might have spotted the tail if he were wearing his glasses.

The screw was being tightened everywhere. When Terence MacSwiney, the Lord Mayor of Cork, imprisoned in Brixton, died on hunger strike on 25 October, Macready blocked the passage of his body from Dublin to Cork by train. MacSwiney was instead transported south by steamer. A few days later the Archbishop of Dublin, William Walsh, came to Macready seeking clemency for Kevin Barry, a teenager arrested during an IRA attack, court martialled and sentenced to death. Macready pointed out that three soldiers had been killed in the same attack while collecting bread from a van. Much had been made in the press of Barry being aged just eighteen. Macready said one of those killed by the IRA was even younger than Barry. He was hanged on 1 November. In the space of a month, Ireland had three more martyrs.

Stories and songs were written and sung for them. Over a year after Soloheadbeg had been condemned as an atrocity, many newspapers reported IRA attacks and casualties in a more sympathetic way. The battlefield had changed, and their shared story had ended a long way from where it began in the hearts and minds of thousands.

PART II

GAELIC FOOTBALL IN DUBLIN AND TIPPERARY, AND THE RISE OF THE GAA 1884–1920

CHAPTER 5

A New Force

The man with the GAA in his hands. Luke O'Toole's battles with Tipperary and the Castle. Striking a blow on Gaelic Sunday. New challenges emerge from the footballers of south Tipperary.

JANUARY 1905–FEBRUARY 1919

Luke O'Toole lived in a small house on Albert Villas on the north side of Dublin beside Croke Park with the future of an entire cultural and sporting movement in his hands. From his back window, he could see the pitch roll out in front of him. The Long Stand was on the left, sitting on top of the solid brick unit that housed his office and the dressing rooms. Behind the goal backing onto the railway track was the Hill 60 terrace, named after a battle involving Irish troops at Gallipoli (renamed Hill 16 in the 1930s to commemorate the Easter Rising). On the other side of the field a bank rose to the wall separating Croke Park from the Belvedere sports grounds. The rest of the ground was growing into a monument to the Gaelic Athletic Association's growth and O'Toole's thrift.

He lived for the GAA. As full-time secretary, his career existed because of the GAA. His wife, Bridget, looked after their eight children and helped in O'Toole's office, doing some typing and administrative work while he travelled the country nurturing and protecting the association's roots. She also took care of the little jobs on the big days. When Croke Park needed extra seating to accommodate demand for the 1913 All-Ireland football final between Kerry and Louth, Bridget borrowed chairs from their neighbours and lined them up along the sidelines. The games were their love and their life. O'Toole had moved to Dublin from Wicklow before he was twenty-five and bought two newsagent's shops on the south side of the city: one on Charlemont Street, the other on Rathmines Road. He played Gaelic football and hurling for Benburbs of Donnybrook before moving to the newly formed Hibernians in 1898. He shared a house on Mountpleasant Avenue with his brother, Hugh, and their sister, Elizabeth. Business was good, but the GAA was already consuming all of O'Toole's time.

The creation of the GAA in 1884, alongside bodies like the Gaelic League and other organisations dedicated to Irish literature and language, was part of a revolution designed to revive Ireland's cultural identity. Its playing rules, written by the GAA's first President, Maurice Davin, and formalised in January 1885, were well established by 1900. Clubs had been formed in parishes everywhere. County boards and provincial councils governing Munster, Leinster, Ulster and Connacht had been elected to run games and competitions and administer the rules of the association. County teams were established in hurling and Gaelic football selected from the best club players in the region. The provincial championships and All-Ireland finals drew extraordinary crowds. By the end of the nineteenth century, the GAA was a visibly distinct expression of Irishness. To progress further, it now had to bring the fight to the competition.

As attendances continued to increase, the GAA needed to develop better venues and push on with the business of recruiting more members. Its first great statement of intent was appointing O'Toole as full-time secretary in 1901. For the first three years his desk at home in Ranelagh teemed with paper. In 1904 the GAA procured offices at 68 Sackville Street. O'Toole moved everything across town, and left his newsagents behind for good.

He travelled the country in those first few years, visiting newly founded county boards and clubs. All-Ireland final gate receipts were breaking records as crowds increased every year. Having started out in 1901 nursing an £800 debt, O'Toole oversaw its transformation into a £670 profit by the end of 1905. He promoted the spread of Gaelic games to America and Britain, Argentina and Australia. Over five thousand people watched England and Scotland play an international hurling game in Liverpool that year. O'Toole refereed the match, and the series was maintained for the next twenty years.

As much as he sought to bring people in, he also advocated keeping some people out. In 1902 the GAA invoked a policy of non-involvement by its members in other sports. 'The ban' threatened a two-year suspension on any member caught playing soccer, hockey, cricket or 'other imported games'. On his trips to London, O'Toole found a kindred spirit in Michael Collins. In 1907 Collins was eighteen, working for the Royal Mail and secretary of the Geraldines GAA club. To him, Gaelic games were the natural companion to his political beliefs. Other sports acted like a Trojan horse, allowing what Collins called 'the peaceful penetration of Ireland' by Britain. The ban helped the GAA articulate things they could never publicly say themselves.

With their finances in a healthy state, the GAA began giving grants to counties organising schools competitions. The playing rules were tightened up even more. Having struggled frequently to run their competitions off within the calendar year, everything was up-to-date by 1909. Even O'Toole's annoyance at the lack of media coverage for Gaelic games was eased by the launch of *The Gaelic Athlete* newspaper in 1912.

Buying their own grounds in 1913 was the great leap forward. Frank Dineen, who had once served as GAA secretary, owned a site on Jones's Road near the Royal Canal on the north side of the city, and already granted the GAA use of the grounds. O'Toole believed investing in this stadium would double as an expression of the GAA's good health and a way to secure their future – but not everyone saw it that way.

In 1913 the GAA also decided to honour the late Thomas Croke, Archbishop of Cashel and Emly and the GAA's first patron, by erecting a monument in Thurles, County Tipperary. O'Toole organised the Croke memorial tournament, a knockout competition in hurling and football between the country's top county teams. He expected to raise between five and seven hundred pounds, but crowds thronged to the matches, pushing the final tally to £2,400.

With so much money, the GAA started thinking bigger than a monument. The purchase of Dineen's grounds on Jones's Road was proposed. The Tipperary County Board were incensed. They demanded the money be spent on the Croke Memorial which had been promised to Tipperary. O'Toole travelled to Thurles for a meeting with the presiding Archbishop, John Harty.

Instead of attending the meeting himself, Harty sent his administrator, Fr Michael Bannon. O'Toole didn't react to this apparent snub, and laid out his own compromise. Instead of a monument, the GAA offered to erect a marble altar and a stained-glass window in Thurles cathedral. The cathedral was already sufficiently stocked with windows and altars, Bannon replied. The clergy had other ideas. In exchange for withdrawing their objections to investing the money in Jones's Road, the Tipperary County Board and the diocesan office wanted a bronze statue of Archbishop Croke erected on Thurles's Liberty Square and a generous donation from the GAA to help rebuild the local confraternity hall which had been destroyed by fire. The original building had been built with the GAA's assistance in 1901. Something between three and six hundred pounds would do, Fr Bannon said.

O'Toole returned to Dublin with their proposal. The GAA's Central Council, its main governing body, agreed to spend some of the tournament money on the statue. Another £300 was set aside for the hall. The rest would be invested in buying their new stadium, which would be called Croke Memorial Park.

The agreement allowed a brief cessation of hostilities. But when construction of the monument was delayed, Tipperary County Board took legal action in January 1914 to stop the GAA spending any more money from the Croke Memorial Fund on Croke Park. It seemed an act borne of raw temper, but O'Toole's previous battle with Tipperary had taught him the value of prudence. In 1902, when Clonmel Shamrocks were refused a £10 payment by the GAA to cover expenses incurred by an overnight stay in Dublin for the All-Ireland football final, they got a court order against O'Toole and seized £7/10d worth of his personal property. This time the GAA increased their donation to £1,200, with the confraternity hall now renamed Croke Memorial Hall. Still, the argument rumbled on longer than the looming war. When the Great War broke out, the use of bronze in Ireland was outlawed except for government-approved initiatives. On top of that, the designer employed by the GAA to create the statue was conscripted for war work. In the end, the foundation stone wasn't officially laid in Liberty Square until St Patrick's Day, March 1920. Tipperary finally had its monument. By then O'Toole also had Croke Park.

O'Toole's fights with Tipperary were only one part of a difficult battlefield complicated by multiple fronts and constantly shifting flanks. Different shades of green had jostled for power in the GAA since its inception. Militant groups like the Irish Republican Brotherhood saw the GAA as the perfect vehicle to gather support and members. The Home Rule movement saw it as an equally potent vote-getter.

Although it adopted an apolitical stance in public, the GAA's very genesis was rooted in nationalism. O'Toole privately saw Sinn Féin as the way forward. Like the GAA, it fostered a distinct sense of Irish identity. Its existence wasn't based on attending parliament or adapting to British law; it lived outside all that. It was Irish and stubbornly independent. When the Irish Volunteers were formed in November 1913 at a monster meeting in the Rotunda rink, O'Toole was the GAA's representative and among those who addressed the crowd.

Soon after, the GAA received a request to support the Volunteers publicly. The GAA's most prominent leaders were all sympathetic towards the Volunteers, and almost every nationalist outlet had issued some support for the Volunteer concept, but none of the GAA's leaders wanted an intrinsically sporting organisation dragged into a political corner. Their solution had O'Toole's fingerprints all over it. O'Toole recognised the need to keep the GAA neutral, thus the GAA wouldn't support the Volunteers in public – but GAA members wouldn't be censured for starting local Volunteer groups either. It satisfied their nonpartisan identity in public, but their roots were entangled with militant republicanism below ground.

Although O'Toole avoided any public connection with the Volunteer movement, a rash of arrests among the GAA's ruling classes after the Easter Rising made O'Toole worry they might come for him, too. Many of the key 1916 leaders were regular visitors to his house. Tom Clarke and Seán MacDiarmada from O'Tooles GAA club had often moved among the crowds during matches in Croke Park seeking like-minded people to fight for independence. JJ Walsh was chairman of the Cork County Board and fought alongside James Connolly in the GPO. Harry Boland played hurling for Dublin and chaired the

Dublin board and also fought in Dublin that week. Collins fought in the GPO and was sent to jail in Stafford.

O'Toole took his family to his homeplace in Ballycumber, near Tinahely in south Wicklow. It was a beautiful place tinged with history. The old oaks in the nearby Tomnafinnoge Woods had been chopped down centuries before to build some of the greatest structures on both islands: the chapel at King's College in Cambridge, Westminster Abbey in London, and Trinity College and St Patrick's Cathedral in Dublin. The family farm was hidden high in the Wicklow mountains, overlooking the valley of Ballinglen. From the side of the mountain he could see all the approach roads in the valley below. A river that threaded around the bottom was only passable at certain unmarked points too. If O'Toole needed to make a quick getaway, the mountain would buy him time.

They stayed three weeks. O'Toole returned to Dublin faced with bans imposed by the railway companies on special trains to ferry extra passengers to GAA matches, and a Castle administration that saw the GAA as an irritant. Political groups were also finding a fresh momentum. In 1917, a year after the Rising, Sinn Féin gathered in the Mansion House for an open weekend forum entitled 'Completely Independent Ireland'. It was a weekend of renewal and rebirth for the party, when the energy generated by the return of prisoners from jails across Britain and the lingering resentment over the killing of the Rising leaders could be harnessed. Croke Park was borrowed for a meeting of the Volunteers, their first since 1915. Over nine hundred people gathered in the grandstand. A small platform was erected using straw bales. Éamon de Valera, Michael Collins and Terence MacSwiney were among those on the platform. Later that year, Harry Boland carried the Volunteer flag in front of the parade around Croke Park before the 1917 All-Ireland football final between Wexford and Clare. If any doubt had previously existed, the GAA was now identified intimately with the political and military wings of the independence movement.

In July 1918 Cumann na mBan, the Volunteers, Sinn Féin and the Gaelic League were all classed as illegal organisations and a new law insisting that all public gatherings required an official permit threatened to upset the GAA fixtures schedule completely. On 28 July matches in Croke Park were stopped by police. Nine boys were arrested in the Phoenix Park for playing football.

The GAA responded by ignoring the new law and issuing its own directive: no permits would be sought by any member or unit of the GAA under threat of indefinite suspension. No member would participate in any event for which a permit had been secured. Every county board was ordered to convene a special meeting inside ten days to arrange a series of matches without permit, all to take place simultaneously on 4 August at 3pm. The GAA called it 'Gaelic Sunday'.

Games were fixed all over the country. Thousands of players and spectators turned out for games and left some vivid scenes behind. In Kilkenny, police surrounded a pitch in Mullinavat before the appointed hour, but the hurling game was taking place two miles away. In Galway, Ballinderreen travelled to Ardrahan for another hurling game. When police surrounded the pitch, players leapt ditches and hurdled drains to escape to another field. The crowd followed, and the game went ahead.

Twenty-four games were played across Dublin at different locations. When the RIC and troops prevented entrance to Croke Park, the crowd were treated instead to a game of camogie on the road outside. The notice published in the newspapers the previous day predicted that '54,000 Gaels will actively participate in national pastimes all over Ireland'. Estimates after Gaelic Sunday put the actual figure closer to 100,000. It was sufficient show of strength for the authorities to allow the GAA the leeway they required.

Three years after the Rising, the visitors to O'Toole's house also reflected the changing complexion of the country's politics. On Sunday nights in the winter Luke often heard a knock on the door around nine. Some nights it was Michael Collins. As time went on, it was Sean Treacy or Dan Breen. Eoin O'Duffy's first meeting with Collins was convened in O'Toole's front parlour. They spent nights swapping gossip and playing Twenty-five. Bridget made tea and the players often ribbed O'Toole that they stayed for her cakes, not the cards.

As the months passed and the country tumbled deeper into conflict, the chats got darker. Some nights an IRA man on the run might tumble in the back yard in Albert Villas looking for sanctuary. Apart from the games, the GAA was always the vehicle for ideas, its direction determined by its members. Many members now stood in open defiance of the law. O'Toole was playing cards with wanted men. Much of the GAA's future was now tied to theirs.

The Tipperary County Board met for their annual convention on 5 April 1919 after a harsh year and facing a difficult future. Soloheadbeg had turned the county upside down. Most of Tipperary was now deemed a Special Military Area. Fr MK Ryan, chairman of the board, addressed the delegates in grim terms.

'The year 1918 has been a year of difficulty for the GAA in Tipperary and elsewhere,' he said. 'No one knew what was going to happen but nevertheless the games went on regardless of obstacles. When we started we had no knowledge whether we would finish the championships on the hurling or football pitch or on the battlefields of Ireland, but we were prepared for the worst. The cloud hangs yet, the country still suffers and is content to suffer with the unflinching courage of the Gael.'

Remarkably, their football team was a shining source of hope.

Although Tipperary had been among the early forces in football after the GAA was founded, they had slipped away from the front of the pack a long time ago. Their last Munster football title was won in 1902 and they had reached only one Munster final since. In contrast, the Tipperary hurlers had won eleven Munster titles since the first Munster championship in 1887 and eight All-Ireland titles. Hurling dominated the county, but in 1918 the footballers had struck a staggering blow. 'To everyone's surprise they turned out [a team] that astonished all Gaeldom,' said Fr Ryan. 'As gallant a team and led by as gallant a captain as ever donned a jersey.'

Their captain, Ned O'Shea from Fethard, was sitting among the delegates. It had been a year that astounded them all. Even him. When the 1918 Munster football championship had begun, Tipperary met Cork in the first round on a boiling hot day in June with everyone making a familiar set of predictions: the game would be a useful test for Cork before playing Kerry in the Munster final; Tipperary could concern themselves with hurling.

But this team was different. A new generation of players had emerged, moulded and steeled by the fierce matches waged in Grangemockler and Fethard, Mullinahone and the other villages and fields of south Tipperary. Dan Hogan had been lost to Monaghan, but others took his place. Gus McCarthy from Fethard played corner-forward for Tipperary, a cerebral genius and the team's inspiration. O'Shea was their captain and anchor at full-back.

Jimmy McNamara from Cahir had declined a chance to play soccer with Glasgow Celtic to stay with Tipperary. Standing at just 5ft4in, his speed and his sidestep allowed him survive the worst intentions of most defenders. He added a body swerve and dummy, and mastered the foot-to-hand solo, sweeping upfield with a panache that quickly made him a hero. Arthur Carroll was a great goalkeeper. Jerry Shelly from Grangemockler was a tough corner-back and, like O'Shea, a leader.

They set about Cork like no Tipperary team had managed for years. Davy Tobin from Mullinahone kicked a good goal and Tipperary won by six points, 1-5 to 0-2. Word spread around Munster of a truly great game. But people still wondered how bad Cork must have been.

Three weeks later Tipperary met Waterford in the semi-final at Clonmel, kept them scoreless and won by five goals. The public still saw Tipperary's resurgence as an aberration. Kerry would correct that. In football's developing landscape, Kerry represented the summit. They were innovators and inveterate winners. In 1903, a year after Tipperary's last Munster title, Kerry had won their first All-Ireland. Ten Munster titles and five All-Ireland titles had followed. Their rivalry with Cork was already formed and everyone else tilted helplessly at them, like a group of Don Quixotes battling vainly against an immovable windmill.

But in 1918, for once, the balance was weighted severely against Kerry. Many of Kerry's best footballers were also Volunteers and had been interned after the Easter Rising. They hadn't competed in the Munster championship for two years. That should have given everyone else a chance, but Kerry still crushed Clare by four goals in their semi-final, matching anything Tipperary did against Waterford.

The Munster final was fixed for Cork in September. While they waited and trained, Ned Egan, Tipperary's great centre-back, picked up an injury. Starting without Egan seemed too much ground to yield against Kerry, but the game turned back in their favour before it even began. The pitch in Cork was heavy. Tipperary were a strong, young team that relied on good defence. A soft pitch suited them. Kerry, with their fast-moving forwards, thrived on hard ground, not boggy, sticky conditions.

It gave Tipperary a foothold in the game. When a ball floated by Tipperary's Dick Heffernan towards the Kerry goal was deflected by Bill Grant to the net, the mood was transformed. If people came to see Tipperary out of curiosity, they now discovered a team ready to win.

Kerry pulled back a point before half-time, but the talk was the same all across the ground. Tipperary had dominated the match. They led by two points and should have been out of sight.

Davy Tobin scored a great point early in the second half to extend Tipperary's lead to three points. Kerry attacked in waves, but each one crashed and dissolved against the Tipperary defence. When the final whistle went, Tipperary had broken out of their own half and were still ahead. They won by Bill Grant's goal, 1-1 to 0-1. The crowd invaded the pitch and engulfed them. Hats were flung in the air. Kerry retreated home grumbling about good players left on the sidelines and chances missed. When the south Tipperary boys returned home that week, they were fêted as heroes.

Then, football stopped again. An influenza epidemic in August 1918 hung heavy over the country like a black cloud. Some scientists said the American soldiers who joined the war in 1917 had brought a bug to Europe that mutated into something much worse; that mutation was brought home in turn by thousands of demobbed soldiers. Young adults were most susceptible. In 1918 the pandemic would kill 10,651 people in Ireland alone, and almost twenty-five million across the world in the first six months.

It was called Spanish 'Flu. The symptoms were dreadful. Those infected lost copious amounts of blood. Their skin turned black. Many suffered signs of dementia. Six of the Tipperary team fell ill. Davy Tobin, who had scored the goal against Cork in the Munster quarter-final that shocked the country and the point that helped beat Kerry in the final, suffered into the autumn and died. In November a challenge game against Kerry was postponed with half the Tipperary team still sick. The 1918 All-Ireland semi-finals were postponed till early 1919 until the worst of the epidemic had passed.

On 12 January 1919, Tipperary finally played their 1918 semi-final against Mayo in Croke Park, but looked sullen and uncertain compared to the exuberant group that had swept past Kerry. Defence was still Tipperary's great strength, but Mayo won enough possession at centrefield to lay siege to the Tipperary goal and put them under severe pressure throughout the game. Despite their troubles Tipperary hacked out a one-point win, 0-8 to 0-7. Maybe playing poorly in a semi-final was no bad thing. No one would give them a chance in the final anyway.

Their opponents were Wexford, whose status as the greatest team football had ever seen was already beyond question. Winning a fourth successive title would gild their crown for posterity. Once again, Tipperary's absence from this stage over the years was produced in evidence against them. Tipperary hadn't reached an All-Ireland final for fifteen years, or won an All-Ireland title since 1900. This was Wexford's fifth successive final. No team had ever won four All-Irelands in a row before. After years in the shadows, Tipperary now faced an awesome footballing force on their biggest day.

The final was set for 16 February 1919. Instead of training regularly through the summer, county teams usually gathered in training camps for an extended spell before any big game. The army and police intrusions made anywhere in Tipperary completely unsuited to their requirements, so the footballers escaped to Waterford for two weeks. They stayed in the Eagle Hotel, trained on the strand in Dungarvan every day and played some practice games against Waterford. A few local players from Kilrossanty helped round out the numbers at training. The team visited Dungarvan in the evenings to stave off boredom. Ned O'Shea and Jerry Shelly were watching the clocks, ensuring they were home at a reasonable time.

Tommy Ryan joined the team from Waterford prison. He had been arrested the day after Soloheadbeg. He knew Treacy, Breen, Hogan and

Robinson well and his connections with the Volunteers were known to policemen and civilians everywhere. The day of the ambush Ryan had got word from Treacy. They wanted to stay the night at his place. Ryan wanted to help but a threshing machine was due that evening to commence work the following day. The neighbours would flock to see that event, and Ryan was already expecting to be arrested for openly drilling his battalion around Clogheen a few days before. He visited Treacy's safe house to talk, but Treacy and the others had already decided to go elsewhere. The following day the RIC came and took Ryan away. His stories now helped pass the nights in Dungarvan. He told one about the prison governor. The morning he was released, Ryan was called to his office and upbraided for the folly of his interest in the IRA. Nothing good could come of it, only trouble. Ryan smirked. The governor reared up. 'Do you think a lot of pups like you can defeat the British Government?' he asked. Ryan was dismissed, and headed for Dungarvan.

Another story went that Ryan, like Jimmy McNamara, had also been offered £8 a week by Glasgow Celtic to leave Gaelic football behind. It was a jump from the eight shillings he earned as a farm hand, but Ryan couldn't leave. Football and the Volunteers had reeled him in. His best friend had joined the British Army before the war and died at the Battle of Mons. His neighbours mourned the boy's death. Ryan mourned a wasted life.

The night the Easter Rising began, Ryan called to his godfather, James Hanrahan, seeking to make some kind of gesture. They took a tricolour to the highest point in Ballylooby, the steeple of the Protestant church. Ryan climbed through the church to the top floor and attached the flag to the steeple. As he descended, the floor in the steeple collapsed. Ryan fell sixteen feet but got up without a scratch. The flag fluttered over Ballylooby for a week.

His mind was always stranded somewhere between football, farming and rebellion. During Tipperary's stay in Dungarvan, even with an All-Ireland final in sight, he noticed one of the barmaids in the hotel was being courted by an RIC officer. He charted their movements – where they walked, where they went. One night he asked Bill Grant to come with him. They followed the barmaid and the policeman and soon found them sitting on a bench. 'Pull your collar up,' Ryan whispered to Grant. 'Pull down your hat.' They looped around and approached the couple from behind. Ryan saw the policeman's revolver lying on the bench. He grabbed the gun. The policeman spun around. 'Don't move!' Ryan shouted. He backed away and disappeared with Grant into the night. For a week, Ryan waited for a reaction, but nothing happened. The policeman still courted the barmaid, and the barmaid never treated Ryan any differently. He couldn't imagine his disguise had been that good.

The players returned home to Tipperary a few days before the game. When two players fell ill, the lingering memory of Davy Tobin's death accompanied them to Dublin. They feared the worst, but they were also liberated by the realisation that, against Wexford, they had nothing to lose.

The newspaper reports that Wexford were also missing some great players also encouraged them. Sean O'Kennedy, their iconic captain, was injured. His brother, Gus, was also hobbled by injury, but would start the final. Fr Ned Wheeler had been central to Wexford winning three All-Irelands in a row, but he was gone. Tom Mernagh and Frank Furlong were also injured, weakening Wexford in defence and attack.

The Wexford team had changed dramatically but for thousands who hadn't seen Tipperary dominate Kerry and Cork, they were still Wexford. Still untouchable. For Tipperary, it was like the Munster final again. Wexford had replaced Kerry as unconquerable foes. Why couldn't this game deliver the same result? Whatever everyone said about Wexford, Tipperary knew they could beat them. They were thinking like champions. Now they had to perform that way.

Over ten thousand people filled the stands and banks around Croke Park. It was clear from the beginning that Tipperary were not racked by tension or fear. They had come to play. The standard of football was high and the pace was fast. Both teams coughed up frees and chances. While Tipperary got two points ahead early on, Wexford shot three wides before responding with three points in succession to lead at half-time 0-3 to 0-2. Another point from Toddy Pierce put Wexford two points up in the second half, but Tipperary refused to yield. A few minutes later Dick Heffernan won a fierce tussle to escape with the ball into the Wexford half and kicked a point, but the whistle was blown for a free in his favour and the score disallowed.

Tipperary kept pressing but they kicked too many wides. Tommy Ryan and Gus McCarthy eventually kicked a pair of points to get them level and despite all the delays that summer, the tragedy of Davy Tobin and their troubles back home, Tipperary were within reach of an All-Ireland title.

The ball was kicked out after McCarthy's equaliser. Wexford won it cleanly at centrefield. Gus O'Kennedy switched the ball to Jimmy Redmond, who put Wexford back in front, 0-5 to 0-4. Tipperary attacked again, but struggled to find their shooting range. Luck wasn't with them either. The Wexford goalkeeper appeared to carry one ball over the line, but Tipperary were denied the goal. Near the end of the game Tipperary were awarded three frees. One hit the post. One rattled the crossbar. The other trailed wide.

While Tipperary tightened up as the game neared the end. Wexford led by a point in a pitched battle. If they kept their heads, another All-Ireland and an immortal piece of history was theirs.

Then Tipperary got a chance. With only a few seconds left, Gus McCarthy found himself in front of the posts. It was Tipperary's last kick in the hands of their best forward. This was the nail on which a hinge of history could swing. McCarthy kicked, but his shot faded wide. The referee blew his whistle. Wexford were historic champions.

Panic and a tinge of fear had overtaken Tipperary's exuberance at the crucial moment. Tipperary had fallen short but not the way everyone expected. They left Croke Park with the luxury of regret. What if Dick Heffernan's point had stood? Gus McCarthy had made an error they would never expect from him. Some players wondered about the ferocity of the training in Dungarvan. Had they done too much? Perhaps those exertions left them leg-weary at the end.

These were the arguments and conversations that followed them into spring 1919. They also recognised the scale of what they had achieved. Wexford were truly great. Tipperary had come close to making them mortal. For all the trouble in the country, the coming few months promised more football matches and more days like this. Tipperary were good and knew they could get better.

CHAPTER 6

Faith Restored

Tipperary lose their way but discover a better path. A tragedy in Grangemockler. A challenge from Dublin. Mick Hogan's first pilgrimage to Croke Park.

TIPPERARY AND DUBLIN, APRIL 1919–DECEMBER 1919

O n 6 April 1919, almost precisely two months after the delayed 1918 All-Ireland final, Tipperary returned to Croke Park to play Wexford in a match to raise money for the Republican Prisoners' Benefit Fund. It might have been just a challenge match, but playing in the shadow of such a dramatic final heightened everything about the game.

Tipperary retreated into a training camp as they had done for the All-Ireland final. Word filtered back that Wexford were doing the same thing. Tipperary's improvement in a year was almost miraculous. Around the core formed by Gus McCarthy, Jimmy McNamara and Ned O'Shea, other players had matured and come forward. Mikey

Tobin, the old red-haired favourite of Master Browne's in Grangemockler, had grown into a powerful player who dominated centrefield. Bill Barrett, who had grown up in a house in Mullinahone that became a haven for IRA men on the run, played at wing-forward. In time, people would write poems about him. Bill Ryan, at right-half-back, was light and willowy but possessed a startling turn of speed. Their success in 1918 had been unexpected. The coming year would tell them whether it was all built on sand.

Wexford had questions, too. Their status as the greatest football team ever seen was already secure, but they couldn't be sure what might come next. Losing to Tipperary now might sow doubts about their future among their own people, and more importantly, among themselves.

The game easily caught the public's attention and the streets around Croke Park hummed with activity from early morning. As Luke O'Toole walked around Croke Park he surveyed the packed stands and banks. The attendance was bigger than the All-Ireland final. O'Toole reckoned maybe twenty thousand people had turned up. Other estimates put the total closer to twenty-five. When the gate receipts were added up, they totalled £1,086, just £98 less than the all-time record for Croke Park.

It was an afternoon wrapped in green and heavy with symbolism. The O'Tooles Pipe Band led the teams out, playing 'The Wearing of the Green'. Harry Boland jogged out as referee. Behind him came Éamon de Valera, who walked to the middle of the field to the tune of 'The Soldier's Song' with Lord Mayor Laurence O'Neill and Alderman James Nowlan, President of the GAA. It was only a few months since Boland and Michael Collins had broken de Valera out of Lincoln Jail. Now he was cheered by the crowds and serenaded by the band, greeted like a folk hero.

The band withdrew. De Valera threw the ball in. Tipperary immediately won a free but within seconds had conceded a free to Wexford. That set the tone. Both teams were racked by nerves. Instead of reaching the thrilling heights of the All-Ireland final, the game was quickly reduced to a dour, niggly struggle.

'It was spoiled by the wild methods of the players,' reported the *Irish Independent*, 'which, we think, might have been checked early in the game and not allowed develop into roughness, which was unedifying.'

Apart from the constant stream of fouls, both teams struggled with their shooting. Tipperary's defence was stubborn and unyielding, but their ongoing quest to find an effective group of forwards remained unfulfilled. Shots skimmed posts and trailed off wide. Good attacks were spoiled by needless fouling and nervous hands. 'The forwards, instead of trying to receive a pass would stand and try to take the rolling ball up on the foot,' continued the *Independent* report. 'Even in this fundamental phase of the game they showed themselves lacking.'

Wexford took an early lead with a point from Toddy Pierce, who caused persistent problems for Tipperary through the first half. Tipperary gradually took over as the game went on and had a goal disallowed, but their failure to convert their chances kept Wexford in front. Jim Ryan finally equalised near half-time but promising attacks withered away as forwards squandered possession, committed careless fouls and blighted their play with a succession of terrible wides.

They reached half-time with a point apiece. De Valera threw the ball in again for the second half. Tipperary's goalkeeper, Arthur Carroll, was forced into a good save early on, but Wexford didn't muster much more in attack. Instead Tipperary camped in Wexford's half, still pounding at the Wexford defence but fluffing their own chances.

As the match drained into its final few minutes, Wexford broke out. Arthur Carroll drew shrieks from the crowd as he tipped Pierce's shot over the crossbar for a point. Tipperary drove downfield again but wasted another easy free. They crafted one final attack, but the final shot drifted in the same direction as the rest. Wexford won by a point.

It was a shattering blow. Tipperary had lost to Wexford again, this time playing badly. They had seven weeks before they played Kerry in the Munster championship. They didn't have Kerry's years of victories, tradition and confidence to fall back on in a crisis, and travelled to Cork for the game on 26 May unsure about what version of themselves might take the field.

Their response was magnificent. The political troubles now engulfing the entire province of Munster reduced the crowd and the number of newspaper reporters at the press table. It would take days before the story of a classic would reach the rest of the country. Even then, it was agonisingly short on detail.

The few paragraphs that appeared recalled a match where the deficit between the teams was never more than a few points, leaving the game in the balance till the end. A year of proper training and games had transformed Kerry into a sharper, fitter, more confident team. Still, Tipperary matched them in the first half, but as the second half unfolded, Kerry's skill on the ball and the swiftness of their movement in attack caused Tipperary problems. Kerry were too quick. Too cute. When the whistle blew, they were a goal ahead, 2-4 to 1-4.

A month after they lost to Kerry, Tipperary took out their temper on Waterford, beating them 5-2 to 1-6. Their reaction to defeat confirmed what they had hoped: though Tipperary's Munster title was gone, the team had a future.

Football in Grangemockler never stopped. The men and boys came together every Sunday afternoon and the club team were moving well. Now aged twenty-three, Mick Hogan had followed Dan's path as a footballer and emerged as a fine defender. The talk went that Mick might even make the Tipperary team before the year was out.

One Sunday in July 1919 he played a match alongside his old friend John Browne. At one point Browne challenged for a ball in the air and took a knock in his side. It took the wind from him. The match finished up and everyone headed home. The aching pain stayed with Browne into the evening.

His mother, Kate, had his dinner ready when he got home. He didn't eat. That night, as the house slept, Kate could hear John tossing and turning in his bed. When he tried to get up the following morning, the pain shot through his body. The doctor was in Grangemockler that day. Kate asked him to call. His examination found nothing seriously wrong. It was a bad muscle bruise, he said. A day's rest would put everything right.

Kate wasn't satisfied. She called another doctor. This time, the diagnosis was more serious. The doctor advised a hospital stay in Dublin. Kate called to John Madden, who owned a Model T Ford car. They improvised a bed across the back seat. Frank Feehan and Mick Kerrigan from the village came with them for company.

The journey was rough. The roads were badly rutted and pockmarked with potholes. In some places the local IRA had torn them up entirely to disrupt the movement of police and military trucks. They reached Dublin that night. When they visited John in hospital the following morning he was in good spirits. Kate felt better for that and set out for home, but as the day went on his condition worsened.

His injury was diagnosed as a ruptured duodenum. A serious infection set in. On 4 July he received the sacraments. He drifted in and out of sleep, rambling into the night about card games with Ned Feehan, Peter Walshe and Martin Bowers, and going to the dances with Kitty Kerrigan. That morning, he died.

The news broke Kate's heart. When the train bearing his coffin arrived in Kilkenny, the local Volunteers collected it and draped a tricolour over the lid. They brought him as far as Callan, followed by a two-mile procession of cars and three hundred people on bicycles.

It was eleven that night before his coffin reached the church in Grangemockler. On the way back, the locals talked about John. Some of the men whispered that if he hadn't died this way, he would surely have lost the rag with a policeman some night and taken one with him. The girls in the villages around Grangemockler always thought him the most handsome of the Brownes, with his hazel-coloured eyes and perfect nose, a cow's lick of light brown hair and the same spark of humour as his mother. Kate wondered if she might ever smile again.

As the Brownes grieved, their friends helped maintain the farm. Mick Hogan cut hay on their five acres of meadow at Cruan and the other boys from the village helped save it in one day. Mick brought his horses down to the meadow again the following spring to plough and sow seed. If they ever talked of John, Kate would talk like he was only gone a while. 'I feel that he is only gone on a short journey,' she said. 'I expect that he'll come back some evening after the cows.' Sometimes she thought she heard his laughter ring out as he raced across the street to the house from Feehan's. But he never came home.

Kate saw much of John in Mick Hogan's kindness and his dry, droll humour. After football practice he would call with some friends and sit by the fireside. They talked of everything but John. Sometimes Kate would sit among them looking mournful and lost, her eyes filled with the sadness of losing her son. Then Mick would crack a joke the same way John would. In those moments and days of great sorrow, no one could lift Kate Browne up and make her smile like Mick Hogan.

Playing games in Tipperary got even harder as 1919 drained into autumn. A hurling tournament near Cappawhite was stopped by a large force of RIC and military. One day, around a hundred police and soldiers prevented access to Thurles Sportsfield for matches.

The Tipperary footballers filled their idle months after defeat to Kerry with challenge matches. On 3 August, they hosted Wexford in Clonmel. Compared to their dull game in April, a much better match unfolded into a fascinating clash of styles. Wexford were more precise with their passing and clever in their movement. Instead of trying to match their science, Tipperary ripped into them. Like the 1918 All-Ireland final, they played the game at a high tempo and hit hard, trying to knock Wexford off kilter.

This time it worked. In front of a huge crowd on a sunny day, Tipperary led 1-1 to 0-3 at half-time and pulled away to win by five points, 2-4 to 0-5. Two weeks later they went to Dungarvan to meet Kerry in another challenge game. They led by 1-1 to 0-2 at half-time and hung on against a stiff breeze in the second half to draw 1-4 apiece.

They reconvened in Tralee for a rematch on 6 September. Playing at home, combined with their traditional superiority over Tipperary, made it Kerry's game to lose, but Tipperary won by a point, 1-3 to 0-5. It all reminded them of how quickly opportunities and seasons can slip by. With Tipperary's hurlers gone from the championship and the footballers starring only in the half-light of the challenge circuit, the *Nenagh Guardian* correspondent captured the essence of a trying summer: 'There is a kind of unpleasant feeling that our own Tipperary might have shown to better advantage,' he wrote. 'In both hurling and football there is, we are convinced, material fit to win the All-Ireland final. It is a pity that through lack of organisation or co-operation, perhaps, or better government by our county board, our teams have not achieved the pre-eminence to which they are entitled.'

Capturing all the frustration of a year that saw them beat Wexford and Kerry but lose their Munster title, he reached for a verse.

Of all the words of tongue or pen,
The saddest are 'it might have been'.

A final request for a challenge game arrived with the Tipperary county board that November. It was from Dublin, seeking a match in Croke Park. A batch of gold medals would be minted for the winners with all proceeds going to the IRA's Prisoners Fund.

This was an attractive proposition. The game was scheduled for December. It was a trip to Dublin for Tipperary and the chance of another serious game against an excellent team. Since Wexford had begun their journey towards greatness, no team had been tortured by their success like Dublin.

In many ways, that greatness could have been destined for Dublin, not Wexford. From the beginning of their existence Dublin drew crowds and produced players different to any other county. In 1914 they had lost the Leinster final to Wexford after a replay that brought thirteen thousand people to Croke Park. Nothing had ever drawn a crowd like that before. In 1917 Dublin lost another Leinster final to Wexford by two points.

They met again in 1918 in a national tournament organised to aid the Prisoners' Fund. This time Dublin hammered Wexford, 1-6 to 1-0. When Dublin were drawn to play Louth in the 1918 Leinster championship, their eyes were already scanning the rest of the championship for Wexford.

It was a disastrous mistake. Solomon Lawlor scored three goals for Dublin in the second half but instead of breaking Louth, his goals only kept Dublin in the game. Louth won 3-5 to 3-3. Having come close to competing with the greatest team of them all, Dublin had been floored by a lightweight. That winter two Dublin players, Peadar Smith and Paddy Lynch, died during the 'flu epidemic. Dublin were grieving and weakened as 1919 began. After seeing how close Tipperary got to winning the All-Ireland final that February, they also sensed Wexford could be waning.

The 1919 Leinster semi-final was scheduled for 17 August but the Wexford players refused to travel to Dublin. Wexford teams had journeyed to Dublin many times in the previous five years, but never hosted Dublin in Wexford. They hadn't even played at a neutral venue. Wexford offered to play at any other neutral ground, or even take a chance with a coin toss for home advantage. Wexford had repeatedly accommodated Dublin and the Leinster Council for six years by playing in Croke Park. As All-Ireland champions chasing their fifth title in a row, they had surely earned the privilege of playing in front of their own people?

Dublin wondered about Wexford's motives. Was this a statement of weakness? Wexford hadn't had any trouble winning in Croke Park since 1914. This match came a fortnight after they had lost to Tipperary. Maybe they needed every advantage they could find? Maybe they were simply flexing their muscles as All-Ireland champions? No one was sure.

Even Wexford itself seemed split. The Wexford county chairman, Sean Etchingham, told the newspapers he hadn't heard about the players' objection to playing the game in Croke Park. Jim Byrne, the Wexford captain, met Jack Shouldice, the Leinster Council secretary, at a game in Wexford Park on 7 August, ten days before the game. Wexford, said Byrne, weren't for budging. If they didn't show in Croke Park, Shouldice said, Dublin would be awarded the game. Wexford offered again to toss a coin for home advantage. Shouldice refused.

Later in the week, he wired Byrne a message: Croke Park on 17 August was the venue and date. Failure to play would result in forfeiture of the game. Leinster Council chairman Dan McCarthy sent another telegram. 'May I make a final appeal that your team travel to Dublin on Sunday week as arranged by the Council. Prestige of the Association is at stake.' Byrne still wouldn't give in.

It was an anxious stand-off. Wexford were the greatest team football had ever been blessed with. Losing their historic All-Ireland title like this was unthinkable. A match involving Dublin and Wexford was also guaranteed to draw huge crowds and the GAA needed the revenue.

There was also the question for Wexford of their reputation. Even though Wexford were All-Ireland champions, Dublin were already considered mild favourites for the game. Wexford knew they could beat them. Failing to fulfil the fixture would leave a question mark over the team, regardless of anything they had achieved. The game was postponed and Wexford allowed to stay in the championship, but they had to come to Croke Park. Sunday, 31 August, was the date.

The weekend started badly for Wexford. The father of two players, the Howlett brothers, died late in the week and was buried on Saturday. Wexford lined out the following day wearing black armbands in his memory. When Jim Byrne kicked a free that went over Dublin goalkeeper Johnny McDonnell to the net in the first minute, all their troubles and discontent looked set to be overtaken by another powerful performance. As the game settled down, though, it was clear that Wexford weren't themselves.

Dublin were better in the air and quicker on the ground. They hit the crossbar twice and missed an open goal, but scored six points to overturn Wexford's lead and got to half-time 0-6 to 1-0 ahead. Wexford tried to come back at them in the second half, but they were drained of energy. Paddy McDonnell's free-taking tortured them and Dublin ran away to win by 0-11 to 1-1. It was the first time Wexford had lost a Leinster championship game in seven years. Their All-Ireland was gone. A great empire crumbled into the dust.

Dublin strode into the Leinster final the following Sunday against

Kildare. It was a match that pitted two great players against each other: Paddy McDonnell of Dublin and Larry Stanley of Kildare. Both of them played at centrefield. Both were captains. Both were revered for their accuracy in attack and their ability to win ball in the air. They were the north stars in their county's sky, guiding their teams for years.

With Wexford gone, both teams had also waited years for this chance. Kildare were smart and well-organised in defence. Dublin had the best forwards in the country. Dublin hadn't won a Leinster title since 1908. Fourteen years had passed since Kildare's last Leinster title. The sun shone brilliantly and the crowds filled Croke Park a long time before the game began. They waited for Dublin and Kildare. McDonnell and Stanley.

McDonnell landed the first punch, hitting a glorious free from thirty-five yards for a point that pulled Dublin level after an early score by Kildare's Mick Sammon. A few minutes later Sammon escaped for a goal. Kildare had grabbed the whip.

Stanley was magnificent at centrefield. McDonnell struggled to match him. John Synnott rose to fist a marvellous pass from Frank Burke to the net, but instead of propelling them into a lead it simply kept Dublin in touch. In the second half Dublin only managed a single point. That came in the final minute of the match. Kildare were ahead at the end, 1-3 to 1-2. Dublin had broken the greatest of them all, but Kildare were Leinster champions. What did beating Wexford mean now?

The crowds leapt the fences around the field at the final whistle and hoisted Stanley onto their shoulders. 'Those who had never heard of him and never saw him in action until Sunday have something to think about for some time to come,' wrote the commentator in the *Kildare Observer*. 'Certainly, Larry, you are a marvel, and the crack Dublin captain has good reason never to forget you. It has been said with truth that it would take three good men to match the Kildare captain.'

That September Kildare beat Galway to win the All-Ireland title. Stanley was immortalised. Dublin were nowhere.

Dublin's December match with Tipperary would finish their season. Word of the match spread quickly and the newspapers latched onto the game. Dublin were favourites but both teams had beaten Wexford that year and were near the front of the pack chasing Kildare. 'They [Tipperary] claim an improvement in all departments in their present team,' wrote the correspondent in the *Freeman's Journal*. 'If this is so, tomorrow's match should provide the most scientific and exciting game seen at Croke Park for a long time.'

In Grangemockler, all the talk was about a new player for Tipperary. On 10 December Mick Hogan took his first steps in Croke Park. The weather was wet and cold. The pitch felt soft under his boots. The freezing frost of the night before was followed by driving rain early that morning, making the ground slippery and boggy. As he lined up on the halfway line with the rest of the team for the throw-in, the wind whipped like a branch across his face.

Frees were plentiful, but both teams battled in bad conditions to keep their balance and get some rhythm into the game. Paddy McDonnell kicked a free for the first point. Tipperary looked jittery. Frank Burke caused them problems in attack. Josie Synnott kept Dublin secure in defence. Tipperary were winning frees but poor shooting was tormenting them again. They needed a stroke of luck. Tommy Ryan made a good run, finding JJ Skinner who sent the ball across the face of the Dublin goal. Johnny McDonnell came out from his goals to gather but Gus O'Dwyer got there first, deflecting the ball to the net.

Tipperary started to relax. Frank Burke had a fierce shot fisted away by Tipperary goalkeeper Arthur Carroll, but a free from Jerry Shelly stretched Tipperary's lead to a goal, 1-1 to 0-1, before O'Dwyer added another point. Tipperary were four up at half-time, 1-2 to 0-1. Dublin were in trouble.

They began the chase early in the second half. A good ball from the wing found John Synnott racing towards the Tipperary goal. He took possession from twenty yards out and fired a ferocious shot. Carroll almost got his hands to the ball, but it flew past his fingers into the net. The ground erupted. Dublin were just a point down. Most of the crowd on the slopes and in the stands surrounding the pitch reckoned the goal would break Tipperary's heart. Dublin looked the better team on paper. With the gap bridged, they would show their class.

But Tipperary were unbreakable. They couldn't match Dublin's skill and dexterity in attack, but they had great defenders and a stubborn streak of resilience running through the whole team. Ned O'Shea, Jerry Shelly and Dick Heffernan intercepted passes, tackled like demons and dominated the skies when Dublin kicked the ball long. Frank Burke still terrorised them in attack and Paddy McDonnell and the Synnott brothers were a constant menace, but Tipperary held them in check and sensed a famous win.

As Dublin threw themselves forward, Tipperary broke out of defence. A long ball found O'Dwyer again. He composed himself, measured his kick and split the posts. Dublin hared back upfield, but it was too late. Tipperary had won, 1-3 to 1-1. That night the teams convened at the Mansion House in the city centre for a reception and a medal presentation to the winning team. For all the disappointment and difficulties of 1919, Tipperary could reflect on beating Wexford, Kerry and Dublin. An All-Ireland was back within reach.

Somewhere in the middle of all the banter and fun, Mick Hogan stood in the wood-panelled great hall of the Mansion House. Five months had passed since John Browne had died. Mick's stories of his weekend in Dublin might even make Kate Browne smile and hold off the darkness of a sad winter for at least one evening.

The following day the team would take the train back to Fethard and head home to their towns and villages across Tipperary. Christmas was a fortnight away. The new year rolled out like an untouched carpet of snow waiting for them all to leave their footprint. A good team could make themselves great in 1920. Mick Hogan was among them all now, looking differently at these men he once knew as neighbours and rivals: Jerry Shelly and Mikey Tobin from Grangemockler. Ned O'Shea and Gus McCarthy from nearby Fethard. Arthur Carroll, the marvellous keeper from the top of the county in Templemore. The Mullinahone boys and Bill Ryan from Loughmore. This was exalted company to keep.

CHAPTER 7

The Brainy Bunch

A club of sportspeople, poets, singers and dancers with a rebel heart. A superstar is discovered in Dublin. A good team begins to become a great one.

DUBLIN, FEBRUARY–AUGUST 1920

Losing the 1919 Leinster final to Kildare meant Dublin had been beaten by the eventual All-Ireland champions three times in six seasons. Eleven years had now passed since their last Leinster title. They hadn't won an All-Ireland since 1908. For all their potential and the mighty crowds that followed them, Dublin were falling painfully short.

It was a state of affairs that almost defied explanation. In every way Dublin appeared to be ahead of the pack on paper. Their defence was sound. In Paddy McDonnell they had a magnificent leader and their forwards matched the best in the country. Since the GAA's creation in 1884, Dublin teams always played a little smarter. Instead of playing the ball away first time, Dublin quickly learned to catch, pause, look, and kick. Their forwards were fast and skilful. Elusive. Some reckoned it was the influence of soccer and the other sports in the city that made

Dublin different: a generous degree of thought seemed to go into every move they made.

Dublin also had O'Tooles at the heart of their team. It was a young, vibrant club that drew its footballers from a small web of streets in the north inner city. Between 1918 and 1920 O'Tooles would win three successive county titles. When Dublin fielded their strongest team, it usually contained at least ten players from O'Tooles.

The club was barely twenty years old and already fostered an inquisitive, progressive environment. Frank Cahill taught in the local Christian Brothers' school near Seville Place, and took boys for training in hurling and football. At a time when weights were found only in circus acts, his players used barbells and dumbbells for training at school, performing all the movements to the rhythm he played on a mouth organ. The players also bought blocks of timber for ninepence from a sawmill in Ringsend, and Cahill showed them how to shape the timber into a hurley, smoothing the rough surface with a spokeshave and glass. He repaired splintered hurleys using a band of hooped iron. He taught the boys to judge the quality of a hurley by the thickness of its handle and the smoothness of the curve down to the *bos*. A hurley had to be well balanced and properly carved, he said. If it didn't feel right in their hands, it wouldn't feel right in a game.

It was a club where artisans and playwrights mixed with men wedded to the work of the docklands, and offered a friendly haven to those from the country marooned in an unfamiliar city. Sean O'Casey was a member. The O'Hanrahan brothers were famous sculptors and hurled with O'Tooles from its inception. Two signatories of the 1916 proclamation, Tom Clarke and Seán MacDiarmada, were O'Tooles men.

Their pastimes were a by-product of their cause. The GAA club itself had grown from the Saint Laurence O'Toole branch of the Gaelic League. A branch of the Irish Republican Brotherhood was also attached to the club. In 1910 Douglas Hyde, a founder of the Gaelic

League, attended the first meeting of the St Laurence O'Toole Pipe Band. MacDiarmada, Arthur Griffith and Patrick Pearse also attended, reflecting the political and militant ends of the O'Tooles constituency. Sean O'Casey was appointed secretary and Cahill its treasurer. Tom Clarke was joint-president.

In May 1912, Pearse officially unfurled a new banner for the pipers. Sean O'Casey accepted it on behalf of the band. In time, the band would lead striking workers to Liberty Hall for a rally during the great lockout of 1913 when their instruments were smashed by police armed with swords, bayonets and batons. They were regulars in Croke Park and serenaded crowds before matches across Britain and Ireland. They were the official band of the Volunteers and led the parade on St Patrick's Day 1916. A few weeks later, seventy-three club members were scattered across the city in rebellion.

With no room for a pitch among the streets and slums of the inner city, O'Tooles played their matches in the Phoenix Park and anywhere else they could arrange. On 26 March 1920, O'Tooles bought premises alongside the Dublin–Belfast railway line at 100 Seville Place for £520. It hosted everything from club meetings to Irish classes and *scóir*, with Irish dancing, music and storytelling. Sean O'Casey would sing 'Down by Mulcreasant at Owen Doyle's Wedding' and Kevin O'Lochlainn 'The Low-Backed Car'. Mick Colgan would sing 'The Old Rustic Bridge by the Mill', and Kitty Keegan sang 'Jackets Green'. And all the time the teacher Frank Cahill was there, playing the fiddle or the tin whistle if nothing else was available.

It was also a regular meeting place for Michael Collins, Harry Boland and the Squad. Soon after O'Tooles took on Seville Place, the Squad used it as their daily base, playing cards, reading and chatting while they waited for a call to arms. Sometimes British troops kept watch on the place for days. On other occasions they called on Seville Place and smashed the clubhouse into pieces.

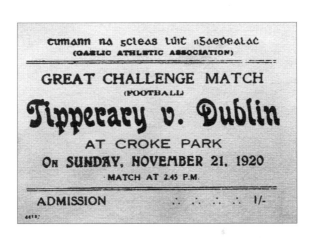

The Bloody Sunday match ticket.

The Dublin team, Bloody Sunday 1920. Back row (from left): Patrick
Hughes, Gerry Doyle, Tom Markham, Tom Carey, Patrick Carey,
Frank Burke, Paddy McDonnell, (capt), Jack Reilly, Jimmy Moore,
Christy Joyce, Johnny McDonnell, Joe Norris, John Kirwan, Charlie
Harris (trainer). Front row (from left): Tom Ennis, John Synnott, John
Murphy, William Donovan, Joe Joyce, Josie Synnott, Jack Carey, William
Robbins, Stephen Synnott, Tom Fitzgerald.

Back row second from right: Patrick Moran, leader of the IRA Squad that carried out an attack on the Gresham Hotel on Bloody Sunday, with the Dunleary Commercials football team later that day at Croke Park.

General Sir Nevil Macready, General Officer Conmmander-in-chief of the British forces in Ireland, 1920-1922.

Luke O'Toole, General Secretary of the GAA 1901–1929 (centre), with
Michael Collins (left) and Harry Boland (right) at Croke Park.

Left to right: Seamus Robinson, Sean Treacy and Dan Breen, with Mick Brennan (Clare IRA)

A troup of Auxiliaries at their barracks in Beggar's Bush, 7 October 1920. Some of these men went to Croke Park on Bloody Sunday.

Dublin firemen, some of whom attended at Croke Park. M Buckley and J Connolly, fourth and fifth from left, back row, were in the ambulance, and E Doyle, second from left, front row, was in the crew that took Hogan off the pitch.

Joe Traynor, in his club football colours. He was killed at Croke Park on
Bloody Sunday – he died on the way to Jervis Street Hospital.

Thomas Hogan, killed at Croke Park on Bloody Sunday.

The bleak scene at Croke Park on the morning after Bloody Sunday.

Relatives of the Bloody Sunday dead and injured, and onlookers, mingle outside Jervis Street Hospital during the military inquiry.

Former Tipperary players and relations commemorate Bloody Sunday in Croke Park in the 1960s; includes Mick Tobin (Grangemockler, 2nd left), Tommy Ryan (3rd left), Jim Ryan (Loughmore, 3rd right), Paddy Hogan (brother of Michael, 2nd right).

The club had committed so many men to the Rising that many more poured into the IRA's Second Battalion in the city after 1918. O'Tooles men were spread throughout some of the IRA's earliest, most intensive operations: raids on Collinstown Aerodrome and the B&I stores at the North Wall in the docklands that yielded a huge return of arms and ammunition. They raided a building at Kings Inns for guns and took part in an attack on a hotel at the North Wall that housed a battalion of Auxiliaries. They stole gelignite from the Northern Railway and captured a British Army store at Portland Row. They ambushed British Army lorries all over the north inner city and set alight the RIC barracks in the suburb of Raheny.

Although many of their players were imprisoned after the Rising, O'Tooles football team maintained its prominent position. In February 1917 the Emeralds club, who were based on Emerald Street within St Laurence O'Toole's parish, refused to play Hibernian Knights in a county senior football semi-final because two members of the Knights had driven British troops during Easter week. Some Emeralds players wanted to play the game. Others wouldn't share a dressing room with them. The split never healed and O'Tooles gathered up the players who cut themselves adrift.

That injection of footballers propelled O'Tooles into a spell of supreme dominance. The Synnott brothers were among those who arrived. Four of the eight brothers played for Dublin, but John, Josie and Stephen were the famous ones. All of them brought something different to the team. Josie was a small, nippy defender. His brothers would tell a story of Josie once escaping a lumbering opponent by ducking down and scurrying between his legs, collecting the ball on the other side. John was a stylish corner-forward. Stephen was a tall, physical full-forward, but also a good finisher. He ran a shop near Seville Place and lived on Russell Avenue. Most mornings he sat on the potato sacks outside the front window, smoking cigarettes and sharing news with the dockers and drovers and coal merchants at the heart of a little village inside the city.

It was a team of famous names and families. Although Johnny and Paddy McDonnell were IRA Volunteers and footballers celebrated across the city and beyond, O'Tooles demanded their first loyalty. When Seville Place was bought, Paddy McDonnell was one of the trustees.

In time, Johnny would match everything Paddy would achieve. Both of them had started out with O'Tooles as children in 1904. They joined the Volunteers together a decade later. Paddy escaped capture amid the flour and chaos at the Jacob's factory after the Rising. Johnny was interned in Frongoch but quickly resumed with O'Tooles and the Volunteers after returning home in 1918.

If O'Tooles provided the Dublin team with its heart, Frank Burke was the twinkle in its eye. He came to Dublin in 1909 from Carbury in Kildare to attend boarding school at St Enda's, Rathfarnham. Patrick Pearse was his teacher. When it came to history and militant republicanism, Burke was a willing student. He was a steward at the Rotunda Rink when the Irish Volunteers assembled for the first time, and he joined a battalion comprising former pupils from St Enda's; it was called Pearse's Own. Pearse was their captain and personally presented Burke with a Lee-Enfield rifle.

In the months before the Easter Rising, Burke spent his evenings at St Enda's making handgrenades and filling cartridges with shot. He also fashioned batons for use against any looters that came loping around. A fortnight before the Easter Rising, the school was shut for the Easter holidays. As a boarder, he watched vans and cars arrive every day for a week collecting boxes of grenades, rifles and bullets and ferrying them to different destinations. The school's arsenal was emptied by Holy Thursday. Burke went to town and bought a haversack and two bandolier pouches, a knapsack and a billy can. He found a pair of green puttees at home. They were the only green clothes he had.

On Good Friday, bad news filtered through from Kerry. The *Aud*, carrying a supply of arms from Germany for the Volunteers, had been intercepted off the coast. The Volunteers' key contact, Roger Casement, was arrested in Kerry hours after making land from a submarine. Burke and his company stood guard at St Enda's. On Easter Sunday they received an order cancelling all operations, but thirty-seven men in the company still decided to march on Rathfarnham church. On the way Eoin MacNeill, the Volunteers' chief of staff, intercepted the leaders of the group. 'You're being led into a trap,' he told them.

Burke went back to St Enda's, unconvinced. On Easter Monday he boarded the Number 17 tram bound for Sackville Street, dressed in his puttees and carrying his rifle. As he passed the Jacob's factory on Bishop Street he saw Volunteers at the windows. He heard the rattle of machine-gun fire at the junction of George's Street and Dame Street. He went down College Street and turned right onto Tara Street, marching briskly along by the Liffey. He crossed Butt Bridge for Liberty Hall, went inside and climbed the stairs to the roof. He saw the GPO away to his right, under fire, but under Volunteer control. He raced downstairs and out onto the street, weaving through the small laneways linking back to Sackville Street, and sprinted across the road to the GPO side. He spotted a small open window at the corner and clambered in. A few minutes later he was on the roof, keeping watch under the newly raised tricolour.

By Wednesday, Clery's department store across the road was in flames. The raging heat burned against Burke's skin. He was relocated downstairs to the front of the GPO building, manning the front and corner windows facing onto Sackville Street. The situation was already desperate. Conditions in the GPO were dire. Burke stared for hours at a civilian lying dead on the street, still clutching a white flag.

On the final day of the Rising, the last remaining troops in the GPO were mustered and sent across Henry Street to try and mount a final stand. Burke survived the hail of machine-gun fire and gathered his thoughts while awaiting one final bayonet charge. He remembered Pearse and better days at St Enda's. He thought of how so many old friends had died that week. He thought of his mother in Kildare, already worried, soon to be left broken-hearted.

Then, instead of charging, everything stopped. Pearse had surrendered. The battle was over. Burke was marched with everyone else to the Rotunda. He saw Pearse and the other leaders plucked from the hundreds of men and taken away. The rest marched through a smouldering city to a boat bound for Holyhead – first for Stafford Jail, then the internment camp at Frongoch.

After being released in 1917 Burke returned to St Enda's as a teacher. The Dublin hurling team immediately asked him to play. He agreed and Dublin won an All-Ireland. As a footballer, Burke was a lethal corner-forward: part-playmaker, part-finisher. He scored spectacular points and burned defenders with his pace. Even if his opponents kept up with him, his mind was usually a few steps ahead. He was the sprinkle of stardust that always made Dublin lethal.

On a Sunday in early February 1920 Dublin played their first game of the year, a challenge match against Kildare in Croke Park. The memory of the 1919 Leinster final had drawn a good crowd. It was heartening to see, but a game that could draw a crowd like that deserved a better stage.

Croke Park had been fully owned by the GAA for seven years now and was already enshrined as the GAA's landmark venue, but it still bore the appearance of a rough, unfinished husk. A few years before, the public toilets on one side of the ground were so poorly serviced a stream of sewage sometimes flowed into the dressing rooms. The story went that the GAA's secretary, Luke O'Toole, had hired a team of architects and experts to draw up plans for a new stand and a fresh sod for the pitch, but progress was slow.

'The need for its proper equipment is a present matter of dissatisfaction and urgency,' wrote 'Camán', the GAA correspondent for *Sport* newspaper. 'It is a national possession; it is a memorial of a great Gael; it is an absolute necessity to a body like the GAA. The nearer and sooner it is brought up to the requirements of players and patrons, the better for all concerned and for the credit of the movement.'

Dublin annihilated Kildare that day. The following week they reduced Louth to rubble in Dundalk, winning by nine points. To Camán, Dublin was already his light in the sky for the year. 'Little need be said of Dublin,' he wrote. 'There is probably not a team in Ireland with a better understanding, greater resource, steadier combination or in better practice than that which captain Paddy McDonnell can now lead onto the field.'

The GAA's accounts published in 1920 proudly recorded the best financial year in its history and began with a profit of £2,500 to spend. O'Toole had created a competition called the 'Croke Park Tournament' to raise more money to fund improvements. In May 1920 the Tipperary footballers were back in Croke Park to play Cork in the tournament's Munster final.

A healthy crowd flocked to a match played at a furious pace, but both teams were rusty. The game was dominated by reckless tackling, fouls and poor shooting. There was little attempt made to keep possession and pass the ball. The kicking was wild. Control of the ball was even worse. Defences dominated, but the quality of the forward play was so bad they didn't need to do much. Camán sat at the press table in front of the old pavilion, jotting down notes and shaking his head. 'Scoring,' he wrote, 'was entirely a matter of luck.'

Only Ned O'Shea in defence emerged with any credit for Tipperary. He even had to come forward and score their opening goal. The rest of the team seemed stuck in a bad rut. Cork held them level by half-time, 1-1 each, and with Tipperary facing the sun and wind in the second half, Cork ran away with victory.

A week later Dublin hammered Offaly in Maryborough in the Croke Park Tournament, 3-5 to 0-3, without even getting near full tilt. Unlike in Tipperary, club games were proceeding briskly across the city. The Dublin players looked fit and sharp as a result. Kildare were waiting at the beginning of June in the Leinster final of the Croke Park Tournament. More than ten thousand turned up to watch. It was fiercely contested and reduced to a familiar battle: Kildare's defence and Dublin's elusive forward line. This time, though, Dublin struggled to find any fluency. With the wind behind them in the first half, Kildare scored a goal from a penalty. Dublin replied with three points to get level by half-time. With the breeze to come, they had Kildare in their maw.

Instead of crushing Kildare, Dublin froze. Two fast points put Kildare 1-2 to 0-3 ahead. They were moving the ball quickly and hitting Dublin hard. The crowd were restless. This had happened Dublin too often in big games when great things had been expected. How would they respond now?

Just as their supporters hoped, Paddy McDonnell and Frank Burke conjured more space. Tom Pierce and the Synnott brothers exerted a greater influence on the game with their kicking and playmaking. Burke kicked a point to get Dublin closer. Then Paddy McDonnell and the Synnotts exploded, hitting 1-4 between them. Dublin won by six points, 1-8 to 1-2. They hadn't just beaten the All-Ireland champions – they had obliterated them.

A month later, June 1920, Dublin swept by Laois in the Leinster semi-final, holding them scoreless in the first half before cantering home 2-6 to 0-1. They were winning tight games and cakewalks alike and looking like champions. Now they were facing Kildare again, this time in a Leinster final.

Although two wins over Kildare suggested the balance had swung to Dublin, beating them in a Leinster final was a different business to the light-hearted caper of the Croke Park Tournament. After beating Dublin in the 1919 Leinster final, Kildare had beaten Galway by ten points in the All-Ireland final. Dublin had lost five finals since their last Leinster title in 1908. Their playing pool was greater than anyone else's, and O'Tooles had shown an industry and innovation other teams had yet to even imagine, but without a Leinster title all that intelligence and dedication was forgotten.

Kildare had beaten Wexford and Westmeath to reach the final. None of their performances, even beating Wexford, had risen a plume of dust, but they were still in a good position. They expected Dublin would make the running from the start. Kildare could soak up that pressure and wait for the seeds of doubt buried in Dublin by years of failure to bloom.

Dublin lined out playing into Hill 60 with the canal goal at their backs. Kildare attacked first and kicked an early point through Frank 'Joyce' Conlan, their devilish corner-forward. Instead of allowing Dublin dictate the pace, Kildare took the reins. Being All-Ireland champions gave them the confidence to try winning the match from the front.

They caught plenty of ball at centrefield and quickly funnelled it to their best forwards with impressive accuracy. In contrast to their usual dash, Dublin were sluggish. Then, for a few moments, Kildare dropped their guard. Frank Burke was already causing problems for the Kildare defence. Having taken possession he sent a beautifully placed low ball to Jack Carey, who rattled the net. Moments later Johnny McDonnell made a great save from Kildare's George Magan. Kildare had dominated the play, but Dublin were a goal ahead. The luck seemed with them.

A point from Stephen Synnott extended their lead to four points. Frank Conlan scored another point for Kildare, but Dublin were mugging them in the tackle and winning more ball in the air at centrefield. Kildare were pushed back and penned into their own half. Dublin led at half-time, 1-1 to 0-2. It was only a two-point lead and Dublin hadn't dazzled anyone, but so far they had played like champions.

Kildare battled hard in the second half but even though Dublin kicked more wides than usual, Kildare didn't have the craft in their own attack to take advantage. Even when they were awarded a penalty, Mick Sammon's kick dribbled wide. It was the kind of miss they couldn't cope with this time. Frank Burke got away for Dublin's final point to seal a three-point win, 1-3 to 0-3.

Beating the All-Ireland champions to win a Leinster title settled plenty of doubts about Dublin's character. When they were pushed back against the wall, Dublin had kept playing and worn Kildare down. From being the team every champion had stepped over, they were now the team everyone had to catch.

Cavan, the Ulster champions, were their opponents in the All-Ireland semi-final, but as the country suffered under the squeeze of military rule, finding a date to play the game was difficult. The match was scheduled first for 12 September, then postponed. Then, on Friday, 24 September, an opportunity presented itself. The GAA's Central Council proposed the game take place in Navan, County Meath, that Sunday. Everyone was taken by surprise. In Cavan town, the *Anglo-Celt* newspaper had already gone to print carrying a story suggesting the match wouldn't be played till the tension created across the country by Terence MacSwiney's hunger strike in Brixton had eased. At the last minute an advertisement was inserted by their printers in Dublin announcing the game that Sunday.

Dublin leapt at the chance to play. Cavan were less enthusiastic. They had already taken their team away for a fortnight's training ahead of the original date, but reconvened in Virginia the day before the game knowing their peak had passed. Two days' notice was hopelessly inadequate; preparation to play a team like Dublin would usually demand weeks in a training camp. Even then, Cavan would have brought little more with them than hope. They had won six Ulster titles in their history and failed to make an All-Ireland final even once. Dublin were now afraid of nothing.

A bright, sunny day drew a big crowd. Roadblocks had cut off many roads around Cavan but people found a way to make the journey. Over ten thousand people thronged Navan for the game, clogging its main street with cars and charabancs. 'Under so unfortunate and discouraging conditions it wasn't much wonder to find everyone down in the mouth,' wrote the *Anglo-Celt*'s correspondent, 'and the most enthusiastic supporters could only hope the team could make a decent show. Victory was out of the question.'

They didn't even get a decent show. Dublin had the wind behind them and the sun at their backs for the first half, and quickly set about taking Cavan apart. John and Stephen Synnott scored two goals in the first ten minutes, while Frank Burke simply caught fire. 'Dublin owes much to this sterling and loyal Gael,' wrote Camán, 'whose work, if not always flashy or risky, is neither timorous or fruitless.'

Stephen Synnott scored another goal in the second half and finished with 2-2 of Dublin's 3-6. Cavan managed 1-1 in the first half but never got near Dublin for the rest of the game. In time they would lodge a complaint over the circumstances of the fixture, but the game also reinforced the gap between Ulster and the rest.

'Physical training is all right,' wrote the *Anglo-Celt*'s demoralised correspondent, 'but intellectual training is just as important. It is nearly time our players, in club and county football, did more thinking and utilised brain as well as bone and sinew. We are not, so far, moving with the time or giving the return which thousands of supporters expect.'

Cavan returned home through roadblocks and unfamiliar roads with nothing from the game to shorten the journey. Dublin were in the All-Ireland final. They would wait nearly two years for an opponent.

CHAPTER 8

The Challenge

Tipperary throw down an unlikely gauntlet to Dublin. A chilling
plan is hatched in the city. The 'man with the cap' goes to war.

JUNE 1920–NOVEMBER 1920

Luke O'Toole reflected on the first quarter of 1920 with relief, despite all its difficulties. The GAA's schedule of athletics meetings and matches was almost on track. The foundation stone for the Croke Memorial had finally been laid in Thurles and celebrated with a hurling match between Cork and Tipperary. That March the Leinster Council reported the formation of sixty new GAA clubs between 1918 and 1919 at its annual convention. O'Toole also unveiled plans to upgrade Croke Park at the GAA's Annual Congress. With that in mind delegates also agreed that all future All-Ireland finals would be played at Croke Park.

His carefully worked-out schedule started losing ground as summer unfolded. Three of the four hurling and football provincial championships were successfully played off by late summer, but a ban on public meetings in July 1920 delayed a string of games in Munster. The Munster Council's annual convention was also called off, with many delegates interned or on the run. In Cork the Munster hurling semi-finals in July were forced out of the Athletic Grounds in the city to a smaller venue at Riverstown.

Tipperary had drawn against Clare in a quickly convened Munster football quarter-final in June. The replay was fixed for Limerick in July, but ended level again. Clare offered to play extra-time at the end of the game; Tipperary refused. Apart from ensuring a match for Clonmel, it was a stubborn, inexplicable decision. With the military clampdown across Munster, the games weren't drawing good crowds. Every delay cost the Munster Council money and wasted weekends the GAA didn't have.

Tipperary may also have been playing for time. Their form was a worry. Kerry had beaten Clare 6-11 to 2-0 in the 1919 Munster final. In the 1918 Munster final, Tipperary had only beaten Kerry by a goal. Now, in 1920, Tipperary were slaving to score two points and draw against Clare.

Their forwards were in terrible form. Mick Hogan was growing into a good corner-back beside Ned O'Shea and the defence was stable as usual, but the rest of the team had fallen off the fierce pace they had set in 1919. The replay with Clare was fixed for 15 August. This time Tipperary played in a temper. After hitting a goal inside the first few minutes they kicked six more points before half-time without conceding a score. The second half was reduced to a stroll. Tipperary won 1-7 to 0-1.

A huge crowd thronged the town before the game, the locals went home pleased and the Munster Council had a few extra pounds to offset the losses inflicted by the replays. Setting a date for the semi-final in Waterford was a more complicated matter.

Time was running out to play off the season before the end of the year.

The Munster hurling final was already postponed into September. The Croke Park Tournament football semi-final between Cork and Mayo was first delayed in mid-July by a railway strike, before being postponed indefinitely. As Terence MacSwiney lay starving in Brixton prison as October began, Cork County Board called off all GAA matches in the county. The Munster Council quickly followed their lead.

On 23 October the All-Ireland hurling semi-final between Dublin and Galway was played at Croke Park in near silence. Hill 60 was empty. A small crowd dotted the banks and pavilion seats. There was no band, only isolated musicians playing their tunes for a few pence around the ground. Dublin won with plenty to spare, but no one expected an All-Ireland final before the end of the year.

With the Munster football championship effectively locked down, teams looked around for any games they could muster. Tipperary's Munster semi-final against Waterford had been fixed for 14 November, but the military refused to grant permission for it to take place. Even with their options for games down to a small handful, Tipperary had to be discerning. Playing matches in Munster under the restrictions was impossible. So they looked to Leinster.

Dublin had invited them to a game in late 1919. Since Dublin had reached the All-Ireland final, Tipperary saw them as the perfect barometer to measure the state of their health. It also offered Dublin a serious game to tide them over before the All-Ireland final. On 1 November, a letter appeared in the *Freeman's Journal*. The same letter was reprinted in *Sport* newspaper on 6 November. It was written to pick a fight.

> *We understand that Tipperary's superiority over Dublin in foot-ball, despite two decisive victories by Tipperary, is being questioned by Dublin. We, therefore, challenge Dublin to a match on the first available date in any venue and for any object.*

Signed on behalf of the Tipperary football team

T Ryan (Sec)

E O'Shea (Capt)

The challenge didn't catch the public's imagination at first. Most people wondered what Tipperary were talking about. Their 'decisive victories' had come in a pair of challenge games. If any pair of teams had created something close to a sustained rivalry that held the public's attention, it was Dublin and Kildare. Camán was still pleased to find something for his GAA column in *Sport*, but couldn't disguise his weariness at Tipperary's arguments.

'We did not think the comparative merit of Dublin and Tipperary football was a matter of very keen current debate,' he wrote, 'for the simple reason that the counties have not met with representative teams for a considerable time. However, as Tipperary is in the mood we are sure the Metropolitans will have little hesitation in obliging them, and there are only too many deserving objects for which the meeting could be arranged, though the difficulty of a suitable date and venue may not prove equally adjustable.'

'The game would be an attractive prospect,' Camán concluded. 'Tipperary would put up a great game. Dublin would need [their] best resources so that their championship prospects might not be prejudiced by defeat.'

Dublin had played one match in October, drawing five thousand people to Croke Park to see them beat Kildare in a game organised by the Irish National Foresters to fund a group of construction workers on strike. Playing Tipperary in Croke Park wouldn't pose a problem. The GAA decreed the game would be a fundraiser 'in aid of an injured Gael', a familiar euphemism to mask an IRA fundraiser for the Volunteers' Dependants' Fund. This time, the cause was more specific. As well as stewarding matches at Croke Park, members of the IRA's Second Battalion in Dublin often helped intimidate and disperse touts and bookies before big games. One of those IRA men had been badly injured during a fracas that summer. The money raised would go to his family. The match was fixed for 21 November.

There was no training camp in Dungarvan this time before the Tipperary footballers travelled to Dublin. They didn't gather together either in Grangemockler or Clonmel, or even on the field in Mullinahone that they often used. Football was helpless against the turmoil surrounding them. On 30 October, Winston Churchill ordered more armoured cars for use in Ireland. On the same day over five thousand people attended Mass in Carrick-on-Suir for Terence MacSwiney, who had died in Brixton prison. A couple of days later Kevin Barry was hanged in Dublin.

On the same day Barry was hanged, a British convoy heading to Thurles for rifle practice was ambushed near Thomastown in Kilkenny. Five were killed and three wounded. That night twenty men returned to Thomastown armed with trench tools and sticks. They smashed shop windows and shutters. Goods were looted. A jewellery shop was almost emptied. Medical supplies were stolen and almost £2,000 worth of damage was done before an armoured car and military picket arrived to restore order. 'We're getting our own back,' shouted one raider.

Around the same time the RIC barracks in Littleton near Thurles was attacked and arms taken. Littleton creamery was burned in reprisal and shots were fired in the village. On 13 November a police lorry came under attack near Aherlow. As IRA men poured fire onto the passing lorry it swerved into a ditch. The policemen trapped inside clambered onto the floor of the truck and returned fire. They eventually wriggled out of the vehicle and took cover on the road beneath the lorry. Fuel was leaking from the truck and it eventually caught fire. One policeman was badly charred. Two more were killed. Another died from his wounds. When the fighting was over the IRA men salvaged arms from the truck.

The reprisals were merciless and immediate. Four lorries of soldiers and RIC men set out for Tipperary town that night. A cottage near the ambush site was burned. Two more houses were burned the following morning. A local nationalist politician, PJ Moloney, was given five minutes to leave his house and pub; both were then doused in petrol and set alight. The fire extended to a shop next door. The final bill for the damage that night totalled £36,000.

It was an endless spiral of atrocity and reprisal, both sides constantly seeking opportunities to spring an attack or inflict their revenge. By mid-November Patrick Butler from Ninemilehouse had been watching the RIC barracks in Glenbower near Grangemockler for weeks. He noticed how a patrol of five or six policemen went out every Sunday afternoon. That left six policemen in the station. It got him thinking. Once the patrol departed, a motor car containing IRA men could pull up at the door of the barracks. Assuming one RIC man would open the door, he could be taken hostage by an armed group of IRA men. The rest could be overwhelmed quickly by a surprise attack executed at speed.

It was an audacious idea that didn't require many people and could deliver a fine return of arms and ammunition. It was also the kind of attack that could energise the IRA in the area. Sean Treacy had visited Grangemockler a few weeks before he was killed in Dublin to drill the local company on field tactics, volunteer organisation and weaponry. Butler and three others had volunteered that October for a new flying column and were waiting to be called. Attacking the barracks in Glenbower would keep them busy.

Butler, John Browne and Mick Hogan were a typical trinity of stories of the time. Butler had attended school with Browne and Hogan, and had served in the British Army for a few years. They all played football with Grangemockler. When Browne helped form the local Sinn

Féin club, Butler became a member and paid his weekly twopence subscription. When the Volunteers were formed they all drilled together in Grangemockler a couple of times a week.

In 1920 their paths started to split. John was dead. Mick was playing football with Tipperary and was also an active Volunteer. Butler was devoted to making war. In August 1920 he helped sweep every farmhouse in the area for arms and secured them beneath the floor of the parochial hall. Later on the same night, fearing the dump might be found, Butler and a few others sneaked back in and exhumed the arms. They hid them instead beneath the floorboards of the school, leaving Master Browne to teach his lessons with thirty rifles hidden beneath the childen's feet.

It was the beginning of a week in late November when Butler visited the IRA brigade headquarters at Rosegreen with his proposal to attack the RIC barracks in Glenbower. Sean Hogan and two others, Jerry Kiely and Sean Hayes, were sent back with him to help organise the attack for the weekend. The three IRA men needed somewhere to stay. They visited Mick Hogan seeking lodgings.

They stayed a few nights, planning their attack and weighing up the risks. The house was busy. Mick had farm work to finish before the weekend. The plans to attack the RIC station had brought the war into his own parlour, but Mick himself couldn't get involved: they had chosen 21 November to attack the barracks, the same day Mick was to play in Croke Park.

SATURDAY, 20 NOVEMBER 1920

The day before the match, Tipperary players gathered on different platforms in different parishes waiting for the train to Dublin. The local newspapers had carried brief despatches all week from the Tipperary camp, capturing the sense of intent and expectation. They hadn't trained much or played many matches, but they knew the value of their team. This was a clash of potential champions.

'There is sure to be an enormous attendance in Croke Park, Dublin, on Sunday next when Tipperary and Dublin football teams meet in a great challenge encounter,' wrote the *Clonmel Nationalist* reporter. 'Considerable interest has been centred in this meeting for some time past and in Metropolitan circles it is looked upon as a virtual All-Ireland final as Dublin have qualified for same and Tipperary are firm favourites for the Munster championship. The selections have been made for some time and it is expected that both teams will take the field fit and well.'

Before Mick Hogan left home that morning Sean Hogan pulled him aside and handed him a set of messages for delivery to Shanahan's bar in Dublin that night. Mick folded them into a tiny square and fixed them inside his shoe. Four Grangemockler men gathered in the village: Mick Hogan, Dick Lanigan and Jerry Shelly were ready to go, but Mikey Tobin's father was dying. His family expected it could happen any hour. Tobin decided to stay.

The other three made for Mullinahone and took a sidecar to Fethard station to meet up with the rest of the team. The mood was boisterous. Wing-back Bill Ryan jumped aboard at Templemore and the train chugged on towards Dublin. A few players were engrossed in a card game, playing twenty-five for a penny a hand.

Jackie Brett from Mullinahone was talking to a priest, Fr Delahunty, from Kilkenny, when a group of soldiers boarded the train at Ballybrophy. As they edged past Brett and the priest, one soldier directed a remark at Delahunty. Brett rose from his seat and swung a punch. A scrum of soldiers quickly had Brett on the ground. Delahunty called for help. Tipperary footballers arrived in numbers from both ends of the carriage. There were fourteen soldiers, giving the footballers a slight numerical advantage. All of them whaled into the brawl.

Bill Ryan had his boots flung out the window. Mick Hogan was in the middle of the fracas, worrying about the despatches in his shoe. When the train trundled into Maryborough, the soldiers jumped off and waited for the next train. Once the euphoria of their victory subsided, some of the players started to worry: word would surely reach Dublin about the fight before the train did. A party of military and police could be waiting for them. Instead of facing Dublin in Croke Park the following day, the entire team could be in jail.

The rest of the journey passed slowly. The train eventually arrived in Kingsbridge Station after five o'clock. An armed guard was waiting on the platform. The players gathered their bags and nervously stepped off the train. They watched a party of Black and Tans walk towards them and prepared to be arrested. But the Tans didn't stop. Beyond them, a man was plucked from the crowd. The weighing machine in Portlaoise station had been vandalised and the money stolen. The Tipperary players watched the man being taken away, change spilling from his pockets.

The team was booked to stay at Barry's Hotel near Croke Park. After the trouble on the train, some made different arrangements. Tommy Ryan joined up with Mick Hogan and headed for Shanahan's in the Monto. They arrived at the bar soon after nine. It was full of Tipperary people in town for the match. Hogan slipped the despatches from his shoe and passed them to Phil Shanahan. Ryan met up with DP Walsh, an IRA man from Fethard. Walsh had news about a big job happening in the city the following morning. He couldn't get into details, he told them, but it was big.

Walsh asked Ryan to follow him down to Shanahan's cellar for help collecting arms and ammunition. They gathered up revolvers and a collection of porter bottles filled with bullets, and headed for Fleming's

Hotel on nearby Gardiner Place. Ryan walked on one side of the street, Walsh on the other. It was a safety device: if one was intercepted by police or military, the other could open fire.

This was Ryan's first experience of Dublin in wartime. On their way back to Shanahan's, they stopped in a church and went to confession. When they returned to Shanahan's, Ryan quietly offered his services for the job the following morning. His soul and conscience were clear.

But the mood in the bar had changed. Someone had been around and heard that the footballers knew something. The job was off, they were told. Head upstairs to sleep. Get ready for the match. Whatever was happening didn't concern them.

Planning this operation had taken almost a month. In October 1920 three of Michael Collins's closest deputies, Frank Thornton, Tom Cullen and Frank Saurin, had begun frequenting Kidd's bar near Grafton Street. Constable David Neligan, one of Collins's most important contacts in Dublin Castle, introduced them to an array of Auxiliaries and agents.

These men, he told the Auxiliaries, were 'touts'. Informers. One day, during a conversation about Collins and his network, an officer engaged them in conversation. 'Surely you fellows know these men: Liam Tobin, Tom Cullen and Frank Thornton. These are Collins's three officers. If you can get these fellows, we would locate Collins himself.' Cullen and Thornton's blood ran cold – they knew Tobin as the head of operations at the IRA's intelligence office a few hundred yards away on Crow Street. Only a lack of photographs, or even a reliable description, stood between them all and imminent discovery.

The authorities also delivered a handful of scares inside the first two weeks of November. Thornton was arrested and held for ten days. Richard Mulcahy, the IRA's chief of staff, escaped capture, but the authorities did find a document listing the names and addresses of two hundred IRA Volunteers. Liam Tobin and Tom Cullen were arrested and questioned before being let go. The British hadn't quite caught up with them, but they were getting close.

Whether or not he wished to risk an operation of such magnitude, Collins felt compelled to track down the agents he called 'the particular ones'. Organising the attack was left to Dick McKee, brigadier of the IRA's Dublin Brigade. He briefed every Squad member and representatives from the four battalions of the IRA's Dublin Brigade, giving names and descriptions of the proposed targets. They gathered information from the usual network of secretaries, typists, civil servants, hotel staff, policemen and maids.

They knew one target, Henry Angliss, was drinking heavily and prone to loose talk. They knew he wore a signet rig on the little finger of his left hand. They also reckoned he had killed John Lynch, the Sinn Féin councillor from Limerick. Two others, Lieutenants Peter Ames and George Bennett, were known from Kidd's. Squadman Charles Dalton spoke to a maid, Maudie, who worked at 28 Upper Pembroke Street. The house was full of Auxiliaries and agents. She outlined their daily routines. One day she brought Dalton the contents of a wastepaper basket. He found documents charting Volunteer movements and torn up photographs of wanted men. The night before the operation he met Maudie again. Everyone was at home, she said, apart from two officers: Ames and Bennett. They had moved to 38 Upper Mount Street. An extra operation was added to the list. To find the right men for the job McKee went back to Seville Place. Back to Second Battalion.

It hadn't been a weekend for Dublin footballer Johnny McDonnell to think about IRA business. True, there was a kitbag of revolvers hidden at home, having been smuggled in from Britain, but it was safe and out of sight. McDonnell's had been an arms dump for the IRA for a while now. No Black and Tans had come visiting yet. Sunday was all about Tipperary and Croke Park.

Then came a sudden invitation to Seville Place on Saturday night. As McDonnell neared O'Tooles, he noticed the military trucks parked on the road outside. A raid.

Word spread quickly and discreetly throughout the city, diverting everyone to Tara Hall on Gloucester Street. A few hours earlier Michael Collins had met there with the IRA's inner sanctum of leaders to finalise the list of targets. They settled on thirty-five different agents. Sean Russell, the IRA's director of munitions and a senior staff member at their general headquarters, now explained the plans for the following morning.

Members of the Squad would lead groups of men to different addresses around the city. Their targets, Russell said, were members of a secret service determined to destroy the IRA. Many of them had ended the war with great reputations as spies. It was vital they were removed. If any man had any moral scruples about the work at hand, he added, they could walk away now. Anyone undertaking this work needed a clear conscience. No one left.

The target agents lived on a web of streets that covered the southside of the city: Mount Street and Pembroke Street, Baggot Street, Fitzwilliam Square, Morehampton Road and Earlsfort Terrace. Others were based in the Gresham Hotel on Sackville Street. Others lived in Ranelagh. Johnny McDonnell was among those gathered to attack 38 Upper Mount Street. Vinny Byrne, who had been included as second-in-command of the group heading for 22 Lower Mount Street, was now promoted to lead the Upper Mount Street attack.

The prospect of the fight wouldn't have bothered McDonnell. He had already survived the Rising. His entire family lived every day with the risks of being in the IRA. He also knew he would be surrounded the following morning by O'Tooles men: Vinny Byrne, Tom Ennis, Michael Lawless. As the IRA leaders dispersed, Collins, Dick McKee and a few others retired to the top floor of Vaughan's Hotel on Parnell Square for a drink. The porter noticed a guest making a phone call before disappearing out the door. It was after curfew. The porter sensed trouble. He ran upstairs to Collins. 'I think, sirs,' he said, 'you ought to be going.' 'Come on, boys, quick,' said Collins.

A few minutes later a convoy of Auxiliaries swept through the hotel and arrested Conor Clune, an Irish-language enthusiast from Clare, who was the only guest not registered for the night. Later on McKee and Peadar Clancy, his deputy in the Dublin Brigade, were also taken to Dublin Castle.

Down in the Monto closing time had come and gone in Shanahan's. The bar was almost empty apart from Shanahan himself, DP Walsh and Jeremiah Frewen, another Tipperary IRA man who was helping Walsh bring his guns to Tipperary. The doors swung open. A tall man swept in. 'Hello, Phil,' he said. This, Shanahan told the other two, was Michael Collins.

He ordered a bottle of stout and made small talk with the Tipperary men. He didn't speak of Vaughan's Hotel or any plans for the morning to come. After a while he turned to Shanahan. 'If any of you are thinking of going to Croke Park tomorrow, it might be safer for you to stay away,' he said. 'There may be trouble.'

Few IRA men slept easy that night. Charles Dalton was seventeen years old and bound for Pembroke Street the next day. He stayed up all night. Frank Saurin took a drive to 38 Upper Mount Street to see the house and the steps leading to the front door. Some men went to Mass and confession. Others slept together in the same bed, huddled up like children warding off nightmares.

Back near Seville Place, Johnny McDonnell's clothes were ready for the morning; his boots, cap and shorts ready for the afternoon. A few hundred yards away Mick Hogan lay in his bed above Shanahan's, tortured by thoughts of Croke Park and his opponent Frank Burke, and praying for sleep, no matter how brief and restless.

PART III

CROKE PARK AND BLOODY SUNDAY, 21 NOVEMBER 1920

CHAPTER 9

Morning – 7am to Midday

An inventory of the killings. Frank Crozier saves an IRA man's life. Nevil Macready plans a trip to Croke Park. A close encounter for Michael Collins.

On Sunday morning IRA men across the city tried to disappear into the maze of streets and alleys. Some of the attacks had gone well that morning. Some had been botched. More hadn't happened at all. Some targeted agents had been killed. Innocent men had died, too.

Of the six targets at 28/29 Upper Pembroke Street, two (Major Charles Dowling and Captain Leonard Price) were killed. Four others were left with severe gunshot wounds, the result of shaking, terrified hands as the IRA men took aim. One of the injured, Lieutenant Colonel Hugh F Montgomery, suffered his injuries for nearly three weeks before he died.

During one operation in the Shelbourne Hotel, a Volunteer was startled by his own reflection in a mirror as he climbed the stairs and opened fire. The target upstairs heard the noise and escaped. One attack in Phibsborough was called off. A target on North Circular Road wasn't at home. The same happened at a boarding house on St Stephen's Green. Two more targets weren't in their rooms at the Eastwood Hotel on Leeson Street. At 28 Earlsfort Terrace, the raiding party asked for 'Colonel Fitzpatrick'; a maid had informed them that Sergeant Fitzgerald, an RIC man, lived there. He was brought from his bed and shot.

Joe Dolan and Dan McDonnell led a group to Ranelagh Road with orders to shoot Lieutenant William Noble and his mistress. When they arrived Noble wasn't there, only the woman and some children. A door opened. Another lodger was met by the barrel of a gun. One of the attackers recognised him. He was their informant. McDonnell and Dolan pushed the lodger and children aside and upturned the house looking for papers and documents, destroying furniture in the process. They wondered what to do with the woman. Their orders specified that she and Noble were to be killed together. Dolan couldn't contain his frustration and pulled a sword scabbard off the wall. He beat the woman and stole her rings before setting fire to the room. The children ran from the flames as the other Volunteers organised all the occupants of the house into a human chain from a tap in the basement, passing up buckets of water to quench the blaze.

Another kind of chaos had unfolded at 92 Lower Baggot Street. Bill Stapleton and Joe Leonard had led a party to kill Captain William Newbury. His wife, who was heavily pregnant, heard them ascending the stairs and forced the door shut. The attackers stood back and fired at the door. When it finally opened, Newbury was hanging out the window, riddled with bullets. Mrs Newbury gave birth to a stillborn baby a week later.

At 117 Morehampton Road a ten-year-old boy answered the door. Moments later his father, Thomas Smith, who owned the house, was dead alongside Captain Donald MacLean. Tom Keogh led an IRA unit to Lower Mount Street and killed the loose-lipped Lieutenant Henry

Angliss. Another man who had been sharing his bed rolled off and hid underneath before the firing started. Lieutenant Charles Peel barricaded his door and survived as seventeen shots splintered the blockade. A truck of Auxiliaries pulled up outside, forcing the IRA men into a brief firefight. Two Auxiliaries, Temporary Cadets Frank Garniss and Cecil Morris, who ran to get reinforcements at nearby Beggars Bush depot, were caught and killed.

Paddy Moran's instructions the night before had been chillingly simple: take thirteen men from D Company of the IRA's Second Battalion in Dublin the following morning to the Gresham Hotel on Sackville Street and kill three targets. Moran wasn't a Squad man, but a captain in D Company. That morning he met Paddy Kennedy, his intelligence officer, on North Earl Street. The rest of his men ghosted out of the alleys and street corners to join them.

Hugh Gallagher stood at the door of the Gresham every morning, welcoming guests and visitors. He opened the door as Moran and the others approached. They brushed past him. 'What business is this?' he asked. 'You'll soon find out,' replied one. Moran looked for the hotel register and the keys for three rooms. One of the rooms was empty, Gallagher told them. He spotted one of the men carrying a sledgehammer to break a door down; there would be no need for that.

Moran and his group stood at the door to the dining room, guns trained on the guests at breakfast while some of his men went to Leonard Wilde's room. Wilde opened the door himself. Four shots echoed through the hotel. They then went to Captain Patrick McCormack's room. He was sitting up in bed reading his newspaper as the door opened. Six more shots rang out. A lorry full of Auxiliaries rumbled past outside. As the men rushed out of the hotel, Moran tore three pages from the register. It was barely ten minutes past nine.

Of the fourteen men killed that morning, six were intelligence agents, two were court martial officers, two were Auxiliaries who came upon an attack and one was an RIC sergeant. Thomas Smith was a landlord. Patrick McCormack had returned to Ireland to buy horses for the Alexandria Turf Club in Egypt. Leonard Wilde was a British civilian with nationalist sympathies. Hugh Montgomery, who died later of his injuries, was a staff officer.

Johnny McDonnell had got away with the O'Tooles boys across the river back to Seville Place before the news had even spread that far. All that was both accurate and misjudged about Collins's plan was contained in their attack. Collins had seen Ames and Bennett as lynchpins in the British intelligence network. They were indeed agents at work in Dublin but their service records listed them as low- to mid-ranking. When McDonnell and the others attempted to make their escape, a hail of bullets rained down from a window across the road. Their assailant was Major Frank Carew, an important intelligence agent who had helped corner Sean Treacy a month before.

It carried all the horror of the other attacks: a maid crying in terror after Ames and Bennett had been killed; Ames and Bennett watching Frank Saurin gathering up their papers as they waited to be killed, realising he was their friend from Kidd's bar. In those few moments the breadth of Collins's web was revealed to them.

Once McDonnell was home he remembered the kitbag of revolvers hidden in his house. He left them for now and went to Croke Park. As for hiding himself, maybe standing out in the open on a football field was the best place. Whatever happened next, the worst of the day had surely passed.

FP Crozier was awake that morning before seven. His day promised a lazy mix of squash, lunch at the Shelbourne Hotel sharing stories and gossip and a stroll in St Stephen's Green. There was a new division of Auxiliaries to inspect and send to Meath before breakfast, and some paperwork later in the afternoon. Outside that, the day was happily his.

The new Auxiliary division was on parade in Beggars Bush at nine. It was November but the weather felt like springtime. As Crozier moved through the ranks, a military messenger on motorbike buzzed onto the parade ground, a nurse following him on foot. He was looking for Crozier. There had been an attack on a house. Two Auxiliaries had been dragged into a back garden on Lower Mount Street and killed. Crozier's face turned pale. The messenger was confused. Beggars Bush was within a few hundred yards of Mount Street. Hadn't he heard the shots?

Crozier shook his head. Revolver fire in Dublin had become as familiar and forgettable to him as night firing in the trenches. He took some men with him to Lower Mount Street. A woman's scream drifted down from the top floor of a house as he drove past. 'Murder! Murder!' she cried.

They reached the house on Lower Mount Street. Crozier went upstairs. One man was lying dead in his bed. Another was hiding underneath. Outside the house an Auxiliary had an IRA man, Frank Teeling, by the throat with a gun to his head, counting him out like a boxer. Teeling had been among the raiding party at the house. Killing one IRA man seemed a fair trade for losing three of their own.

Crozier stepped between them and knocked the Auxiliary's gun to the ground. He saw that Teeling was injured. Crozier put him in the back of a Crossley Tender and despatched it to the nearest hospital. He then pointed his own transport towards Dublin Castle.

He started piecing the story together along the way. A group of off-duty Auxiliaries had been on their way to catch a train west when they heard screams coming from the house and stopped to help. The two Auxiliaries apprehended by the IRA had been on their way to Beggars Bush to raise the alarm and gather reinforcements. The others had broken down the door and survived a shoot-out.

When he arrived at Dublin Castle, Crozier headed directly inside with news of the three killings on Mount Street. The office was full of secret service men, all of them in civilian clothes, some of them still eating breakfast at their desks. Crozier was in his full military uniform having been on parade that morning. They looked up from their plates of eggs. Crozier told his story, watching their mouths widen as their breakfasts got cold. Then a telephone rang. An official answered. 'What?' he said. 'In Leeson Street? Yes. Yes … hold on.' His face had turned white. His hands gripped the sides of the table. 'About fifty officers are shot in all parts of the city,' he said. 'Collins has done in most of the secret service people!'

Dublin Castle was soon gripped with panic. A jam of cars clogged the main gate. Officers and secret service men brought their wives and families, seeking refuge. By the end of the day every room in the Castle was full. More troops were packed into City Hall next door. Officers were accommodated in the Central Hotel on Exchequer Street and the Royal Exchange Hotel on Parliament Street.

Strange, disturbing stories drifted through the Castle offices. One officer had shot himself in his room. The rumour went that the dead man thought he had accidentally betrayed one of those killed by revealing his address. Another officer wounded himself in a café on Dame Street, then claimed he was attacked and received compensation.

As Commander in Chief of the military in Ireland Nevil Macready didn't care for spies but he knew Collins's audacity demanded a response. The city itself was shut down. Trains and trams were immediately suspended and checkpoints set up to monitor every other form of transport out of the city. The match in Croke Park would give the opportunity to send a message to the killers, and maybe weed out a few. If the GAA wasn't explicitly identified as a political movement, it certainly provided a playground for those who were. To Macready, it seemed a good place to start the search.

A map of Croke Park was produced and assessed. Its boundaries and entrance gates were well established. A railway line ran along the north end of the ground behind Hill 60. A canal bordered the ground along the south end. Jones's Road ran along the western side, and the Belvedere College sports grounds were adjacent on the eastern side of the ground, separated by a seven-foot-high wall topped with barbed wire. The drop from the top of the wall onto the field alongside was twenty feet.

The fencing around the rest of the ground was equally robust. A wall blocked the railway line behind Hill 60. Another wall ran along the rest of the terrace with a patch of waste ground outside. The Jones's Road side of Croke Park was well protected by walls separating it from the back gardens of the nearby houses. As well as the stand that housed the pavilion, Luke O'Toole's office and the dressing rooms, a set of concrete steps stretched towards Hill 60.

There were four main entrances: a shilling entrance at the Canal bridge that allowed access to the canal end and the bank that stretched out the length of the field on the Belvedere side; a two-shilling entrance near the middle of Jones's Road that allowed access into the pavilion and the sideline seats; another one-shilling gate at the north-eastern corner of the ground, allowing access to the bank alongside Hill 60. The fourth entrance stood at the corner of Jones's Road and Clonliffe Road, allowing entrance to Hill 60. Macready sent a message to Lieutenant Colonel Robert Bray at Collinstown Aerodrome, where the 2nd Battalion, Duke of Wellingtons (West Riding Regiment) were stationed.

There is a football match between a Tipperary team and a Dublin team taking place at Croke Park at 1445hrs this afternoon. You will surround the ground and picquet all exits.

Two points at the Railway End. Point C on the eastern side; D and E on the Railway Southern and Canal side, and the three known exits.

No picquet should be less than one officer and 15 men.

A reserve of not less than one platoon should be at Exit Y. Two armoured cars under an officer will meet your party on the Lwr Drumcondra Rd at the junction with Fitzroy Ave at 1515hrs.

About a quarter of an hour before the match is over a Special Intelligence Officer will warn by megaphone all people present at the match that they will only leave the grounds by the exits. Anybody attempting to get away elsewhere will be shot.

All male persons will be stopped, searched. Special Party 'O' will meet you at the same point as the armoured cars to assist in search.

Crozier had returned to Beggars Bush. The Auxiliaries bound for Meath were ordered to stay in Dublin that night. He fulfilled his appointment for a game of squash and reclined in the tub afterwards. Then he dressed for lunch at the Shelbourne.

Despite the news, and the shooting incident that morning in the Shelbourne itself, the mood was jolly. Crozier was in the company of military and political men. None of them had much sympathy for spies and agents. Crozier described his visit to Dublin Castle that morning and how he left the agents' faces pale and their eggs cold. 'A superior intelligent crowd,' he said, 'mostly hoy-hoy-la-di-dahs in mufti [civilian clothes].'

More interesting to him was what the politicians might do now. Macready would most likely be replaced by a commander-in-chief with the sea legs to withstand the political turbulence in Ireland. Then much floor-stamping in anger would follow and the branding of Shinners with every name under the sun. None of those around the table expected a fragment of practical, helpful aid.

An MP joined them for lunch. Ireland was a political playground for those opportunists in Westminster, Crozier told him. On one side you had the humbug of the Liberal coalitionists. On the other were the die-hards, depicting their opposition to a Home Rule solution for Ireland as loyalty to the Crown when they were really exploiting the scene for their own political gain.

'The worst of all,' said Crozier's staff officer, 'are the country gentlemen and retired soldiers in the House. A peculiar brand of incompetence, procrastination and laziness.'

They had no grasp of Dublin or Ireland. An Irish newspaper proprietor once visited Crozier and produced a list of atrocities and reprisals instigated by the IRA and British forces over the previous year. Crozier had seen the abiding horrors of the Boer War and the cruelty of an empire overthrown in Western Sudan, the bloodied mud and futility of Thiepval and the Somme. Even all this paled, he felt, against the wanton violence and excess he saw in Ireland on both sides. The lack of discipline among his own men cut to the bone. Like Macready, Crozier was a soldier. He believed in the sanctity of duty and respect even for the most scurrilous opponents but the uneven and uncertain implementation of the rule of law in Ireland went against that. His own Auxiliaries were almost completely out of control. By November 1920, Crozier had already fired over fifty Auxiliaries for indiscipline. Word came from London: no more dismissals. The risk of more negative press from those sent home wasn't worth the price of trying to knock some gumption into a few rotten apples. When thinking of Westminster and Ireland, Crozier often recalled the old story of what the Turkish officer said to his Australian counterpart at Gallipoli, when a lull was called in the fighting so the dead could be gathered and buried: 'God bless all good soldiers and God damn all politicians.'

The post went round. Crozier received a memo listing orders to make available to the military a company of Auxiliaries to assist at Croke Park that afternoon. He passed the details to his Staff Officer. The new company, initially intended for Meath, would be despatched to Croke Park under Major EL Mills. Mills had served with Crozier during the war and followed him to Lithuania in 1919 when Crozier tried to reorder the army there. He was solid. Reliable. Dealing with such a large crowd in Croke Park would need his steady hand.

Up around Drumcondra and Phibsborough near Croke Park at midday, people were being stopped at police checkpoints and searched. Patrick Berry was a warder in Maryborough jail and sympathetic to the IRA. He was with two Volunteers on Cross Guns Bridge a few hundred yards along the canal from Croke Park, waiting to deliver a set of despatches from the prisoners. He saw a tall, familiar figure striding towards him. It was Michael Collins.

They shook hands and began walking back towards Phibsborough, straight into a checkpoint. Berry's nerves were jumping. If Collins was caught, the blame would fall on him. An Auxiliary pointed his gun at Collins. Both of them put their hands in the air. 'We're all right,' said Berry. He slipped his hand into his coat pocket and produced an old pass for Ship Street (military) Barracks. 'We're out of Mountjoy [Jail],' he said. The Auxiliary took the pass and studied it. He growled. 'All right, you bastards. Pass on.'

They walked a short distance to an off-licence. Berry spotted the owner, Bill Connolly, heading in the door and quickened his pace to catch him. Berry tapped him on the shoulder. 'You were always pretty anxious to meet Mr Collins,' he said. 'Now I have the honour of introducing him to you.' Connolly brought them inside, flushed with excitement at the glamour of his guest. His hand scrambled along the top shelf for a bottle of his best sherry. A whole row of bottles fell, smashing on the floor. Collins and Berry drank a drop, settled themselves and then headed as far from Croke Park as they could, wading through the tide of people going the other way.

CHAPTER 10

Afternoon – 11am to 3.25pm

The story of Jane Boyle. A life-changing decision for Luke O'Toole. A crowd gathers in Croke Park. Mick Hogan prepares for Frank Burke.

11.00AM

The morning sun glinted against Jane Boyle's bedroom window like an unexpected gift. The smell of freshly baked bread wafted up the street from the Elliman's Bretzel Bakery a few doors down on the corner, the soft scent of 'Little Jerusalem'.

Home was a red-bricked two-storey house on Lennox Street at the heart of the Jewish neighbourhood in the middle of Dublin. The nearby Grand Canal was flecked with gold by the sun. The southern suburbs of Ranelagh and Rathmines were just over the humpback bridge. Her neighbours were a mix of strange accents and oddly spelt surnames. Most had escaped the pogroms that swept across Russia and Lithuania in the 1880s, travelling as far west as they could. They settled in such numbers around Portobello that many residents filled in the form for the 1901 census in Hebrew.

Over the years the Jewish community had stitched itself into the everyday fabric of city life. Many Jews became involved in politics. Some took up arms in the struggle for Irish independence. Local children and domestic help earned a few shillings lighting fires and helping out in Jewish homes on the Sabbath. On Sundays men made their way to the local Jewish clubs to play cards and share news.

Nearby Clanbrassil Street was lined with kosher butchers, moneylenders, tailors and synagogues. Sometimes Jane would hear the children playing on her road speaking a harsh, unfamiliar language before being admonished by their parents: 'No Yiddish on the street!'

Jane was twenty-six years old and lived with her sister, May, and May's husband and children. Every morning she walked a few minutes to catch the tram to Sackville Street and worked in Speidel's butchers on Talbot Street. She was a charge girl, serving customers and taking money behind the counter. Other girls worked out back helping bone and cook the meat. They made sausages using pork, rusk and Speidel's own seasoning. They cut bacon rashers, drained the blood and helped render down the pig fat for black pudding. The pigs were slaughtered out the back of the shop. Out front, customers would come in to buy pig's feet wrapped in paper, then eat them in the local pubs.

Talbot Street pulsed with all the good, bad and desirable of life. The Masterpiece Cinema next door to Speidel's did a busy trade in matinees and feature shows. The Monto bordered the end of the street. Living in the centre of a city meant trouble had often visited the Speidels. The family had survived the 1916 Rising sleeping and eating for the week in their sitting room. They covered the windows using mattresses and listened through the skylight in the second-floor ceiling to snipers spotting targets in the GPO shouting orders to each other on the roof.

The Republican Outfitters store was a few doors up. Jane knew the IRA men who hung around outside it. Most of them were Collins's men. Some of them were barely grown boys clutching their guns tightly and burying their fear. One day she saw three of them, Paddy O'Daly, Joe Leonard and Tom Keogh, walking past Speidel's. The police were searching people for guns further up the street. Jane came to the front door and called them back. If they had guns, she said, give them to her. They followed her through the shop and out the back door where she hid the guns. After the police left the men came back for their guns and continued up the street.

They walked with a swagger and talked about their favourite weapons like pets. Their light Mauser pistols were nicknamed Peter the Painters. They made holsters that sat neatly inside their long jackets. She read in the newspapers of the frequent killings everywhere, in the city and the country. These were the things they did. The things they saw.

Jane had been working in Speidel's the day Sean Treacy was killed. He fell outside their window. She heard the bullets peppering the Masterpiece next door. A bullet had flown through the window of Speidel's and embedded itself in the ceiling above the staff behind the counter. A newspaper man spoke to one of the girls. It all appeared in the *Freeman's Journal* the following day.

'Two bullets came in quick succession through the window and whistled past me but to save my life I could not move,' she said. 'One bullet went upwards and struck the ceiling, knocking the plaster off the moulding. No one in the shop was hit, but we had a remarkable escape as the bullets came on our side of the window and not on the side where the customers stood. Some of the latter were so startled by the suddenness of the affair that they did not seem to realise it until it was all over.'

Jane had run onto the street with everyone else. She spotted Paddy O'Daly, Joe Leonard and Tom Keogh coming back from lunch. 'Don't go down there,' she said. 'Republican Outfitters has been raided. There was an awful lot of shooting.' She asked them if they wanted to hide anything again in the butcher's shop. They declined. They had been carrying guns all day. Now, they didn't know how soon they might need to use them.

She had heard gunshots at home before and seen bodies on the streets near Lennox Street. On 22 March that year, a group of soldiers was strolling home along Camden Street from the theatre singing 'Rule Britannia' when a group of people began throwing stones at them. The soldiers retreated up Lennox Street, past Jane's house. Shots rang out. One soldier fell, shot in the chest. Then two civilians were killed. One was a nineteen-year-old domestic servant. The other was a van driver who lived a few streets away from Jane on Charlemont Street.

The following month Harry Kells, a plainclothes detective with the DMP who lived near Lennox Street, was shot dead by Collins's Squad having just left home. Kells had been sifting through line-ups of Republican prisoners in Mountjoy Jail, seeking suspects in different cases. The RIC and its new divisions of Black and Tans descended on the Jewish quarter that night and rounded up over a hundred suspects.

This death dance between the IRA and the authorities shrouded the city in fear, but people still found happiness in simple, familiar things. Jane walked to Mass that Sunday morning in St Kevin's Church on Harrington Street, a few hundred yards from home. On Friday she would return here to marry Daniel Byron. She would stand at the same altar she knelt before now, wearing her carefully embroidered dress, her short black hair crimped and shaped into a neat bob beneath a delicate veil. Her wedding trousseau was a thing of great pride, filled with linen and crockery, plates and all the cutlery and trinkets that would make her new house with Daniel a home.

She looked forward to seeing him that afternoon for their outing to Croke Park. Only the billboards proclaiming the news in the stop-press editions of the morning papers worried her. Fourteen British officers killed. IRA attacks across the city. The churchgoers chattered about the killings. Most of the houses of the dead were clustered around the same area, a few bridges down the canal from Portobello. From the IRA men she knew, to Daniel and the family that would gather round them on Friday, she had a choice of souls to pray for.

MIDDAY

News of the killings had reached Luke O'Toole at Croke Park early that morning as Central Council delegates from across the country gathered for a meeting to debate the ban on GAA players playing soccer and rugby. O'Toole pulled aside Dan McCarthy, chairman of the Leinster Council; Jim Nowlan; Andy Harty, a Dublin GAA representative; and Jack Shouldice, Leinster Council secretary, an IRA veteran of the Rising and the man in charge of managing the gate receipts that day.

They all expected a reprisal. They knew Croke Park could be a target. Should they call the game off? Once again O'Toole duelled with the contradiction of what the GAA believed in private and how they wished to be seen in public: if the game was cancelled because of the killings, the GAA would be acknowledging the impact on their organisation of a violent, political act. That was an arena they didn't wish to inhabit. They couldn't call off the match.

A crowd was already milling around. Ticket sellers were doing a brisk trade. The fruit sellers strolled along the road outside and around the pitch with baskets of apples and oranges. Hawkers sold badges and colours for the game. Before the Tipperary–Dublin match, Dunleary Commercials and Erin's Hope were to replay their drawn Dublin county intermediate football final.

After completing his work at the Gresham Hotel, Paddy Moran had headed for Croke Park. As chairman of the Dunleary club, this Sunday had already meant a lot. The club was barely a year old and chasing their first ever title. He arrived in time to stand in for the team photograph, still wearing the broad flat cap that had shielded his eyes that morning. Dunleary had the breeze at the beginning. Two early goals got them seven points up at half-time. Erin's Hope charged at them in the second half, but their shooting was bad and Dunleary's defence was good. Dunleary even scored another goal to win 3-2 to 0-2. Moran mingled with his team, then quietly disappeared into the crowd.

A few other Squad members came to Croke Park with the same idea of blending in. Behind the goals on Hill 60, Tom Keogh stood with Joe Dolan and Dan McDonnell. Keogh had been in the party that killed Henry Angliss at Lower Mount Street. He had even made a date with one of the maids before they left. Dolan and McDonnell could share their story of the burning room in Ranelagh Road, if not the woman scourged with a sword and scabbard.

McDonnell scanned the crowd. He was restless. He had little interest in football. Croke Park held even less attraction than usual for him this afternoon. Dolan was edgy, too. Vinny Byrne had already mentioned to a couple of IRA men that he thought the idea of going to Croke Park was madness. 'Something might happen,' he said. Just like Luke O'Toole, they all waited, and wondered.

2.30PM

Before the Tipperary team gathered at Barry's Hotel at lunchtime Tommy Ryan left Mick Hogan at Shanahan's and went to Mount Street for a look. There was no sign of any shootings. The police had moved on. Every doorway looked untouched and undisturbed by violence. He returned to Shanahan's around eleven o'clock. There was a message waiting for him. It was Dan Breen. He was leaving for Tipperary as soon as he could. If Ryan wanted, he could join him. Staying around for a match and going to Croke Park, said the message, wasn't a good idea. Ryan still decided to stay.

In Barry's Hotel, amid all the news from Tipperary and of the killings that morning, news also drifted around about the Tipperary team. Monsignor Maurice Browne and Mick Kerrigan stood with their neighbour, Mick Hogan, in the foyer. They already knew that Mikey Tobin hadn't come because of his father's imminent death. Their great goalkeeper, Arthur Carroll, was replaced by Frank 'Scout' Butler from Mullinahone. Beyond that, it was a familiar-looking team. Mick Hogan, Ned O'Shea and Jerry Shelly were the full-back line in front of Butler. Bill Ryan was in his usual position at right-half-back, alongside Jim Egan at centre-back and Tommy Powell at left-half-back. Tommy Ryan and Jim Ryan partnered each other at centrefield. Bill Barrett and Jimmy Doran were right and left-wing-forwards, flanking Jimmy McNamara, Glasgow Celtic's old flame. Gus McCarthy started at right-corner-forward with Jack Kickham at full-forward and Jackie Brett in the other corner. It wasn't a team picked with another day in mind: there were no experiments, no gambles. This was the team that had brought Tipperary level in the pack with Dublin, and within reach of an All-Ireland. They didn't see this as an idle challenge match, filling a weekend before Christmas. Tipperary had travelled to make a point. They had come to win.

Browne checked the time. It was ticking quickly towards throw-in. They wished Hogan luck and edged through the thinning crowd in the foyer towards the door. Before he left Browne looked around and saw footballers laughing and chatting with their neighbours and friends. Years later, this was how he would always remember them. 'They were happy as sandboys,' he wrote.

A few hundred yards away, across Mountjoy Square and down Fitzgibbon Street onto Jones's Road, thousands of people now streamed into Croke Park. Three IRA men – Harry Colley, adjutant to the Dublin Brigade, Sean Russell and Tom Kilcoyne – slipped quickly through the cracks in the crowd. They were looking for Luke O'Toole to give him a message. Word had reached Kilcoyne from a DMP sergeant that a force of Auxiliaries and military were being mobilised for Croke Park.

O'Toole met them with Jack Shouldice of the Leinster Council at the entrance gate by Hill 60. The IRA's message was simple: call the game off. The men from the IRA's Second Battalion, who usually stewarded these fundraising games, had already been pulled out. The Auxiliaries and the military were heading for Croke Park. Close the gates now, Russell said. Stop any more people from entering. 'Imagine if the machine guns open fire,' he said. 'What an appalling thing.'

It wasn't that easy, replied O'Toole. Shouldice agreed. Put aside the politics; the difficulty now was in the timing. The game was due to start in fifteen minutes. What about the difficulty of moving so many people out of the ground now? Those who had already paid would probably want their money back. Imagine the panic of a public announcement like this. The stampede to leave might lead to deaths all by itself. They also reminded the IRA men that the match was being played to raise money for a member of Second Battalion who had been injured in a fight while acting as a steward at Croke Park. That couldn't be helped, replied Russell. Play the match at a later date.

The Dublin players were arriving while they spoke. O'Toole and Shouldice consulted again with Dan McCarthy, Shouldice's colleague on the Leinster Council. As a compromise, O'Toole agreed to close the turnstiles to try and limit the crowd. As the IRA men walked down Clonliffe Road, Colley noticed the lack of stewards around the ground. Who would tell the turnstile men to stop allowing people in? He nipped across to the stile at the corner of St James's Avenue and told the turnstile operator there to close his gate. A few minutes passed. The crowd outside the entrance swelled and grew impatient. The turnstile man disappeared for a moment and returned in a temper, swearing at the IRA men. This was madness. He opened the turnstile and let the crowd in. Russell, Kilcoyne and Colley looked at each other. There was nothing they could do.

Billy Scott peered out his living-room window on Fitzroy Avenue at the people strolling towards Croke Park. He was fourteen years old, with the greatest playground in the city at the end of his street. Wasn't he lucky? Any day he liked he could stand on his front doorstep and see Croke Park. There was no tramping up from the dirty city below or sitting on trains coming from places far away.

Today he would eat his dinner before young Daly from a few doors up called in for him. They would go to the match and find a good spot, maybe in the trees at the corner of the pitch or along one of the high walls, or pressed down in the front row behind the fence at the canal end that separated the crowd from the pitch.

Dublin and Tipperary. There had been articles in the paper and great promises for the match.

GAA Challenge Match

Tipperary (challengers) v Dublin (Leinster champions)

An All-Ireland test!

At Croke Park tomorrow, 21st at 2.45pm

A thrilling game expected!

'A good, scientific game should result,' said the *Sunday Independent*. 'Considerable interest is centred on the game. As Tipperary defeated the Metropolitans in their last two friendlies, it will be interesting to see, in view of future engagements, how they shape in the game under notice.

'The Dublin team is just now in good fettle and they should prove a difficult lot to defeat on home ground. Tipperary have a good, strong, young team and as they were chief parties to the match they are certain to leave nothing undone to gain honours.'

When he came home from the match, Billy would have all the news for his father to take with him to work the following day. Billy could replay the game in school and the other boys would wish they had been there to see the Synnotts, the McDonnells and Frank Burke. Daly called in, and they walked together until they were lost in the milling crowd.

Up the road from Barry's Hotel in a small, shabby cottage down a muddy laneway, Michael Feery pulled a comb through his sandy brown hair. He did up his old army boots and buttoned a cardigan over his green undershirt. He was small and frail. His surviving front teeth were brown and rotted. All his years as a soldier, since long before the war, had left him with few possessions and lots of time to sit on the kerb. Home was the first damp, cold cottage in a row of seven on Gardiner Place, with his wife and son. They lived in perpetual hunger and penury, cheek by jowl with fine hotels and flea-bitten doss houses. The young shop apprentices employed by Clery's department store were billeted around the corner. They had jobs and futures and a route away from Gardiner Place. On Sundays like this, Croke Park was Feery's escape hatch.

It was the same for thousands of others. Down on Green Street in the tenements of the Ormond slum near Sackville Street, James Teehan from Tipperary wished his brother, John, good luck around half-past two and closed the door of his pub behind him. James strolled past the ruins and tenements, smelling the freshly cut lumber stacked in the yard of Tickell's timber store before striding out onto Sackville Street and up towards Croke Park.

William Robinson was eleven years old and lived on Little Britain Street, a few doors from Teehan's pub. Everyone called him Perry. His father, Patrick, made a living as a labourer. Sometimes he bought and traded any spare stock he could get at the Ormond fruit market. Like his father, Perry possessed an eye for an opportunity. He knew Croke Park. He had a good spot in mind for this game, the crook of a tree at the corner of the canal end on the Jones's Road side, looking across the pitch above the heads of everyone.

As throw-in time drew close, Daniel Byron and Jane Boyle found an equally good place on the halfway line across from the main stand. Perry Robinson was sitting in his tree. Billy Scott squeezed in among the men behind the canal goal. Ten-year-old Jerome O'Leary, from Blessington Street near the Rotunda Hospital at the top of Sackville Street, was perched nearby on the back wall.

The Dublin team were in their dressing room. Johnny McDonnell was there, his cap fixed. Ready. Tom Ennis, one of McDonnell's comrades that morning on Upper Mount Street, slipped in the door, looking for Paddy McDonnell. They talked about the events of the morning and about the possibility of the game being postponed. Paddy shrugged. The Dublin boys wanted to play. Twelve of the twenty players in the dressing room were O'Tooles men. Whatever came that afternoon they could take it, good or bad.

Frank Burke had seen O'Toole, Shouldice and the IRA leaders talking by the entrance gate as he arrived. He had set out that morning from St Enda's school with his friend Brian Joyce and caught a tram to Parnell Square. Burke saw a newspaper placard and its headline about the killings. It was the first they had heard of it. He turned to Joyce. 'There'll be a raid some place today.' Croke Park never crossed his mind.

3PM

After leaving the Tipperary team in Barry's, Monsignor Browne and Mick Kerrigan hurried along Mountjoy Square, down the hill past the Mountjoy brewery towards Croke Park. They had got lucky. The crowds milling outside had forced a delay of the game. Instead of 2.45pm, the match would now start at 3.15pm. Even then, Browne and Kerrigan had barely slipped through the turnstiles and found a place on the sideline by the time the teams lined up.

Mick Hogan's nerves hadn't stopped twitching. He had asked Bill Ryan again in the dressing room to change positions and spare him from Frank Burke. But Ryan grimaced. 'It's these boots,' he explained. 'They're just too loose.'

Hogan went to his bag and felt around inside, producing a spare lace for Ryan to tighten around his right boot. At least one of them could ease the other's nerves. Everyone else seemed so calm as they jogged out onto the field. Jim Egan from Mullinahone was at the sideline talking to a priest from home, Fr Crotty. Some of the players even smiled for the team photograph. Hogan stood in the back row and sheepishly poked his head out between Bill Barrett and Jimmy McNamara.

He jogged to his corner and waited for Frank Burke. The serious business of the day was upon him. No matter what way he tried to avoid it, Hogan would have to face Burke. Frank of the blistering dash and dancing feet. Frank, who could thread a kick through any gap you liked. Frank, who loved to score.

Then again, plenty had gone right so far this weekend. Hogan had survived a brush with the soldiers on the train and successfully delivered his message. He had seen something of the Monto on Saturday night and successfully hidden his nerves from Monsignor Browne and Mick Kerrigan. Now he was in Croke Park on a bright November afternoon with neighbours and friends in the crowd and a great football match to play. Whatever happened, he would have stories for Kate Browne and the boys by the fireside for the week and plenty to shorten the evenings between now and spring. If Frank Burke was the height of his problems, maybe they didn't amount to much. Maybe everything would work out fine.

CHAPTER 11

The Bloodied Field
3.25pm to 5.30pm

Lieutenant Colonel Robert Bray's watch ticked past three as he rolled his troops out of Collinstown Aerodrome for Croke Park. The infantry trucks joined two armoured cars at the junction of Drumcondra Road and Fitzroy Avenue, which led directly to the ground. Another armoured car led the convoy further up Drumcondra Road to the next junction and turned down Clonliffe Road. They drove a few hundred yards, passing behind Hill 60 until they reached the next junction with St James's Avenue. Bray was in a third armoured car and stopped near the entrance gate at the corner of Jones's Road and Hill 60. The soldiers jogged into their positions along Clonliffe Road. He checked his watch. It was 3.15pm.

His military unit was there to control the crowd; the RIC's role, including the Black and Tans and the Auxiliaries, was to detain and search them. On arrival at Croke Park the unit would split up and cover every exit gate, making the crowd file out in single queues. A cheer rose inside Croke Park. The game had finally begun. An aeroplane passed overhead, firing off a flare. That was a rare thing. Bray heard the familiar whine of a Crossley Tender and saw an RIC truck crest the canal bridge at the other end of Jones's Road. Over a dozen more trucks lined up behind them stretching back up the hill towards the Mountjoy brewery. Bray checked his watch again. It was 3.25pm. They were early. The RIC forces weren't due to arrive for another ten minutes. He would wait. It was almost time.

About a hundred Black and Tans had left the Phoenix Park barracks for Beggars Bush where the new force of Auxiliaries, originally bound for Meath, had joined the convoy. Major EL Mills led the Auxiliaries. Major George Vernon Dudley was in charge of the Black and Tans. Dudley was a man who liked a drink and a bet. He had worked all over the world, serving as a policeman in Rhodesia and with the North West Mounted Police in Canada, gathering strange, instructive stories of colonial life everywhere he went. He had once refused to use artillery to shoot wild game and scatter a bloat of hippos in Rhodesia to allow clear passage along the river for a sculling race. He often boasted of boxing in Canada against Tommy Burns, who later fought Jack Johnson for a world title, and of surviving a fight against a boxer named Pelkey, who had once killed a man. Ireland offered him work, but it was different to every other place he had been. He had met gangsters and toughs before, but saw a different cruelty in Ireland that pushed men into the darker shadows of themselves.

His Black and Tans would handle the bulk of the searches, along with the Auxiliaries. One of them, Roland Knight, sat in the second truck of the convoy. He was not in his Auxiliary uniform but carried his glengarry cap in his pocket, to be used to distinguish him in the crowd. He was barely twenty years old and from Fareham, a small market town on the south coast of England, the son of a silk merchant. He had worked as a grain merchant's clerk before war took him away to Europe as a captain in the Essex Regiment. He had been in Dublin since September. The morning's killings had inflamed his temper. If the Black and Tans and Auxiliaries were seen as ruthless and cruel, Ireland had driven them to that extreme, he argued. If British officers couldn't feel safe in their beds, why should the enemy feel safe at a football game? If the Irish wanted war, they would get war.

The trucks had swept up Sackville Street, blared across Mountjoy Square and down the hill past the Mountjoy brewery on Russell Street, heading to Jones's Road. People saw the trucks as they passed by and wondered where they were going. Some said a quiet prayer. When the first truck reached the crest of the bridge over the canal, the ticket sellers outside Croke Park started running. 'The Tans are coming,' said one. 'Ambush!' shouted a Tan. Dudley leapt down from the lead truck and directed six vehicles further up Jones's Road. The rest of the Tans poured out of the trucks and hurtled down the dip from the bridge towards the turnstiles.

Out on the field Tipperary had started brightly. The wind was blowing from the canal end into Dublin's faces, forcing them to weather a storm. The first couple of attacks required two smart saves from Johnny McDonnell. The game was almost ten minutes old before Dublin finally broke out.

Frank Burke immediately got on the move. Mick Hogan chased him like a hound hunting a hare. Jane Boyle clasped Daniel Byron's arm. When he heard the rumble of trucks on the bridge behind him, Perry Robinson turned around from his seat in the crook of the tree. A shot rang out. The bullet whizzed through the air into Perry's chest and through his right shoulder. He fell from the tree.

Jerome O'Leary looked back from his perch on the wall behind the canal goal. A second shot rang out. O'Leary fell to the ground, shot through the head.

More RIC men as well as Black and Tans and Auxiliaries, sprinted towards the turnstiles at the corner of the canal end. A ticket seller, Thomas Doyle, stood behind a table, his hands gripping the edges. An RIC sergeant stepped forward. 'Open the gate!' Doyle hesitated. 'Open the gate or we'll shoot you!' Doyle stepped out of the way.

Splinters of brick and mortar struck Roland Knight's face as he reached the turnstile. He climbed the wall and landed inside the ground on his feet. He watched the crowd scramble towards the wall behind the canal goal, and aimed his revolver at a knot of men. Fire. He turned to face the rest of the pitch. He picked a moving target and took aim. Fire. Again another. Aim. Fire.

Joe Traynor was in the middle of the knot of men with his friend PJ Ryan and a handful of others who had cycled in from Ballymount that morning. Now Ryan had lost him in the crowd and Traynor was hanging onto the wall. A bullet hit him in the back. He slumped over the other side.

A row of Black and Tans took positions along the bridge looking into Croke Park and started firing into the ground. People surged onto the pitch trying to escape the line of fire. In the corner of the ground near Luke O'Toole's house, Michael Feery tried to pull himself over the top of the wall. A sharp pain stabbed through his leg like a knife. A spike on top of the wall had cut through his left thigh, the point protruding out through his trousers on the other side.

After being knocked aside by the police, ticket seller Thomas Doyle went to the boy fallen from the tree. Perry Robinson's jersey was blood-stained near the right shoulder. 'Take me to Mother,' he said. Doyle picked him up and carried him away from the ground. He met an acquaintance, JJ Byrne, and handed Robinson to him. An RIC man ordered Byrne to take the child away. 'My name is John Byrne,' he told the boy. 'What's yours?' 'William Robinson. Will you tell my da I'm hurt?' Robinson told him his address. Byrne hailed a cab and ordered the driver to take Perry to Drumcondra hospital. Byrne headed for Little Britain Street to find Patrick, the boy's father.

Auxiliaries and Black and Tans swept the field again with gunfire. Some took aim. Others fired randomly from the hip. One man had the heel of his boot blown off by a bullet. Another man's hat was shot from his head. One ricocheting bullet hit a constable, passing through his cigarette case and pocket book, denting his whistle. Another ricochet pierced Billy Scott's chest, ripping through him so badly people thought later he had been savaged with a bayonet.

Roland Knight turned from the crowd by the canal wall to the people on his left heading for the main exit. He ran to the gates and joined the other policemen pushing them back in. People clogged the exit gates at the other end of the ground near Hill 60. The crush was unbearable. One gate was flattened and hundreds stampeded over the fallen, making frantically for the passing trams outside.

Up on Hill 60 itself Squad men Joe Dolan, Dan McDonnell and Tom Keogh went in different directions when they heard the first shots. After all the planning and the care and caution of the previous twenty-four hours, they were in danger of getting trapped like rats. McDonnell sprinted through the crowds. His hat flew off. As he stopped to bend down and pick it up, the man in front of him was shot. He kept running across the waste ground along the back of Hill 60 to the St James's Avenue gate at the north-eastern corner of the ground.

Once outside, he looked back at the gate. The crowd was swelling. The crush was getting worse. Those people who had squeezed out onto St James's Avenue were met by an armoured car. Inside the vehicle, the machine-gun operator heard the order to fire and sprayed fifteen rounds into the air. The crowd wheeled backwards into the ground, colliding with those trying to escape. Along the east side, hundreds braved the twenty-foot drop into the Belvedere grounds. Patrick O'Dowd was on top of the wall ready to jump when he spotted someone behind him struggling to pull himself up on the wall. O'Dowd extended his arm and dragged him up and over. As he landed on the other side, O'Dowd was shot in the head. He fell to the ground, landing on the man he had just helped. Some onlookers pulled the man out from underneath O'Dowd, and kept running.

People took refuge in nearby houses. One soldier opened a front door to find about eighty people inside. They were packed into corridors and on staircases, in the parlour and the bedrooms. Everyone was completely silent. Some had fainted and needed water. One young man ran in the door having returned from a presbytery where he'd been looking for a priest. Bullets raked the street outside. Everyone was trapped.

Daniel Byron and Jane Boyle had struggled a few feet up the hill towards the Belvedere wall and the St James's Avenue gate when they were caught in the crush heaving towards the exit. The crowd surged again. People were falling beneath their feet, their screams muffled by the mass of people trampling over them. Daniel felt Jane's fingers gripping his arm. They slipped and scraped the sleeve of his jacket. He felt her nails gripping tighter. More shots rang out. A bullet pierced her back. Her grip loosened. Then she disappeared beneath the people, swept away from him by a wild, unstoppable wave.

When the shots had begun Johnny McDonnell's Volunteer training told him what to do. Hit the dirt. At first, McDonnell thought he recognised the sound. 'Don't worry,' he shouted. 'They're blanks!'

At the other end of the field in the canal goal, the Tipperary goalkeeper Frank 'Scout' Butler was also lying on the field, his hands outstretched. A policeman kicked his arms and legs. 'You're one of those gunmen who killed our lads,' he said. Butler looked at him as he rolled up his sleeve to reveal a regimental tattoo. Butler was a survivor of the Somme. 'The last gun I fired was in Europe,' he said.

Mick Hogan lay flat on the ground right beside Frank Burke. Stephen

Synnott of Dublin was nearby. When the shooting had started, Synnott, Hogan and Burke had run towards the centre of the field. Burke could see the chips exploding from the railway wall as the bullets bounced against it. 'They're shooting at someone in the crowd,' Burke shouted. He whispered an Act of Contrition and began rolling towards the sideline. Their choices were terrifyingly stark: stay on the ground and risk being killed or run the few yards to the picket fence, mingle with the crowd and make their escape. Bullets still flew over their heads. In front of them men were climbing the wall that separated Croke Park from the Belvedere playing fields. Some made it. Others were knocked from the wall like empty bottles.

Hogan saw Burke wriggling towards the line. He did the same. And Synnott. 'We'll lie in here close,' Hogan said. 'We might get some protection.' They lay by the edge of the field. The picket fence was close. Beyond the fence, the crowds were rushing towards Hill 60. Hogan wasn't tired from the game. After all the worry about Frank Burke, he hadn't even broken sweat. He could make that short sprint. If he got among the people he could grab a coat and get away to Barry's Hotel or Shanahan's, or anywhere safe.

Synnott, Burke and Hogan kept crawling and rolling towards the picket fence. They reached the cinder cycling track that circled the pitch. Hogan had played in Croke Park a year before when the pitch was churned up like a ploughed field. This time the grass was beautifully trimmed. The ground felt firm beneath his belly. A few minutes before, Croke Park had captured Hogan at his most vivid and joyous, playing football for Tipperary in the biggest ground against the best team and their greatest player. Now the ground around him was being ripped up by bullets.

Another volley of fire echoed through the air. The pain shot through Hogan's back. Burke heard a groan. 'I'm shot.'

A spectator ran to Hogan. His name was Tom Ryan, born in Glenbrien near Enniscorthy, now working for the gas company in Dublin. Some knew him better as an IRA man. Those men had a different name for him; they called him 'More Rope'. A year before, when the IRA had raided Collinstown Aerodrome for guns, Tom Ryan was in the group. When they reached the guard room, Ryan helped tie up each soldier. He was impressively methodical, turning each man over onto his stomach on the floor and tying his hands behind his back before tying his knees together, then swinging the rope from the rafter overhead. 'More rope!' he kept shouting. 'More rope!'

As an IRA section commander, Ryan had already received word at home in Stoneybatter about the killings on the other side of town that morning. Don't even think about going to Croke Park, said the messenger. His two brothers were already up from Wexford. His parents were Tipperary people and had bred a family of boys who hurled for Wexford. Now the day had made him Simon of Cyrene, dropping to his knees to aid a stricken man. He bent down and whispered an Act of Contrition into Hogan's ear. As he did, a bullet hit Ryan. He slumped onto the ground.

Barely ninety seconds had passed since the shooting began. Out on Russell Street Major Mills ran two hundred yards from his truck at the back of the convoy to the crest of the bridge. He glared at the RIC men lined along the bridge. 'What's all this firing about? Stop firing!' Inside the ground Major Dudley rushed around the field shouting the same order. The firing stopped.

Frank Burke took his chance, stood up and ran. He vaulted the railings and mingled with the crowd, pleading for an overcoat. No one stopped. No one helped. A Black and Tan intercepted him. 'Who are you playing for?' 'Dublin,' replied Burke. Another Black and Tan struck Burke on the back of the head with a revolver. 'Where's your dressing room?' Burke looked across towards the Long Stand and pavilion. 'Over there on the far side,' he said. 'Well, double up!' said the Tan.

Burke jogged along by the railings to the dressing rooms. People were packed inside, gasping for air in the heat. Children clutched onto adults' legs and the hems of coats, crying. Monsignor Maurice Browne and Mick Kerrigan were among them. The bullets had rattled off the galvanised roof above them. Browne and another priest tried to calm the crowd. They asked the people to recite an Act of Contrition and gave them all general absolution.

Browne was jammed just inside the door and had watched the stampede: people tripped and fell over each other; others trampled them; they pulled themselves up walls and through barbed wire. A tall man was knocked to the ground. Another man tried to drag him away; his hands and clothes quickly became covered in blood as another bullet caught his hat and carried it away.

The fruit sellers dropped their baskets. Apples and oranges were strewn everywhere. Umbrellas and hats covered the field, lost and forgotten in the panic. Croke Park was transformed. This place of happy memories and simple pleasures was now darkened by fear, blood and death.

A Black and Tan came to the dressing-room door. Smoke wafted from his gun. He lifted it to Browne's head and cocked the trigger. 'Here,' he said, 'we avenge our fallen comrades.' The policeman then pointed his gun at the ceiling and fired. 'All come out with hands up,' he instructed.

They emerged from the dressing room onto a field packed with thousands of people, their hands in the air. All of them were marshalled into ranks. Machine guns were trained on them from the armoured cars. 'Come forward three paces,' came the order. The crowd shuffled forward. 'Now, back three paces.' They moved back. The guns swivelled along the lines of people, sometimes stopping on one, then moving along. 'Keep your hands higher,' shouted one policeman, 'or by God I'll blow your bloody heads off!'

Burke and the other Dublin players were corralled in the dressing room. All of them were searched. Their watches, cigarettes and money were taken. 'You can thank your Tipperary friends for this,' said one policeman.

Major Dudley was out on the field moving among the civilians. 'Get your hands up,' he said, and started forming lines. The searching could finally begin.

Having delivered the IRA's warning to Luke O'Toole before the game, Harry Colley had sat down for dinner with his mother at home on Clonliffe Road beside Croke Park just as the firing started. It all happened like O'Toole had been warned. Colley went out to the front of the house. A cordon of soldiers lined the road. He watched people walking past. Some were bleeding. Some were cut and bruised. Others were limping. Those who were unhurt made for the trams.

He spotted Tom Keogh in the crowd. His arm was bleeding. 'Tom!' he called. Colley brought him into the house. His sister, Gertie, administered first aid. As she did, Colley noticed a body on the street a few yards from his gate.

The injured knocked on doors everywhere, seeking refuge. Local people came out to help the wounded. The Ring family had run to Croke Park from their home on Sackville Gardens when the shooting started. They saw Joe Traynor on the ground bleeding badly and carried him through the Belvedere sportsfield to their house on the other side. Tom Ryan, Billy Scott and Michael Feery lay on different tables in different houses along Jones's Road and Russell Street, clinging to life. Others all around Croke Park waited their turn for an ambulance to come.

Gunshots still echoed around the streets outside. Inside the ground people held their hands up as the searches continued, praying for their lives. Patrick O'Dowd lay dead by the Belvedere wall. James Teehan had been crushed to death. He lay on the ground, wisps of foam caking his lips like milk.

The Tipperary players were gathered together against the railway wall on Hill 60. They saw two men on the ground away to their left. Both were in Tipperary jerseys. One got up and walked towards them, his face, hands and togs covered in blood. It was Jim Egan from Mullinahone. 'Mick Hogan is dead,' he said. 'Could we get a priest?'

Twelve Tipperary players out of the eighteen that travelled to Dublin were held at gunpoint along the railway wall. Gus McCarthy had escaped. Jack Kickham had slipped through the crowd and jumped the wall into the Belvedere grounds. Bill Ryan had disappeared into the crowd escaping Hill 60. He barely went fifty yards before he was marched back in by a group of soldiers.

Tommy Ryan also disappeared into the wave of people that escaped Hill 60 onto Clonliffe Road, his shorts and jersey hidden by an overcoat. He slipped into a house already full of spectators and waited for the panic to ease off. A few minutes passed. There was a knock on the door. A group of policemen forced their way through. An old man made a remark as they passed by and was hit with the butt of a gun. One of them spotted Ryan. Two policemen drew bayonets. They started picking at his clothes, tearing them. His socks and togs were ripped off. An officer appeared. 'Bring him back to Croke Park,' he said. 'We'll shoot him with the rest of them.'

Ryan was marched along the road. People were still running out of Croke Park. He saw one man impaled on the spike of an iron railing; others used his body to step over the spikes. A man standing with his girlfriend came over to Ryan and threw his overcoat on him, taking a hit from the butt end of a rifle. Ryan saw priests giving the last rites to the wounded and dying. People all over the ground still held their hands aloft, waiting to be searched. He was marched to the railway wall and joined the others on the team.

Ned O'Shea was picked from the players to identify Hogan's dead body. A girl put her hand on his shoulder as he crossed the pitch and placed an overcoat around him. A nurse accompanied them. Jim Egan looked for his neighbour, Fr Crotty. 'You weren't so anxious to have our fellows get the last rites when you were shooting from behind the hedges in Tipperary,' a policeman said.

Fr Crotty was still standing nearby with thousands of others, his arms aloft. A Black and Tan brought him out from the crowd. They turned Hogan over, his face to the sky. O'Shea confirmed it was him. Crotty knelt by Hogan and said an Act of Contrition. As the scale of the horror around him was unfolding, the priest took refuge in the simple rituals. He whispered the prayers for conditional absolution and asked if he could depart for holy oils. The Tan walked him to the gate. He returned from Clonliffe College a few minutes later with another priest, Fr O'Brien.

They crossed Hogan's hands on his chest. A Black and Tan came over to them. 'Where are you from?' he asked. 'Tipperary,' replied O'Shea. 'Well, you'll find it is a long way to Tipperary,' the Tan said.

O'Shea was brought around to the other bodies nearby: one was the crushed, bloodied remains of Jane Boyle; another was a man who was shot dead on the embankment opposite Mick Hogan. He didn't know them. One of the policemen picked up a walking stick from the field and handed it to O'Shea. 'I don't want it,' he said. 'Keep it,' replied the policeman, 'as a memento of the day.'

A couple of hours had passed. As the last people were searched, the Tipperary team still stood by the railway wall. One Black and Tan had a picture of the team. 'Look at them well,' he said. 'You won't see them again.'

An officer appeared from nowhere. It was Major Mills, the Auxiliary commander. He walked along the line of players, speaking softly. 'They intend to shoot every one of you. Something must be done instantly.' He stopped at Bill Ryan. 'How long was the game on?' he asked. 'What was the score? Are you cold?' He called over a spectator and took his overcoat. He draped it around Ryan's shoulders and turned to the Tans. 'These men are under my care. I'm taking them in a body to their hotel to have their belongings searched.'

The Tans dispersed, some of them seething with rage. Mills ordered the players to the dressing rooms. He told them to put on their overcoats. Mills asked one of the Tipperary officials what he knew about the shootings that morning. 'I saw them reported in the stop-press editions,' the man said. 'That's it.'

Jack Shouldice was also in the dressing room. When he was searched, his diary had aroused suspicion. Mills flicked through the pages. He handed Shouldice his diary. 'I don't see anything worth special interrogation here,' he said, before leaning in to Shouldice. 'There's been enough shooting and bloodshed here today,' he whispered. 'I advise you to get away as quickly as you can.'

Mills looked around at the rest of the players and officials in the dressing room. 'Search them and let them go,' he said.

They all walked out of Croke Park into the half-light of evening. The players wore their jerseys and togs under their overcoats, their minds still clouded in fright. Shouldice collected any surviving money bags from the ticket sellers and found only one was missing. The day's takings still amounted to over £160.

Some of the Tipperary players headed for Barry's Hotel. Others dug into their pockets to find their money was gone. Many of them went to O'Tooles club on Seville Place where some Dublin players were waiting. Jack Kavanagh of O'Tooles produced £50 to split among the others to get them home to Tipperary.

Tommy Ryan and another Tipperary player, Tommy O'Connor, headed for Stephen Synnott's house. Four others stayed in a policeman's house. Johnny McDonnell had already bolted for home. It was a night when every player could get raided. He had a kitbag of revolvers to shift.

The evening was getting cold. Ned O'Shea pulled on the borrowed overcoat that was three sizes too small for him, gripped the walking stick still in his hand and headed for Barry's. The rest left for home with nothing but their overcoats and their lives.

CHAPTER 12

The Aftermath

Sorrow and outrage across the city. A city is shut down. The death toll begins to rise.

As the searches dragged on, women, children and the clergy were eventually allowed to leave the ground. Monsignor Browne walked a short distance before turning to look back into Croke Park. He watched the long queues of people, their hands raised in the air, waiting to be searched. He saw men beaten to the ground with rifle butts. A man was on his knees in a corner of the field with a Black and Tan standing over him waving his revolver until the man's nose touched the ground. Bodies lay motionless all round him as the afternoon darkened. Browne recalled his readings from classical Greek history and the words of Virgil depicting the sacking of Troy.

Crudelis ubique luctus, ubique pavor et plurima mortis imago.
Everywhere is relentless grief, everywhere panic and countless shapes of death.

Browne went to the house of Canon Moore, an old friend from Grangemockler. His home was always a meeting point for any Grangemockler people visiting Croke Park. Browne tried to tell him the story, but the Canon found it all too fantastic. Canon Moore asked instead about home and the familiar parishes around south Tipperary. He asked after Browne's other brothers in the priesthood and recalled happy days spent fishing the River Lingaun in Grangemockler. Mick Kerrigan finally arrived with news: Croke Park was almost empty and Mick Hogan was dead. His body still lay on the field.

The news cut through Browne like a winter chill. A stream of images rushed through his head: Mick Hogan on his first day at school, crying for home and finding consolation in his penny package. Mick saving hay and sowing crops for the Brownes after John died, laughing and joking in the kitchen with their mother. Browne owed it to her, and to the Hogans, to find Mick's body. His last act of friendship must ensure Mick wasn't left alone now.

Browne and Kerrigan returned to the top of Jones's Road. The convoy of Tenders still extended back beyond the canal bridge. Some of the Tans seemed drunk, their rifles still cocked and ready. Browne headed straight for the field. A DMP officer on patrol rushed over. 'Come back! Come back! You're mad to walk down that street! You'll be shot!' 'I won't come back,' said Browne. 'I want to find Mick Hogan's body. He's lying on the field.' 'If you're so bent on going,' said the DMP man, 'I'll accompany you.'

They walked along the footpath towards Croke Park. Some of the Tans were singing, others cursing the 'blasted Irish'. The tricolour that normally fluttered from a flagpole over Croke Park was tied to the back of a truck. Browne entered the field.

'The place looked like a battlefield that had been abandoned by the combatants,' he wrote later. 'The ground was strewn with empty cartridge cases. Lifeless bodies were on the sideline and on the sward. Not a living soul was in sight. The silence of the tomb reigned supreme.'

As the trucks finally pulled away people began returning to the field to collect their belongings and look for friends and loved ones. Browne began searching for Mick Hogan, but didn't know where to start. Then someone called out: 'Here's the footballer!'

Hogan's body was covered by a fawn coat. The grass around him was red with blood. All the bodies were carried towards the main entrance and laid side by side. Ambulances ferried away the wounded to the Jervis Street and Mater hospitals. When it was time to move Hogan's body to Jervis Street, Browne got in the back of ambulance. Mick was among friends now.

The same tragedy unfolded in houses all around Croke Park. Joe Traynor lay on the Ring's table in Sackville Gardens. His friend PJ Ryan was still with him. Traynor was awake but blood oozed from two wounds in his back. The Rings went outside to look for an ambulance and worried what might happen if the police came along as well. Instead of bringing the ambulance to their door, they carried Traynor down a laneway away from their house and left him on Sackville Avenue. Shortly after the ambulance arrived at Jervis Street Hospital, Traynor was dead.

On Fitzroy Avenue, John Scott had heard the shooting and the screams from Croke Park. He took fright about his son Billy and went to look for him. When word eventually reached home that Billy had been shot, John was directed to St James's Avenue, to Mrs Colman's house.

The house was silent, and smelt stale from all the people who had taken refuge there. Mrs Colman met him at the door and brought him in. Billy was gone. An ambulance had already taken him. She told his father the story, how Billy had been carried into her house bleeding from the chest and in terrible pain. The same men carrying him sought shelter and as they laid Billy on the table, Mrs Colman and her daughter dropped to their knees and said some prayers. They saw Billy's lips move to the responses. He asked for his mother. 'Pray for me,' he whispered. Billy needed water but no one could safely get out and fetch some. He held on for forty-five minutes, moaning and gasping. Then he died. When the military came to the house they took the body but left him on the kerb. Mrs Colman had covered him in a blanket before the ambulance arrived.

But was she sure? Scott asked. Was it really Billy? Maybe it was another child. Maybe this burden was another parent's to carry? Mrs Colman reached into her pocket. Here was the tie pin he wore. These were his glasses. John Scott took them. His son was gone.

When the shooting was at its worst Major Dudley, the officer leading the Black and Tans, had stopped beside the body of a boy near the Canal wall. It was Jerome O'Leary. He called to a spectator, James Evans. 'Take him away,' he said. Evans carried Jerome to his own house. He called an ambulance as it drove past, but it couldn't stop. It was needed at the field. That evening Jerome O'Leary lay dead in the Mater hospital, unknown and unclaimed.

No one knew the man lying dead in Mr Forsyth's house on Russell Street either. Three RIC men had carried him to the door. He might have been forty, maybe fifty? His dark hair was turning grey. His thin moustache was sandy-coloured. He looked small and frail. He wore army boots and an undershirt that were dirty and worn. His grey shirt bore the writing AF192, printed in black ink. The letters MF were sewn in red thread on the shirt and on his undershirt. His coat, which was once dark grey, was badly faded. His cap was soiled. His army boots were worn down at the heels. There was a leather tobacco pouch in his cardigan jacket. His body was finally removed at 6.30pm and taken to

Jervis Street Hospital. Four days would pass before anyone would come for Michael Feery.

John Byrne and Patrick Robinson sat in Drumcondra Hospital, waiting for news of Perry. When the surgeon arrived the matron told Byrne to fetch a priest, pressing a letter into his hand. The surgeon spoke to Patrick. The bullet had entered Perry on the left side near his shoulder and exited on the right. It could have killed him immediately, but it didn't. His son was alive, but his wounds were extremely severe.

As the light faded on Croke Park, a priest prayed over Jane Boyle's broken body that still lay where she had fallen. Two more men, James Burke and James Teehan, lay crushed to death a few yards further up the hill near the north-east gate. The military finished their search of the neighbouring houses and gardens, and returned with one revolver. The owner of the house had seen a man drop the gun as he raced through her backyard, a policeman said.

Word about the killings at Croke Park was filtering through the city. Robert Brennan, Sinn Féin's first Director of Propaganda, was on a tram with his wife and children after a day on Dollymount strand. A day at the beach with his family was a rare blessing even though a cold wind had forced them home early. He looked out from the top of the tram as it trundled through Fairview. Hundreds of people were running from Croke Park. Some of them were bleeding. Most of them were leaping frantically onto the trams. He saw Paddy Devlin, an old acquaintance and journalist who wrote about Gaelic games. Brennan asked him what happened. 'The Tans drove into Croke Park and opened fire on the crowd,' Devlin replied. 'Some of the players were killed and a lot of the spectators.'

Brennan was stricken with shock but knew it was a story Sinn Féin needed to track carefully. He kissed his wife and children goodbye as the tram stopped at Nelson's Pillar on Sackville Street and headed for the offices of the *Freeman's Journal* across the road. The first reports were coming in. The firing had lasted ten minutes, said the despatches. More than a dozen people were dead and hundreds were wounded. Many more had been trampled in the stampede.

Henry O'Connor, the *Journal*'s chief leader writer, told Brennan that fourteen British officers had been shot that morning and seven others had escaped. As they spoke, word arrived of an enormous fire raging on Sir John Rogerson's Quay. They looked out the window in that direction. Wisps of smoke were visible in the distance. Were the Tans setting the city alight? They quickly clarified that the fires weren't the result of arson but an industrial accident. The city was aflame in every way.

General Crozier was back in Beggars Bush when Auxiliary Major EL Mills asked to see him shortly after five. Mills was furious. 'A rotten show,' he said. 'The worst I've ever seen.' Crozier asked what happened. 'The military surrounded the hurley ground according to plan and were to warn the crowd by megaphone to file out of the gates where they would be searched for arms. A rotten idea anyhow, as of course, if anyone had a gun on him, he'd drop it like a red-hot poker. Well, would you believe it, suddenly the regular RIC from the Phoenix Park and Black and Tans arrived up in lorries, opened fire into the crowd over the fence without reason. They killed about a dozen and wounded many more. I eventually stopped them firing. What do you think of it?'

'Rotten,' Crozier replied. 'Sit down here and write a report to me. I'll forward it to the Castle.'

Mills's report, written within a few hours of the killings, was damning and potentially incendiary, and bore stark contrast to the despatches being prepared for release in Dublin Castle.

Shooting at Croke Park, 21/11/1920
Report from Major EL Mills
To: Adjutant, Auxiliary Division, RIC, Beggars Bush Barracks,
Dublin

At 1.30p.m. 21st inst. I was detailed to take charge of a mixed force of RIC and Auxiliary Division to hold up and search people at CROKE PARK.

I arranged with Major Dudley, DSO, MC, who was in charge of a party of 100 RIC, to split up the two forces so that there would be an equal number posted on the 4 gates of the ground to search people as they came out.

The method to be adopted was that as soon as possible they were to make the onlookers file out of the ground.

I was ordered to leave the Barracks at 3.20pm and arrived at the gate in Russell Street at about 3.35pm.

I was travelling in a car in rear of the RIC leading the Auxiliaries. As we approached the railway bridge in Russell Street near the SW corner of the ground I saw men in the tender in front of me trying to get out of their car and heard some of them shouting about an ambush. Seeing they were getting excited I stopped my car, jumped out and went to see what was the matter. At this moment I heard a considerable amount of rifle fire. As no shots were coming from the football field and all the RIC Constables seemed excited and out of hand, I rushed along and stopped the firing with the assistance of Major Fillery who was in the car with me. There was still firing going on in the football ground. I ran down into the ground and shouted to all the armed men to stop firing at once and eventually the firing ceased.

The crowd by this time was in a state of panic.

After considerable trouble we got the people into more or less of a queue and they filed out as they were searched.

I went round the ground and found two children being carried out apparently dead. I found one female who had been trampled to death, also a man who had apparently died the same way. I saw a few wounded men and I got some sense into the crowd. I got the

*DMP to get ambulances for the wounded. We found no arms on any
of the people attending the match. After the ground had been cleared
and all the buildings had been searched I returned to the Barracks.*

*I did not see any need for any firing at all and the indiscriminate
firing absolutely spoilt any chance of getting hold of any people in
possession of arms.*

The men of the Auxiliary Division did not fire.

*The casualties I personally saw were 6 dead and 4 wounded, two
of the dead were apparently trampled to death.*

Signed

EL Mills

Major, 1ˢᵗ DI,

Adjutant, Auxiliary Division,

RIC

Beggars Bush Barracks,

Dublin.

In Dublin Castle, typewriters clicked and telegrams tapped into the
night. Finding the words to describe the day's events posed a challenge.
It was easy to describe the IRA's actions that morning as the crimes of
a murderous rabble, but the incident at Croke Park looked bad from
every angle.

The first drafts painted the scene of a police force reacting to extreme
provocation. The hawkers and ticket sellers that ran into Croke Park as
the trucks pulled up were described as scouts. The first shots, said the
report, came from inside the ground. This episode wasn't depicted as
a reprisal, or even a botched search. This was self-defence against a vil-
lainous foe that dressed like a civilian and hid daily among them.

That was the story the first statement fed to the newspapers. Spectators had been killed and wounded by police fire, it read, but police were
also 'fired on by Sinn Féin pickets when they were seen approaching,

and returned the fire, killing and wounding a number of persons'. A second statement followed later that night and featured in most reports on Monday. 'Details are not yet to hand as to what actually followed,' it read, 'but fire was returned, and a number of casualties were sustained by people among those watching the match.'

A curfew imposed that night from 10pm till 5am trapped hundreds of people in the city for the night. All trains were cancelled. All trams stopped running after nine. The roads emptied of motor traffic and guards were placed on all the bridges. Any traffic that did brave the streets was stopped and searched.

The theatres and picture houses were empty. Searchlights swept the streets. The roads were busy with troops and little else. The military and the Auxiliaries took up positions around Dublin Castle, City Hall and the City Treasurer's Office, and set up a checkpoint near the Royal Exchange Hotel, near Capel Street bridge. The people who did venture out congregated there, watching the Auxiliaries perform house searches and drag suspects into trucks. When the crowd around Capel Street got too big, a group of soldiers and Auxiliaries fired their guns to clear them away. A seventy-one-year-old man and a fourteen-year-old boy were killed.

Bill Ryan, the Tipperary player, stayed with his brother on Wexford Street on the south side of the city. He had never tasted alcohol in his life. That night he drank his first three bottles of stout and slept through the spatters of gunfire outside. Mick Hogan's bootlace was still in his bag. He kept it for the rest of his life.

More shots rang out on Blessington Street where the O'Learys and O'Dowds mourned their dead. Back near Seville Place, Johnny McDonnell got home that evening to find his mother in tears. She had been told her son had been killed. Tommy Ryan was a few streets over, sitting with Tommy O'Connor in Stephen Synnott's house. Synnott's wife, Molly, had been walking along the banks of the Royal Canal around the time the match had begun, heading towards Croke Park with her baby son, Sean, in her arms. A man passed her as she got closer. 'Woman, I wouldn't go any nearer that place,' he said. 'There's been quite a few shots fired.' She hurried home, and worried all night about Stephen. He finally arrived home at ten with Ryan and O'Connor. Mick Hogan was on all their minds. Synnott had been barely a few feet away, crawling on the ground beside him to the safety of the picket fence. The bullet that killed Hogan, Synnott thought, could easily have killed him instead.

They heard a bell ringing outside and the sound of a truck stopping. The three players leapt up. The Auxiliaries' Crossley Tenders always carried a bell in the front cabin. The three men ran out the back door and into a field behind the house. They crouched behind a pile of manure in the darkness and listened for the Tender to move off. A house three doors up had been raided. They heard another rattle of gunfire. Someone had been shot. No one called to Synnott's.

The political fallout was already taking shape in Dublin Castle and London. To Macready, Crozier and the other military men, Croke Park was an inevitable result of a flawed political approach to Ireland. The politicians would publicly mourn their fallen dead in the coming week. Privately Lloyd George and others had little time for agents and spies. Winston Churchill met with Henry Wilson, Chief of the Imperial General Staff, that evening. The killings of the agents in Dublin had shaken Wilson but Churchill found little reason for sympathy. That night Wilson poured his anger into his diary.

'Tonight Winston insinuated that the murdered officers were careless, and ought to have taken precautions. This fairly roused me, and I let fly about the Cabinet being cowards and not governing, but leaving it to the Black and Tans etc. No Cabinet meeting, as the Cabinet do not think that anything out of the way has happened! I urged on Winston, for the hundredth time, that the Government should govern, should proclaim their fidelity to the Union, and declare martial law. I told him I had not intended to speak on Ireland, as it was useless. But I was angry at the ministerial attitude about these poor wounded officers, and I frightened Winston.'

On nights like this, Ireland felt like an overwhelming problem. *The Sunday Mail* ran a piece that day by G. Ivy Sanders, describing his Halloween in the Wicklow Mountains. Sanders had spent a lot of time in Ireland, but didn't recognise the country anymore. Ireland had given so much to the bloodstream of the empire over the years it seemed inextricable from Britain. That relationship was now toxic.

'The dark days of Ireland completely overshadowed the evening, persistently creeping into conversations and checking laughter on the lips,' he wrote. 'So it was everywhere. Visitors to the hotels are few and subdued. The hotel dining rooms and restaurants are strangely quiet ... Levity is rare and disapproved.

'Theatres, music halls, and cinemas are still open, but the general feeling of depression, combined with the early curfew hours, during which no one must be out of doors, is seriously affecting the attendance at these places. Friends doubt each other. Paid and voluntary 'informers' are employed by both sides. Suspicion has raised a barrier of distrust and reserve which it is hard to break down. The wise absolutely refuse to talk to strangers. Most conversations, no matter how innocent, are now, by force of habit, carried on in hushed tones. Even among trusted acquaintances doors are locked and voices are lowered.

'I find myself regarded as a possible spy. Few talk in trains or other public conveyances or places. Only twice during the many long journeys I have taken have I found a responsive fellow passenger. Even the outside car drivers, the famous "jarveys", who have a worldwide reputation for wit and volubility, are uncommunicative. Is it to be wondered why that many are leaving Ireland today?'

News that Joe Traynor was hurt had reached his home in Ballymount on the fringe of the city around five o'clock. His family knew he was dead by nine. John Teehan stood over his brother James's body in Jervis Street Hospital. James's lips were blue. A small scar behind his left ear was the only visible sign of injury. It was the crowd that crushed him. Michael Feery's body also lay on a slab in Jervis Street, unknown and unclaimed.

Tom Ryan, who whispered prayers in Mick Hogan's ear, had been placed in an ambulance that took him to Jervis Street. Blood poured from his stomach. That night his two brothers sat with him. They had grown up in a family of labourers. The monuments around their home in Glenbrien told a story of rebellion in 1798. On a bright day Vinegar Hill, the site of the rebellion's last stand in Wexford, was visible on the horizon. Tom had come to Dublin years before with an idea of a job in Powers Distillery. He had been in the city during the Rising. His brothers had hurled with Wexford. Now they sat with Tom for his final hours. That evening, a man in a Volunteer uniform came in and stood to attention at the end of Ryan's bed, offering a brisk salute. He looked to the brothers. 'There's one man lying there,' he said. 'But there's hundreds would fall for him tonight.' Ryan was dead within two hours.

James Burke, Billy Scott and Patrick O'Dowd were all dead on arrival at the Mater Hospital. Jerome O'Leary died within an hour. Mick Hogan's body lay in the morgue, apparently unblemished by blood or bullet. No one could see the three bullet wounds on the left side of his back or how his left lung was perforated by a shattered rib.

Jane Boyle's brother, James, stood over her broken body in the Mater Hospital. There was a small bruise over her left eye. The left side of her face was distorted by her broken jaw. A bullet had pierced her back. The happiness of the morning was shattered. Instead of a wedding, Daniel Byron would bury his fiancée in a few days.

That night, Commander Crozier sat with his diary. The death rattle of bullets still echoed across the city. IRA men sat in safe houses planning revenge and retribution. Some of them mingled among the crowds gathering outside both hospitals. Crozier picked up his pen and scratched out a few final words. 'The worst day in history,' he wrote. Then he turned out the light.

PART IV

THE BLOODY SUNDAY INQUIRIES AND THE SEARCH FOR TRUTH, 1920–1921

CHAPTER 13

The Violence of Truth

MONDAY, 22 NOVEMBER TO THURSDAY, 25 NOVEMBER 1920

Bones in Croke Park. Speculation in the newspapers. Fist fights in Westminster.

The Monday morning after Bloody Sunday, a reporter from the *Freeman's Journal* called to Albert Villas to walk through Croke Park with Luke O'Toole. It was a chilling scene. A mist spread like a veil over the field, softening the outlines of the pools of blood and the bullet holes on the walls, hiding the walking sticks and fragments of human bone scattered all over the pitch. A trail of blood streaked the ground outside O'Toole's own house where a wounded woman had been carried.

Bloodstains marked the ground where the bodies had lain. A small group had gathered to pray at the spot where Mick Hogan was killed. The pitch was still covered in hats, umbrellas, apples, oranges and fruit sellers' baskets. The ground was torn up and rutted. The wall at the Clonliffe Road end was pitted with bullet holes. The parapets around the ground were chipped by bullets and ricochets. Blood streaked the walls where people had climbed over, seeking safety. The avenues along the back of the Belvedere grounds were spattered with blood. Up the road, the outside walls of Cotter's pub on Drumcondra Road were pockmarked by stray bullets. Nowhere and no one had escaped.

O'Toole took the reporter to meet the man employed to pick up the shards of human bone left on the pitch. They also visited Mrs Gallagher, one of O'Toole's neighbours. When the Tans had first arrived, she told them, she had heard people shout 'They're coming'. A man staggered into her backyard and collapsed in a puddle of water, blood streaming from a wound in his leg. She called a priest and tried to staunch the bleeding. One cadet, she said, told her it was reprisal for what had happened that morning.

The truth of what happened was already a tangled knot of different accounts and eyewitness testimony. Mrs Gallagher told the reporter she hadn't heard any shots from inside the ground, and had watched what she thought were soldiers scale the turnstiles. Then, she said, the shooting started. But a policeman who had been among the crowd said he heard shots fired before the Black and Tans appeared. O'Toole explained how the ticket sellers outside the ground had probably given the first warning and run back towards Croke Park. There were no IRA lookouts, he said, and no guns on the field. The army had stood by, he said – the police did all the shooting.

The reporter left Albert Villas and crossed the road to Billy Scott's home on Fitzroy Avenue. His father, John, described the diamond-shaped wound just over Billy's heart and the horrendous damage inflicted on him. It could only have been a bayonet wound, John said. Mrs Scott said her boy had been found on the street, brought to a house and laid on a table. He had just enough energy, she said, to ask those around to pray for him. Then he died.

All the newspapers carried vivid eyewitness accounts the following day. The headline on the *Freeman's Journal* recalled the massacre of nearly a thousand people at a public meeting in April 1919 by British troops in India and stirred fear among Macready's men that they might be tainted in a similar way: 'AMRITSAR REPEATED IN DUBLIN.'

The *Journal* reporter himself had been in Croke Park, seated at the press table in front of the pavilion near the dressing rooms. 'Suddenly at the canal end of the ground, a volley rang out from uniformed forces who had entered the park.' The first and only shots, he wrote, came from 'uniformed men'.

'They rushed in as though they were attacking the Germans and began firing straight away,' another spectator told him. 'People rushed off the banking onto the pitch and some succeeded in getting inside the pavilion. Others sought cover under the banking that surrounds the playing area and were huddled up, one on top of the other. It was a scene of terror. No one appeared to be able to speak to anybody else. Many were trampled underfoot as the forces rushed forward at different points in the park. I received a knock, apparently with the butt of a rifle, on the head, and was knocked down. Others fell around me including one man who seemed to roll down the banking as if he were dead.'

The span of opinion and blame varied from title to title. The headline and story in the *Times* of London stayed loyal to the version favoured by Dublin Castle.

RED SUNDAY IN DUBLIN. RIOT OF DEATH. FOUR-
TEEN OFFICERS MURDERED. FOOTBALL FIELD
BATTLE. 9 KILLED. 50 INJURED.

Fourteen Army officers and ex-officers were murdered in their homes in Dublin yesterday, many by gangs of armed assassins, and five others were wounded.

A serious affair occurred in the afternoon. Crown forces drove to Croke Park where a crowd of about 15,000 people had collected to witness a Gaelic football match. Many of them had come from the country. It is alleged that when the Crown forces entered the field they were fired at by scouts who were posted all over the field. They returned fire, then people stampeded and one woman was crushed to death at the gates. It is reported that 12 persons in all were killed and over 100 wounded. Afterwards 30 revolvers were found on the field.

'Hell Let Loose in Dublin,' screamed the *Daily Herald*. 'Fierce Scenes in the Street and at Football Match. Heavy Death Toll. Railways Stopped. Streets Cleared of Motors. Docks Ablaze.'

The *Daily Telegraph* followed suit, claiming 'at least 200 men involved in Sunday morning's murders'.

'The circumstances under which these brave men met their death,' wrote the *Daily Mirror* of the agents killed that morning, 'was equal in horror to any of the incidents that stain Irish history since the days of Elizabeth or Cromwell.'

Other British newspapers like the *Daily News* and *Manchester Guardian* had embedded correspondents in Ireland and took a more sympathetic view. In their pages over the years both newspapers argued that Britain's apparent inability to govern Ireland was an extension of the ruling classes' failure to rule the empire in a fair and equitable way. The sooner Ireland was left to the Irish, they argued, the better for Britain. The *Daily News* coverage on Monday reflected both sides of the same coin: outrage at the atrocities committed on Sunday morning, shadowed by a troubled scepticism at the British response.

DUBLIN'S DAY OF MASSACRE; 12 DEFENCELESS
BRITISH OFFICERS KILLED IN COLD BLOOD; TOTAL

DEATH TOLL OF 24; TERRIBLE SCENES FOLLOW
PANIC AND STAMPEDE AT A FOOTBALL MATCH

*The greatest outbreak of terrorism yet seen in Ireland occurred in
Dublin yesterday. Simultaneously in at least eight separate parts of
the city, armed men entered houses where British officers were resid-
ing. In almost all cases the officers were in bed, and 12 were merci-
lessly murdered without a chance of defending themselves.*

*It is described as the worst massacre of British civilians since the
Indian Mutiny. Five other officers and one civilian were wounded.
Two police cadets were killed.*

*Yesterday afternoon a joint force of troops and police with
armoured cars attended a football match. Shots were fired, a panic
ensued and 10 persons are reported killed and 60 wounded. Last
night it was announced that, from today, a 10pm curfew will come
into operation.*

Another *Daily News* piece, by Hugh Martin, questioned the coverage afforded those killed on Sunday morning in comparison with those
killed in the afternoon. Where in this narrative, he asked, were the
Croke Park dead? 'The most ominous fact about this Irish tragedy is
the way in which the scene at the Croke Park football ground is being
allowed to be passed over with the most off-hand notice. Is it to be
held the usual thing for soldiers, or armed auxiliaries, in the delicate
official language – to fire volley after volley upon a football crowd? We
have to go back to Amritsar to find anything resembling the scenes
at Croke Park as described by the correspondents. Unfortunately the
resemblance in this case is close.'

His assault on the official version of events continued. Martin said
he found little confirmation for the official assertion that IRA men had
fired first on the police, and he illustrated the strange, complex battleground faced by British forces in Dublin: 'Prominent government offi-

cials, police officers and military men with whom I have discussed the position at length have seemed to have no conception of the intense bitterness and fanatical hostility of the people among whom they lived. While believing that no alternative existed to the scheme of ruthless repression … they yet saw no reason for going the "whole hog" and imposing a system of legalised frightfulness.

'Thus it happens that officers are left at the mercy of a gang of desperadoes fighting with their backs to the wall to avoid capture, and determined as the pressure intensified day by day to take as many lives as possible before sacrificing their own.'

The ripples that began in Dublin quickly touched every part of the country. Thirty-six people were arrested in Queenstown, County Cork, that evening and more across Munster. More arrests followed in Galway city and Athlone. A police lorry drove through Cork city centre firing random shots that night at the buildings it passed – one young woman narrowly escaped death as a bullet passed through a window.

The IRA also retaliated. An intelligence officer was killed in Ballincollig, near Cork city, while riding a motorcycle. An RIC man in Leap, West Cork, and the head constable in Newry, County Down, were also killed. A young man was killed in Dolphin's Barn, Dublin city. An RIC constable and a soldier were shot in the Phoenix Park.

Police and military parties raided the offices of the *Irish Independent* and the *Freeman's Journal*. The Irish Transport and General Workers' Union headquarters at Liberty Hall and the Painters' Union Hall were also targeted. On Tuesday, 23 November, the GPO was raided by the police and mail confiscated. The east side of Parnell Square was closed off while hotels in the area and the offices of Dublin County Council were searched. The residence in Drumcondra of the Archbishop, William Walsh, was visited by police and his valet arrested. Searches on Lower Mount Street went on for two hours that morning and yielded a lorryful of suspects.

Opinion in England remained sharply divided. At a rally in Birmingham that Tuesday, Sir John Simon, Liberal MP, described his fears that all hope of reconciliation between Ireland and the empire was in vain. TP O'Connor from Liverpool, the Irish Party's only MP elected in Britain, offered his sympathies to the families of all the victims, and, with the passing of a Home Rule Bill close to completion, spoke directly to Sinn Féin and the IRA: 'England will give you your freedom if you are wise,' he said, 'if you avoid crimes that do no good, either to the name or the honour or the interest of Ireland.'

MPs had convened in Westminster on Monday morning. The chatter in the lobby was about martial law in Ireland and perhaps attaching the death penalty for unlawful possession of arms in certain areas of the country. News was also emerging from Dublin Castle of three more deaths the previous night: Dick McKee, Peadar Clancy and Conor Clune. All of them had been in Castle custody. The official explanation insisted all three had been killed trying to escape. No one in Ireland believed it. Either way, fourteen servicemen lay dead in Dublin but the press were still pulling both ways about the weekend's events. Something needed to be done.

Chief Secretary for Ireland Sir Hamar Greenwood was asked that afternoon in Westminster about the prevailing state of affairs in Dublin. All outward trains from Dublin had been cancelled and motor transport was still severely restricted, he said, but no fresh disturbances had been reported. 'I shall give now,' he said, 'just as I have received them, the details of, I think, one of the most awful tragedies in the history of our empire.'

He listed the fourteen dead servicemen and six injured, 'including one assassin, and three assassins captured redhanded with arms [McKee, Clancy and Clune].' He read deliberately and slowly through the list of the dead.

Captain Baggally, court-martial officer. Shot dead at 119 Lower Baggot Street. 'This gallant officer had lost a leg in war and was a barrister by profession,' said Greenwood. 'He had been employed as Prosecutor on Courts-Martial.'

Captain Fitzgerald. Killed at 28 Earlsfort Terrace, found in a pool of blood, his 'forehead shattered with bullets, another through heart and one through wrist which [he had] held up to ward off shot. All fired point-blank.'

Mr Mahon [Angliss's alias] and Mr Peel, 22 Lower Mount Street. Mahon killed. Peel escaped uninjured. Auxiliary cadets had heard shots as they passed on their way to the train station and attacked the house.

The two cadets, Morris and Garniss, who were despatched to Beggars Bush for reinforcements, 'both of whom were assassinated on the way. The officers chased the assassins through houses and captured one, whom their fire had wounded, and three others, all of whom were armed. These men will be tried for murder.'

Mr Smith and Captain MacLean at 117 Morehampton Road. Both in bed with their wives. A party of between twelve and twenty men knocked at the door. 'It was opened by a boy of ten years,' Greenwood said. 'Captain MacLean and Mr. Smith were dead before an ambulance could arrive. Mr [John] Caldow was seriously wounded. Mr Thomas Henry Smith, who was the landlord, was about forty-five years of age, leaves a wife and three children.'

Captain Newbury of 92 Lower Baggot Street, a court-martial officer.

Major Dowling and Captain Price, murdered at 28 Upper Pembroke Street. Four wounded.

Lieutenants Ames and Bennett at 38 Upper Mount Street. Twenty armed, masked men let in by the servant, Catherine Farrell, who 'unwillingly outpointed the rooms'.

Two murders at the Gresham Hotel. Ex-Captain Patrick McCormack and Lieutenant LE Wilde. '[Wilde] opened and asked: "What do you want?"' reported Greenwood. 'For an answer, three shots were fired into his chest simultaneously.' Five shots were fired into McCormack's body and head. 'Bed saturated,' said Greenwood. 'Body and especially head horribly disfigured. Possibly a hammer was used as well as shots to finish off this gallant officer.'

Greenwood's depictions were lurid and united the House in revulsion. Conservative MP Sir William Davison asked if the police and military had sufficient powers to deal with this menace. Was there need for urgent legislation to empower them further and 'enable persons found in possession of arms or ammunition without a permit in any disturbed area in Ireland to be shot?'

Prime Minister Lloyd George rose to address a question that directly proposed martial law. 'We are convinced, in spite of recent outbreaks, that the Irish authorities are gradually succeeding in their gallant efforts to break up the gang of assassins who have been terrorising Ireland,' he said. 'Should, however, experience show that the powers with which the Irish Government are equipped prove insufficient for that purpose, they will have no hesitation in asking Parliament for such further authority as may be necessary to achieve that end.'

The clock struck four o'clock. Croke Park hadn't been mentioned all afternoon. Joe Devlin, an Irish Party MP from the Falls Road in Belfast, stood up. 'May I ask the Prime Minister why it is, when a question is put to himself and the Chief Secretary to recite all the horrible occurrences that have taken place last Sunday in Dublin, that we have heard nothing about the appearance of the military forces at a football match at which ten people were killed?'

A chorus rose from MPs. 'Sit down!' they shouted.

'I will not sit down,' replied Devlin. 'I want to know from the Prime Minister why the House of Commons has not been made acquainted, in the recital of these other things that have occurred, with the onrush of the military into a football field, with fifteen thousand people, indiscriminate shooting, and ten men killed. Why was the House not told that when the other story was being told? May I ask for an answer?'

'I was never asked that question referred to by the honourable member,' Greenwood replied, 'but I am prepared to answer it now.'

Greenwood rummaged for a moment among his papers. Government MPs were on their feet, still shouting at Devlin to sit down. Greenwood whispered something to Major John Molson sitting nearby. Molson suddenly turned around and reached back towards Devlin, grabbing him by the neck and attempting to pull him into the row below. As Devlin wriggled loose from Molson's grip he dodged a volley of punches from other MPs. Cries of 'Kill him!' came from both sides of the House.

'This is a fine expression of your English courage and chivalry to attack one man among six hundred,' Devlin shouted.

TP O'Connor and James M Hogge of the Liberals tried to restrain Devlin. Labour MP Jack Jones forced himself between Devlin and the rest. 'If there is a fight,' he said, 'I'm in it.'

The speaker suspended the sitting at five minutes past four and closed the public galleries. Most MPs filed out of the chamber, but Devlin, Lloyd George, Andrew Bonar Law, Winston Churchill and Austen Chamberlain stayed in their places. Greenwood and Conservative MP

Sir Laming Worthington-Evans stared coldly back at Devlin. No words passed between them.

The House reconvened at twenty minutes past four. Molson apologised and Devlin accepted, but he continued to prod at Greenwood. 'The question I put was, I think, a perfectly legitimate question arising out of the answer given by the right honourable gentleman, the Chief Secretary for Ireland. It was this: Why was it that he did not recite all the incidents that took place in Dublin and tell the whole story and not part of the story? He said that the reason that he did not answer it was because the question was not specifically put to him.'

Greenwood's eventual answer echoed the despatches from Dublin Castle the previous evening. 'The authorities had reason to believe that Sinn Féin gunmen came into Dublin on Sunday under the guise of attending a hurling match between Dublin and Tipperary, but really to carry out the Sunday morning's murders. A mixed force of military, Royal Irish Constabulary, police etc, therefore surrounded the playing fields at Croke Park on Sunday afternoon to search for arms, etc. This force was fired upon and they fired back, killing ten and wounding others. About three thousand men were searched. Thirty revolvers and other firearms were found on the field. I regret to say that a woman and a man were crushed to death in the crowd.'

Lt Comm Joseph Kenworthy (Liberal): 'Is that the total casualty list?'

Greenwood: 'Ten killed, a number wounded and a man and woman crushed to death in the crowd.'

Jeremiah McVeagh (Irish Party): 'Does the right honourable gentleman think that there was any discretion shown by his officers in attempting to search a crowd of sixteen thousand people?'

Greenwood: 'Three thousand men were searched. As to the total crowd on the ground I have no information.'

Devlin: 'Was there a single incriminatory document found on any of the three thousand people searched?'

'Revolvers!' cried some MPs.

Sir William Davison (Conservative): 'Does not the fact that thirty revolvers were found scattered over this football field impress upon the right honourable gentleman the extreme urgency of getting hold of the arms as the crux of the whole question wherever they are. If the right honourable gentleman has not power to do it by proclaiming martial law, should not legislation be introduced immediately to enable these arms to be taken?'

McVeagh: 'Begin with Carson,' he began– [referring to the 1914 gun running by the Ulster Volunteers]

Sir Edward Carson (Irish Unionist Party): 'You are a liar!'

McVeagh: 'I presume, Mr Speaker, that you heard the observation made by the right honourable member for the Duncairn Division.'

'And the provocation given,' shouted some MPs.

Speaker: 'I did not hear it. I was speaking myself at the moment.'

The MPs cried with laughter. The moment passed and all the anger dissolved in a cheerily familiar round of heckling between Nationalists and Unionists. Afterwards Devlin apologised to Charles Higham, who was accidentally hit during the earlier fight. 'It's always the wrong man who suffers in reprisals,' said Devlin.

The debate stretched into Tuesday as Greenwood gave the final official depiction of events at Croke Park. It offered more detail than any previous explanation and laid the blame for all Sunday's atrocities definitively with the IRA. The authorities, he said, had attended the match to secure 'Sinn Féin gunmen' who had been part of the raiding parties that morning.

'Events at the football ground go to show that this belief was well-founded; that a considerable number of men among the football crowd were carrying arms is proved beyond doubt. Their presence and their efforts to escape had effects of fatal consequence to a number of innocent people, and police were detailed to surround the ground, and to search.

'The military were due to surround the field and an officer announced, using a megaphone, that a search would be made. As the police approached the field and the military encircled it they were observed by civilians evidently posted to watch the approaches to the field.

'The police were fired upon from two corners of the field. Simultaneously, men rose from their places on the grand stand, and fired three quick shots with revolvers into the air. Of this there is indisputable evidence. It seems quite clear that these shots were a pre-arranged signal of warning to certain sections of the crowd. A stampede was caused not by the firing alone, which caused considerable alarm, but also by a rush of men seeking to make their escape from the field.

'They hurried mostly to one side of the field, where a corrugated iron railing was the only barrier to be surmounted. Through its fall a number of people were crushed. Meanwhile the armed pickets outside joined, no doubt, by gunmen escaping from inside the ground, were maintaining a fire in the direction of the police, who returned the fire.

'The firing lasted not more than three minutes. About thirty revolvers, thrown away by men who had formed part of the spectators, were picked up on the ground. Twelve persons lost their lives, eleven were injured seriously enough to warrant their detention in hospital, and about fifty persons sustained slight hurt. These casualties include perfectly innocent persons, whose death I deeply regret. The responsibility for them, however, rests entirely upon those assassins whose existence is a constant menace to all law-abiding persons in Ireland.'

His explanation was never going to sail unhindered past a house of sceptical MPs. Greenwood's reputation for bending the reality of the Irish battleground to fit his own political needs was well established. 'A mythical personage,' wrote Macready of Greenwood's presence in Ireland, 'about whom one read in Hansard but who was rarely seen in the flesh in the land of his appointment'. By Tuesday, every newspaper had also published such a span of differing accounts, Greenwood's official version was freighted with weaknesses.

Further questions were asked in the House of Commons. 'May I ask if the right honourable gentleman is aware that many eyewitnesses are prepared to swear that no shots were fired at the police?' began Lieutenant Commander Kenworthy. 'Is he also aware that the so-called pickets were men selling tickets outside the field? Does he justify firing into a struggling mass of people, including women and children–'

Thomas Moles (Irish Unionist): 'What about the 'so-called' revolvers?'

Kenworthy: '–in an attempt to pick out a very small minority of armed men?'

Edward Kelly (Irish Party): 'Can the honourable gentleman explain at what stage of the proceedings it became necessary to turn a machine gun on the people, and how it happened that a little boy ten years of age was bayoneted to death? Was that done by gunmen?'

Greenwood: 'I am not aware that any machine guns were used, nor do I believe that a boy of ten was bayoneted.'

'You never do,' an MP shouted.

'I have stated, in answer to the question,' Greenwood continued, 'the facts which have been put before me. I believe they are accurate. It is impossible for the Government to lay down rules governing the action which the police and military are compelled to undertake in the necessary duty of searching for arms.'

Questions rained down from the benches. Was the attack on Croke Park part of a preconceived plan or was it formed after the murders that morning? How were the officers faring who had been wounded on Sunday morning?

'I will answer that question at once,' said Greenwood. 'My latest information, I am glad to say, is that none of the gallant men who were wounded are other than improving.'

Joe Devlin asked why wasn't anyone in possession of a revolver arrested, as the official statement declared revolvers were taken from persons at Croke Park?

Jeremiah McVeagh pressed Greenwood further. 'If the Government, according to a statement by Greenwood to the House, were aware these attacks were to be made on these officers, from information received, by men under the cloak of a meeting at Croke Park, can he explain why the officers were allowed to remain in private houses and hotels? May I also ask whether any shots were fired from the aeroplane which was hovering over Croke Park?'

'I will ask my honourable and learned friend to put down those questions,' Greenwood replied. Laughter and cries of 'order!' echoed around the chamber.

Viscountess Nancy Astor stood to ask a question, looking shaken. 'May I ask then if the right honourable gentleman will look into the terrible allegation that a British soldier bayoneted a boy ten years of age? No one can believe it. It is a terrible thing for anyone to say it has happened.'

She never received a reply. The autopsy reports that confirmed the damage done to Billy Scott came from a ricocheted bullet never erased the horrifying image of a boy being bayoneted to death. Nor did Winston Churchill's subsequent insistence that the aeroplane spotted over Croke Park that day was performing routine patrol duties around the city, and that its gun was partially dismantled, ever dismiss the idea that its passing over Croke Park was the signal for an attack to begin. Back in Dublin two inquiries were being organised at the Jervis Street and Mater hospitals, but truth and fiction were already mingling inextricably and indecipherably into one.

CHAPTER 14

The Funerals

*A final handful of victims cling to life. Conspiracy theories grip
Britain. A series of sad journeys home.*

MONDAY, 22 NOVEMBER–
MONDAY, 29 NOVEMBER 1920

As Luke O'Toole guided the *Freeman's Journal* reporter around
Croke Park that Monday morning, crowds continued to gather outside the Mater and Jervis Street hospitals waiting for news of the dead
and wounded. One of the injured, Daniel Carroll, lay in bed in Jervis
Street wondering at his terrible bad luck. His leg was bandaged all the
way up to his waist having been operated on the previous evening. The
surgeons had found a bullet embedded in his thighbone. The muscles
around his thigh were badly lacerated and many of the blood vessels
had been severed.

Martin Kennedy and his wife sat with Carroll. Kennedy owned a
pub in Drumcondra that Carroll had managed for the previous three
years. Carroll, originally from Tipperary, lived with the Kennedys on
James's Street near Christ Church cathedral. They never knew him in
trouble or as anything other than a reliable worker and a friend.

The day of the match alone told them that. It was Carroll's day off, but he still opened the pub that morning and made everything ready. He was still there at 2.30pm. Croke Park was so close and Tipperary were playing. It seemed a sin not to go. 'Wasn't it misfortunate I went?' he said to Martin.

He was even out of Croke Park when he was hit, he told them. The shot came from a lorry while he walked up Russell Street on his way home. The Kennedys gave him their sympathy and good wishes, and left him to rest. They would call on him again soon. His wounds were severe, but he had other things to consider now. What about Mary, his sister? They had both come to Dublin from Templederry in Tipperary after their parents died. She had worked in the Food Control Department for a few months during the war and the Ordnance Clothing Department in Islandbridge, but hadn't found work since June 1919.

She had relied on Daniel's kindness ever since. Of his £120 annual salary from Kennedy's, Carroll gave her £8 10s a month. It was her only income. His brother Denis had only started work in Gibney's grocery shop in Lucan a fortnight before. He was living with Mr Gibney and his family, and needed all his £30 salary for himself.

Their other brother, Joseph, was in Tipperary working as an accountant for the Munster and Leinster Bank in Carrick-on-Suir. He had fought in the Great War as an infantry man before joining the Royal Flying Corps where he received the Croix de Guerre, a medal bestowed by the French government for acts of bravery in 1918. He was still a pilot in January 1920 but illness forced him to leave. His salary as an accountant was good, even if the work was a little duller. With a family and a life to rebuild in Tipperary, he hadn't been able to help Mary either.

Mary and Daniel had stayed close through their time in Dublin. If Daniel ever went to Croke Park he always called to her house in Drumcondra. She never knew him to consort with politicians or rebels. Any spare time he had was spent with her or watching matches.

Tom Hogan lay in bed down the corridor. He had come to Dublin from Tankardstown near Kilmallock in Limerick, escaping a house that heaved with seven children, to work as a mechanic. His father was a farm hand, but had died before Tom turned ten. Watching the Tans streaming over the walls in Croke Park and hearing bullets clack against concrete and bone was nothing new – all his brothers were in the Bruree Brigade of the IRA. When Hogan came to Dublin he also joined an IRA company. Their home in Tankardstown was a known safe house. They hid IRA messages in the hollowed-out statues on their mantelpiece. Soldiers and police raided the house on a regular basis but never found anything.

Sunday was a blur. He could remember being shot and the ambulance driver asking his name. His arm was gone, amputated by the surgeon when they saw the damage done by a bullet wound to his shoulder, but gangrene had set into his wounds. Losing an arm might save his life, but he remained in grave condition. He was nineteen. Too young to be trapped in a hospital bed, waiting for death.

Over in Drumcondra Hospital Perry Robinson clung to life into Tuesday morning, 23 November. His family walked the corridors waiting for news. It had already been a terrible month. On 16 October his cousin, William Robinson, was out near home with three friends. It was just before midnight. As they strolled past the corner of Capel Street and Mary Street, two men stopped them. Both were dressed in matching navy blue suits with soft shirt collars. The one that spoke wore a velour hat. 'Are ye Sinn Féiners?' he asked Robinson, 'because we're Republican police.' 'What do you want to know that for?' Robinson replied. 'We need to see written proof that you're Sinn Féiners,' he said. 'Even if you are, we have to see proof.'

If they recognised him, they would have known Robinson wasn't cut from the same cloth. He didn't play Gaelic games but was a well-known soccer player with Jacobs FC. He was twenty-six years of age and had fought for the British Army in the war. He was tall and well-built. Nothing and no one scared him. These streets around the Ormond slums were his home place. Republican police didn't own him, or his city. 'What proof do you want?' said Robinson. 'Come across the road and I'll show you proof.' The two Republicans followed Robinson and his two friends across the road to an unlit part of the street. As they walked across, one of the Republicans pulled a gun. Robinson and the others ran. One shot skinned his friend's shin. Just as he reached the corner of the street, another shot rang out. Robinson fell. The Republicans ran the other way. Robinson's friends lifted him from the pavement and carried him to Jervis Street Hospital. He died the following night.

A couple of days later, his coffin was carried from his parish church on Halston Street to Glasnevin Cemetery. His widow and four children followed the hearse.

What happened to the Robinsons reflected vividly the fortunes of their city and the history of the previous decade. Perry's grandmother had lived on Moore Street during the 1916 Rising. While his cousin William had fought for the British Army, his younger cousin, Sam, occasionally kept watch when Collins's Squad were holed up at their base near Jervis Street Hospital.

Sam would eventually grow into a better soccer player than William, win an FAI Cup with Bohemians and play twice for Ireland. Perry's father, Patrick, was a champion handball player. Perry followed Gaelic football and the Dublin team. He passed his days playing football on the streets with a ball made from paper and socks, even though playing on the street was barred by law. The girls in the tenements played house with boxes, dolls made from discarded wood and other odds and ends thrown on the street. They all played Tans and Shinners, like children on another continent played cowboys and indians.

Boys scavenged for jam jars and old stout bottles to sell as scrap and collected discarded food to sell to the pig raisers and make a few pennies. Sometimes Perry might pull enough together for the cinema or a trip to Croke Park. Other days he could take his chances pitching pennies on the streets and playing cards. Now he lay in hospital, damaged by a violent, adult world. A doctor finally emerged with news. Perry had died before noon.

Word of Daniel Carroll reached the Kennedys and the Carrolls around the same time. He had endured a terrible night before finally yielding to death at ten that morning. Tom Hogan clung on for days. At 12.30pm the following Friday, 26 November, he took his final breath. Croke Park had claimed its final life.

The morning after the match Ned O'Shea had wired news of Mick Hogan's death home to Grangemockler and asked Fr O'Leary, a local priest, to deliver the news to Mrs Hogan. Talk of the shootings on Sunday morning in Dublin had reached the village by nightfall. Had something else happened in Croke Park as well? No one was certain of the details. None of the story had travelled as far as Aughavaneen.

Fr O'Leary brought another local priest, Fr Fitzgerald, to call on Mrs Hogan. Margaret was in delicate health. They gently broke the news of the shootings, of the Tans and the chaos in Croke Park. About Mick on the field and how he had been shot.

The old woman's eyes shrank. 'It can't be true,' she said. 'It couldn't be.'

Maggie, Mary and Patrick were at home to comfort her. Dan Hogan came from Monaghan to oversee the removal of his brother on Tuesday to the Pro-Cathedral in Dublin where he lay overnight.

On Wednesday his body was moved to Kingsbridge station for the journey to Clonmel. His teammates were with him. The train stopped in Thurles on the way down. A delegation of local councillors met O'Shea and the team, consoled them on their loss but also congratulated them on their own escape.

Every business and shop in Clonmel was closed at one o'clock before the train arrived. A crowd had gathered around the station, marshalled by the local Volunteers. As they waited, a group of soldiers arrived and took up positions inside the station, bayonets fixed. The local RIC were with them. 'Who's in charge?' asked the head constable. A Volunteer stepped forward. 'We are,' he replied. The soldiers held their positions as the constable consulted their commanding officer. The soldiers were ordered to fall out. Most of them were gone when the train arrived. Those who stayed mingled with the crowd and saluted as the cortège passed.

Maggie, Mary and Patrick waited on the platform for Mick. His coffin emerged from the train carriage draped in a tricolour. A hearse was waiting outside but the coffin was borne instead by his friends and neighbours down Gallows Hill and through Gladstone Street, along Mitchell and Parnell streets. A few soldiers saluted as the cortège passed the army barracks on Davis Road. A hearse was waiting at the end of the procession. It was time to take Mick home.

The Tipperary players followed the coffin, along with representatives of Clonmel Corporation and the local council. Members of Cumann na mBan and the Volunteers lined the route. The blinds were drawn on all the houses. The convoy arrived in Grangemockler church that evening. The tricolour was removed to reveal a glass lid. Inside, Hogan was dressed in a Tipperary jersey, shorts and socks unstained by blood or dirt, donated by his teammate Jack Kickham.

That night Patrick Butler was among the Volunteers who stood guard over Mick's coffin. It was barely a few days since he had sat with Sean

Hogan in Mick's kitchen, planning his attack on Glenbower RIC barracks. They were ready to strike on Sunday, around the same time Mick Hogan was playing in Croke Park, but the attack was called off.

After assessing the plan for loopholes, Sean Hogan had found too many questions. The entire plan hinged on the barracks being left undermanned after a six-man patrol set off on Sunday afternoon. Could the IRA men be sure the RIC men would open the door if a strange car pulled up outside? Was it certain that the barracks would be left under-strength? What if they were recognised before they even reached the front door, and were met instead with a volley of fire? Butler was infuriated. To prove his point, he still took a spin to the barracks on Sunday with his brother, Jimmy, and two other Volunteers. When they stopped outside the barracks, a solitary policeman opened the door.

The Volunteers guarded Hogan through the night, one each side of his coffin, each pair passing a two-hour shift. After all the prayers had been said in the morning and people had headed home, Margaret Hogan sat in her cottage broken by grief, gathering her strength for the funeral mass. All her children were home. Relatives came from Waterford city and Tramore, and across the fields from Windgap. Nearly twenty teammates and friends queued to carry Mick's coffin and help lower him down beside his father.

Four Volunteers stood over the grave and fired three volleys into the air. The dirt fell on the glass lid, the noise punctuating the sobbing and crying. Rosaries were said. Eighteen wreaths were laid around his grave near the front of the church. The flowers carried notes from his family and Tipperary County Board; from Cumann na mBan and the Sinn Féin club; the local IRA company in Grangemockler; the football clubs of Mullinahone and Clonmel; Carrick-on-Suir hurling club, the Tobins of Clonmel and the Laurence family of Ninemilehouse.

One wreath bore a note: 'Heartfelt sorrow from your friend, Dick'. Dick Lanigan had played football with Hogan, grown up alongside him and joined him on the Tipperary team. They had travelled to Dublin together that weekend. Lanigan had been a substitute for Tipperary in Croke Park. Like them all, he had lost a teammate and a friend.

The Brownes stood together nearby. Monsignor Browne remembered Mick's first day of school and his cries to be let home. Finally, he thought, Mick was gone 'home to see Da'.

On the same Thursday morning other families of the Bloody Sunday dead gathered in churches and around cold graves in Dublin and beyond. The rules stipulated for the gravesides were the same for them all: family and friends only; and no flags, banners or public displays were permitted.

Most families simply wished to quietly bury their dead. Jane Boyle's funeral Mass began at 11.40am in St Kevin's Church on Harrington Street, the same place she had knelt the previous Sunday morning. The church was full, and more than a thousand people also stood outside on Synge Street. A note of sympathy came from the Irish Automobile Drivers' and Mechanics' Union: Daniel Byron and the Boyle brothers were members.

From there the funeral cortège travelled across the city to Glasnevin cemetery. Her brothers, Peter, James and Thomas, helped Daniel carry her coffin to the plot purchased by her uncle James. A young Volunteer called Henry Coyle lay in a nearby grave, killed during the Easter Rising. He was aged just twenty-eight. Jane was twenty-six. There were too many young people in this place.

Five more were buried in Glasnevin that day. Patrick O'Dowd, who was shot on the wall overlooking the Belvedere Grounds, was mourned by his son John and daughter Mary, and his old work friends from Clarke's Builders in Fairview. Billy Scott was laid to rest that morning. James Matthews, who was killed in the gunfire, was brought from the Pro-Cathedral where his funeral had filled the mighty church. Daniel Carroll and Tom Ryan, who whispered an Act of Contrition into Mick

Hogan's ear, were all buried there.

Jerome O'Leary, the boy shot at the canal end, had been buried in Glasnevin on Wednesday. James Burke was taken south of the river to Holy Cross Church in Dundrum and buried there. James Teehan, the publican from Tipperary who had choked and suffocated in the crowd as they tried to escape, was taken home and carried to Ballinalacken cemetery outside Glengoole village in the rich, green folds of country-side between Thurles and Killenaule.

Joe Traynor, who was carried by the Rings to their home to die, was buried on the outskirts of Dublin in Bluebell. People remembered Joe as a good footballer with Young Emmets and a great captain. His father remembered the bright, friendly child he scolded for dancing around the edge of the limekiln where he worked. Although he had friends in the army, Traynor had joined the Volunteers. A group of them emerged from the crowd that day in the cemetery and fired a volley over his grave.

As the dead were buried in Dublin and Tipperary on Thursday morning, Hamar Greenwood gave the House of Commons details of the funerals of the officers killed in Dublin. Nine bodies were being brought from Dublin that day. They would arrive at Euston Station the following morning, Friday, to be conducted on gun carriages along Euston Road and Tottenham Court Road to Charing Cross Road, from St Martin's Place onto Whitehall and into Parliament Square.

The procession, Greenwood continued, would comprise massed bands, four battalions of guards and two squadrons of the Household Mounted Troops. The king would be represented at Westminster Abbey and Westminster Cathedral. The Protestant funeral service would be performed at the Abbey. The Roman Catholic dead would proceed along Victoria Street to Ashley Place to the Cathedral.

Businesses in Dublin were ordered closed that morning as the coffins of the officers moved from George V Hospital on Arbour Hill down along the north quays towards Sackville Street. Black and Tans and Auxiliaries moved among the crowds that lined the street. Those who hadn't removed their hats as the cortège passed had them thrown into the water.

At the North Wall the coffins were placed on a destroyer that sailed for Wales. Bigger crowds gathered in London on Friday morning to witness the procession of bands, armies and gun carriages to Westminster. As the carriages passed near Euston Station an elderly flower seller in a cloth cap, white apron and black shawl emptied a basket of faded violets and chrysanthemums onto the road beneath their wheels.

'I came right through the war without a scratch,' said a young man standing beside her. 'Then I got pipped outside Dublin Castle. That's what they do to us. Shoot us in the back.'

The crowd chattered with talk of typhoid plots and Irish plans to incinerate England's cities. The *Daily Mirror* reported that captured IRA files revealed plans to attack Liverpool and Manchester. Those on the Irish side quickly refuted any such suggestion. Rumours of a plan to infect the British water supply with typhoid were dismissed by Arthur Griffith as 'a ridiculous lie'.

The newspapers reported Greenwood's claim that the IRA paid £100 for every policeman and military man killed. The *Illustrated London News* carried pictures of the police with a black box containing paper allegedly injected with typhoid and pictures of searchlights strafing the streets of Dublin. Cotton warehouses and timber yards in Liverpool, according to the *Daily Mail*, were set on fire by Irish agitators. Barriers went up to protect Downing Street, and the Houses of Parliament were closed to visitors. According to the *Sunday Pictorial* on 28 November, a Sinn Féin plot to destroy Downing Street was the reason for this shutdown. 'An attack by a fleet of motor cars had been planned for tomorrow [Monday, 29 November],' said the report, 'and that intention was to wreck Downing Street.'

Public sorrow was being churned into resentment, distrust and hate. The *News of the World* carried a cartoon that Sunday on its front page depicting Kathleen Ní Houlihan, the traditional embodiment of Ireland, as a broken, terrified vision crouching and cowering beneath a cloud in the shape of a gunman. It was titled 'Within the Dread Shadow'.

O'er Ireland, fair Ireland, a black shadow's cast;
Nor shall Ireland know peace till that shadow is past.

That day seventeen Auxiliary officers were ambushed and killed by the IRA on a lonely stretch of road near Kilmichael in the Cork countryside. The war went on.

The tension in Dublin hadn't eased. Ironplated gates were erected to protect the entrance to Dublin Castle. Early on Friday morning the RIC arrested Arthur Griffith, then acting President of the Dáil while Éamon de Valera toured America. When word reached Downing Street, Lloyd George contacted General Macready in a rage: Daniel O'Connell and Charles Stewart Parnell had only been arrested on foot of a Cabinet decision, he said. At such a delicate time, with a Home Rule bill in motion and a desperate need to react without privately discomfiting the Dáil, why Griffith? Macready pointed out that getting Griffith and other Sinn Féiners off the streets had a calming effect on the public mood. Whatever about Sinn Féin, he said, the RIC and Auxiliaries also needed handling. Imagine if General Boyd, the Commander of the Dublin District, or General Tudor, head of the RIC, were killed next? Another atrocity could trigger a sacking of the entire city by its own police. At least with Griffith in custody, the IRA wouldn't be bold enough to try such a thing.

While the Bloody Sunday killings might have shaken the will of some politicians, Macready believed a steady military hand was now required. Croke Park didn't cause him any concern. It was simply, he wrote years later, 'a failure on the part of the police to adhere to the exact timetable'.

Families continued to bury their dead. Tom Hogan was borne by train from Kingsbridge that weekend home to Kilmallock and onto Bruree. The funeral drew Volunteers from across Limerick. All Hogan's brothers turned out with the Bruree Brigade. At the graveside three Volunteers dressed in green tunics and bandoliers emerged from the crowd. The RIC officers on the road outside chose not to interfere.

On Friday, 26 November, the Robinsons repeated the bleak journey from Halston Street church to Glasnevin and buried Perry. Michael Feery's body lay in the Pro-Cathedral that morning, the mystery of his identity finally solved. When charting the state of the wounded and dying, the newspapers had made a story of the unknown man in Jervis Street Hospital. 'One man, middle aged and sandy haired,' said the *Dublin Evening Mail* about him, 'of the labouring class.' 'Dark brown hair turning grey,' reported the *Irish Independent*, 'long sandy moustache. Believed to be an ex-soldier wearing an army undershirt and boots.'

On Thursday morning Bridget Feery turned up at Jervis Street Hospital to confirm the body was her husband's. From the grandeur of the Pro-Cathedral he was lowered into a mass grave at Glasnevin, his memory buried in dirt and wood, lost among the bones of strangers.

CHAPTER 15

The Inquiries

NOVEMBER 1920–JANUARY 1921

A thorough examination of the Croke Park massacre draws uncertain conclusions. A series of stories lost to history.

By the time the newspapers hit the streets the morning after Bloody Sunday, confusion and counterclaim had already descended on the events at Croke Park. Although Hamar Greenwood's statements in the House of Commons insisted the police had retaliated having been fired upon from the ground, even the most conservative newspapers in Britain doubted his claim. Auxiliary Major EL Mills's report that Sunday night had given a significantly different account: there had been no shots from the ground before the police opened fire, he said. If that account hardened into accepted fact, Britain truly would be facing another Amritsar.

Two courts of inquiry in the Mater and Jervis Street hospitals were convened over eighteen days by Major-General Gerald Boyd, commanding officer of the military in the Dublin district. Major BG Bromhead of the Royal Berkshire Regiment chaired the Jervis Street Inquiry; he was joined by two other officers, Captain RW Braide and Lieutenant

EJ Barrett. The Mater Hospital Inquiry was chaired by Major RS Bunbury and completed by Lieutenant LH Winterbottom, Lieutenant BJ Key and Major TW Browne.

They began their deliberations barely two days after the massacre, with the bodies taken from Croke Park still in the hospital morgues. The inquiries were bogged down in controversy from the beginning. Because military courts of inquiry had replaced public coroner's inquests under the Restoration of Order Act, Boyd could choose the conditions of inquiry: the inquiries would be heard in private; there would be no public gallery. On the first morning at the Mater Hospital, representatives of the Lord Mayor of Dublin and Dublin Corporation were refused entry.

The families of the deceased gathered outside as a flurry of legal applications was submitted. Having been allowed to appear for the Lord Mayor and the Corporation, Patrick Lynch, KC, insisted the court be instructed to hold the inquiry in public in the same manner as a coroner's inquiry. A lawyer representing James Teehan's next of kin supported Lynch's application and also requested the release of Teehan's body for burial in Tipperary. Given that Teehan wasn't a member of any political organisation, there seemed no need to delay the family further.

His application was granted. Everything else was stonewalled. Later that week the inquiry received a letter from Jane Boyle's family, and the following Monday Michael Comyn, KC, read a statement on behalf of Daniel Byron and the Boyles: 'I decline to produce witnesses on the ground that this is not a public inquisition and I have express instructions not to produce witnesses except in an open court,' he said. 'I protest against an inquiry held behind closed doors into a tragedy which is one of the most awful in the annals of our country and so much opposed to the British ideal of sport.'

The pressure to open the inquiries to public scrutiny came from all sides. In the Commons on 25 November Irish Party MP TP O'Connor asked Hamar Greenwood if the inquiries would remain a military exercise and closed to the public. 'The court of inquiry will be opened or closed according to the judgment of the court itself,' Greenwood replied.

'The criminals!' shouted Joe Devlin.

'When the honourable member calls officers of the British Army "criminals" I do not think he will carry many honourable members with him in this House,' Greenwood replied. 'It is because of the publicity and knowledge of the personnel of some of these courts that several courts-martial officers were murdered on Sunday last.' The issue was never raised again.

The week after Michael Feery was buried, Bridget Feery returned to Jervis Street Hospital to confirm his identity under oath. She wasn't sure of his age. She hadn't seen him alive since midday on Sunday, 21 November. 'My husband was an ex-soldier,' she said, 'discharged from the Royal Marines about a year ago. He was living with me but out of regular employment, and had no work since his discharge, but we earned a few shillings doing odd jobs.' He had been with the Royal Engineers at the beginning of the war, she said, and in the Royal Irish Rifles before that. 'I am destitute with a delicate son and have to support him. The funeral cost me £12 10s and I only got £10 from the Refuge Insurance Company. His age was between forty-four and forty-five years. He drew no pension.'

A relative of every victim went through the same process. These were the forgotten testimonies, fourteen lives reduced to a few lines of recollection calculated into lost pounds and shillings. The documents record the bare anatomy of a tragedy: the last sight of the person alive, a forgotten pouch of tobacco in a jacket pocket, a kindness about them remembered in death. Piecing together these shards of evidence offers a vague outline of those who died. The rest of the testimonies gathered during the hospital inquiries speak directly to the tragedy of the day.

Evidence was gathered briskly from thirty-five witnesses ranging from RIC and DMP constables and commanding officers and Auxiliaries to ambulance attendants and spectators. Twenty-eight witnesses testified before both inquiries.

Major EL Mills was called as the first witness in the Mater Hospital. A few days had passed since his memo. 'I was in charge of a mixed force of RIC and Auxiliary Divisions,' he said. 'We left Beggars Bush barracks at 3.20pm. I was in the 13th car of the convoy. Two hundred yards from Croke Park I heard firing … I shouted at my men not to fire. By the time I reached the gate the firing had ceased. I superintended the searching. I saw about four dead and five civilians. Some were apparently trampled to death. I saw the body of the woman who had apparently been trampled on. I searched the ground for arms and found none.'

Auxiliary Cadet Anderson followed Mills. He recalled hearing a couple of shots and running after Mills to the ground. As they searched the spectators he heard more shots from the direction of the stand. 'I went with Major Mills in that direction … we couldn't find out who was shooting.'

Captain Bartlett, an officer in charge of the soldiers lined along Clonliffe Road, confirmed that the search in Croke Park and the surrounding area yielded one revolver, refuting the account enshrined in Parliament of thirty guns scattered around the field. As the military withdrew around 5.30pm, he recalled a civilian named Norton stopping him on the field to tell him there was a boy lying wounded on St James's Avenue. He took a Ford Box car around the corner and gathered up Billy Scott's body. 'No rifles were fired except one,' Bartlett concluded, 'which was fired accidentally near me.'

An ambulance driver recalled gathering Patrick O'Dowd's body from the field next to Croke Park. 'His face was covered with blood,' he said.

George Dudley, the troubled head of the RIC force, was next. Shots were fired before his men released their volley of fire from the canal bridge, he said. Whatever the papers said, and the eye witnesses insisted, the Black and Tans hadn't started this fight. 'I heard shots and saw two Dublin Metropolitan Policemen running to take cover. Some of my men immediately opened fire from the bridge by the gate. After getting six cars away I went into the grounds and told everyone within hearing to put their hands up and keep still. From that time there was no shooting on my side of the ground. I then started to search. I found no arms … the first shots fired were not fired by my men who were all in the cars at the time. The firing lasted three minutes, with a few odd shots after that. Most of the casualties I saw were in the northeast corner. None of my men were shooting in that direction because they were expecting more of my party to come around there.'

RIC Sergeant Clarke put more meat on the bones of Dudley's evidence. 'My men ran through the gates and commenced firing,' he said. 'The people were told to put their hands up. On this being done, the firing ceased.'

A picture was forming. No haul of revolvers had been retrieved from the ground. Even if the first shots hadn't been fired by the military and the RIC, their riposte hadn't been as a result of a firm order from any army officer, Dudley or Mills.

James Evans, a spectator at the match, recalled lifting Jerome O'Leary onto the wall behind the canal goal and the first shots. One of them hit Jerome. All of them came from the bridge. 'I saw men come in the gate firing. These men were in uniform: RIC cap and coat, and khaki trousers. They were firing rifles and revolvers. They came close to me, firing. I saw the officer in charge [Dudley]. He was in uniform, that is to say, an officer's khaki uniform and a bonnet. He was not firing to the best of my belief. I did not see any men in this uniform firing. The officer gave orders for the firing to cease. The officer ordered me to take O'Leary's body away. Some men were firing over our heads. More of them were firing into the field. I took O'Leary to my house. A corporation ambulance came to the house but refused to take him as he was wanted at the field.'

After Evans, Luke O'Toole stepped forward. Of all thirty-five witnesses in both inquiries, O'Toole's was the only voice from the GAA. Even a month later, when the GAA's Central Council convened for their monthly meeting, any mention of Bloody Sunday was either stricken from the records or not recorded at all. His evidence was typically meticulous and carefully rendered to avoid any implication of the GAA. He was on the stand side of the pitch as the game began, he said. He saw the aeroplane passing overhead, circling around and flying away in the direction of the Phoenix Park. 'A moment or two after that, a man came across the ground to where I was and told me an armoured car was at the entrance gate leading into the sideline seats. I left the gate open after me and went onto the high bank facing and just inside of the main gate. I was looking at the armoured car for four or five seconds when firing commenced at the canal side of the ground. I saw the driver of the car. I took cover under the wall by the entrance gate. I saw police come into the ground through the main gate. They were not firing. People were collected together and police fired some shots up in the air. It seemed to me the police fired to prevent a rush at the gate.'

Finding who shot first remained a murky business. RIC Constable Gordon was in the second lorry of the convoy that stopped on the canal bridge. He noticed the ticket sellers running away from them towards the ground as the trucks arrived. 'By demeanour and formation they gave me the impression they were a picket. As they ran they turned and fired at the first car. They were the first shots I heard ... I immediately jumped down from the car and the other constables followed me. We went straight to the canal entrance gate and entered the ground, climbing over the turnstiles. As soon as we entered I heard firing from the mound in the far opposite corner of the ground. I ran in that direction, going round the fence on the south side of the playing field. I got about halfway round when I was hit by what I thought was a ricochet.'

When he got back to the barracks, Gordon found a bullet in his left breast pocket. It had passed through his cigarette case and pocket book, and dented his whistle. 'I'm wearing the same tunic now,' he said, displaying the ragged hole and the bullet, the perforated pocket book and dented whistle.

Three RIC men insisted shots had been fired from inside the ground – Gordon, Head Constable Lynch and Sergeant Daly. Daly was in the first truck and recalled the event as a shoot-out, not a massacre. 'I observed several men rushing back from the top of the bridge towards the entrance gate of the park,' he said. 'I observed three of them turning backwards as they ran, discharging revolvers in our direction. Almost immediately the firing appeared to be taken up by members of the crowd inside the enclosure. Members of our party were jumping out of the cars. Most of them rushed down the incline towards the entrance gate. Knowing there was another entrance further up Jones's Road, I took cover around the corner and shouted at my men to come along with me. About a dozen followed me and rushed towards the other gate. When we arrived we were met by a rush of people endeavouring to come through. When they observed us armed they rushed back. We called upon them to put their hands up. Every man was searched for arms. We found none.'

Constable Lynch was in the second lorry on the bridge and saw 'some of fifteen to twenty men' firing at the arriving convoy. 'I led my men on foot to the main gate near the railway bridge. [Sergeant Daly] was just behind my party. The gate was closed. As I opened one picket, bullets struck the wall to left of the picket on the inside. I ordered the men to come in. I heard two or three shots behind me after the men came in.'

Each version of events was compromised in some way. Dudley hadn't made any mention of shots being fired at them from the ground. Two

DMP constables patrolling on the canal bridge before the police trucks arrived also rejected the notion of a group of civilians on the street. One of them, Constable Healy went further. 'As the men got out of the car there was no shooting … until after the men had time to run down to the turnstiles.'

His colleague, Constable Harten, backed his story up. 'I saw three men on Russell Street selling tickets,' he said. 'About two minutes after the men jumped out of the cars I heard firing from the entrance to the park.'

It also seems unlikely that Lynch or Daly took their men into Croke Park through the main gate. Constable Healy recalled Lynch and his men pausing on the bridge. 'He [Lynch] said "my party, fall in here quickly".' Some of his men fell in, but before all of them fell in properly, they also ran down the passage leading to the ground.'

Lynch also claimed he arrived at the main gate first, even though Daly's group arrived in a truck ahead of him. Dudley didn't mention seeing a party of men running to that entrance. Lynch didn't mention Dudley's trucks trundling up the same road either. Daly's evidence didn't even mention a second party of men.

The fourteenth witness at the Mater Hospital was Lieutenant Colonel Bray who was at the main entrance where O'Toole was. He saw the police trucks pause at the canal bridge while another group rattled up Jones's Road towards him. 'At exactly that moment I heard three separate shots fired inside the enclosure. One was fired, then a pause. Immediately after, two more. A fusillade began immediately. The first three shots were fired at nearly 1525 hours. I had just purposely looked at my watch to note the time of arrival of the police cars. I had given no orders to the police with regard to firing on civilians.'

Martin White was the thirty-second witness and a spectator on the Jones's Road side of the ground. His evidence appeared the most damning and placed the burden of the responsibility squarely on those inside the ground. 'I was close to the fence around the playing field near the main gate,' he said. 'Someone said "the military are coming". I saw three men in civilian clothes standing in the grandstand near the front. They fired several shots in the air.'

The evidence of a spectator confirming the discharge of shots inside the ground seemed conclusive, but newspaper reports from journalists and eyewitness accounts taken from other spectators in the same area as White didn't mention anyone stepping out from the stand. When over seventeen hundred statements were gathered by the Bureau of Military History between 1947 and 1957 from a variety of IRA Volunteers, organisers and others involved in activities before World War One up to the end of the Civil War, many of them featured brief recollections from Croke Park on Bloody Sunday. None mentioned a shot being fired inside the ground.

Most police witnesses avoided detail of the scene once the firing started, but not all of them. Roland Knight's evidence was remorseless and raw. He recounted the ricocheted bullet off the wall he insisted sent splinters of mortar into his face. He swore the shots came from inside the field. Having entered the field he described fixing his targets. 'I landed on my hands and feet. A group of men – between twenty and twenty-five – were stooping among the crowd away from me between the fence and the wall. I pursued and discharged my revolver in their direction. I had my glengarry cap in my pocket for identification by my own men if necessary. I aimed at individual men in the crowd, trying to conceal themselves. I chased them across the field nearly to the wall on the east side. I then saw a number of people going towards the main gate by which I came in. I rushed to the gate to try and carry out the duties of formal identification.'

Cadet Thompson was in the fourth police car behind Knight. He heard shots from the ground and an order to enter the field and take positions. 'I climbed through the turnstiles. We were fired at. I returned fire, three rounds, at a party of men I thought fired at us. I was armed with a .450 revolver. I saw a party of men running towards the crowd who gathered in a body near the gate. I was in plain clothes with an Auxiliary cap for identification.'

When all the evidence was distilled, it produced a story different in tone and detail to the version produced by Dublin Castle. The suggestion that shots had been fired from within Croke Park at the police was debatable, and on the balance of evidence and information from other sources, unlikely. Only one gun had been found, not thirty. No significantly incriminating documents were found either.

The authority of the commanding officers had been overruled by the rash actions of a handful of Black and Tans and Auxiliaries. Ticket sellers had been mistaken for armed IRA men. Orders to fall in and form ranks had been ignored. Autopsy reports from the hospitals showed the shots that killed Jerome O'Leary and Perry Robinson had come from outside the ground, not inside. The shooting that followed had been equally random and uncontrolled.

Both inquiries had sufficient evidence to overturn the prevailing theory that the attack was a reprisal and that the firing on spectators had been sparked by initial fire from the crowd. The instinct to protect the reputation of the RIC and army, however, was overwhelming. Both reports were completed on 8 December. Both fall short of absolute clarity, and absolute truth.

The Mater report began by listing the causes of death among those housed at Jervis Street Hospital and Perry Robinson in the Drumcondra Hospital.

The Court find that all the above wounds were inflicted on the deceased persons [who] were spectators at a football match, the said crowd being raided at the time by a mixed force of RIC, Auxiliary Police and Military. The Court find that the firing was started by civilians unknown, either as a warning of the raid or with the inten-

tion of creating a panic.

The Court further find that the injuries on the deceased persons were inflicted by rifle or revolver fire, fired by members of the RIC from the Canal Bridge and the Canal Bridge gates of Croke Park football ground, and by civilians in the football ground; that some of the RIC fired over the heads of the crowd and that others fired into the crowd at certain persons who they believed were attempting to evade arrest.

Further that the firing by the RIC was carried out without orders and was in excess of what was necessitated by the situation.

The court further find that no firing was carried out by the Auxiliary Police or by the Military except that the Military in an Armoured Car fired a burst of fire into the air to stop the crowd from breaking through.

The Jervis Street report listed its findings in the same cold, clinical detail.

The firing was started by certain civilians in the football ground, thereby causing a panic to ensue among spectators.

[There was] no firing by the Auxiliary Police or the Military forces of the Crown except from an armoured car in St James's Avenue which fired into the air in an effort to prevent the crowd escaping.

That in order to prevent certain civilians escaping from the football ground, without orders an indiscriminate and excessive fire was opened by the RIC from the Canal Bridge.

That certain civilians opened fire at the RIC who were at the time near the Canal entrance gate. This fire was returned by members of the RIC.

On 25 October Arthur Henderson MP, a former Labour Party leader, had announced the formation of a commission under the party's auspices 'to inquire into the whole question of "reprisals" and violence in Ireland'. A delegation of twelve Labour politicians, military experts and officials left for Dublin on 30 November. Newspaper reports and accounts of atrocities, reprisals and lawlessness on the part of those forces charged with restoring order was their starting point. Before heading into the country, the commission spent the first five days in Dublin meeting union officials and members of the Irish Labour Party. They visited Balbriggan, Skerries and other locations in the city to examine the damage done by Black and Tan reprisals. They visited Croke Park to reconstruct the incidents of Bloody Sunday, inviting an array of witnesses to return to the ground.

Their evidence, hidden in the appendices of a long report published in January 1921, presents a starker picture than the official inquiries into the Croke Park killings. Instead of police and military personnel, the Labour Commission concentrated on eyewitnesses among the spectators and those working in Croke Park that day. Some of these had also testified at the hospital tribunals, but for most of them it was their only chance to speak out.

The ticketseller Thomas Doyle remembered wrestling at his table with Sergeant Clarke and the police sweeping past him into the pitch. 'I was taking tickets at the turnstile entrance when I saw a boy fall from a tree close by. I then saw the Black and Tans coming from the direction of the bridge. They were firing. One of them ordered me to open the gate and threatened to shoot me if I did not. I opened the gate and as soon as the Black and Tans got in they began to fire towards the hill on the other side of the ground.' Doyle remembered bringing Perry Robinson from the ground and handing him to JJ Byrne who placed him in the cab on the North Circular Road.

Daniel Byron also returned to Croke Park to meet the commissioners. Jane was only buried a few days. After being frustrated by the closed nature of the hospital inquiry, he felt that the commission offered a chance to tell his story at least once. 'We were standing near the centre line of the ground opposite the grandstand,' he said. 'The match had been in progress about a quarter of an hour when I saw an aeroplane approach, hover over the ground, and then go away. Almost immediately afterwards I heard the sound of shots coming from the direction of the bridge outside the ground, and my fiancée, who had hold of my arm, was shot dead. A few seconds after this Black and Tans rushed into the field through the gate near the bridge, and people became panic stricken. I saw the Black and Tans ordering people to put up their hands. I saw no shots fired from the crowd.'

The detail of the evidence captured the final forgotten moments of many of those who had died. A man walking home from work towards Russell Street came across a dying man, probably Michael Feery, his left hand gripping the railings. 'An army officer went up to him and then called to me and asked for water. I procured for him a jug. I saw the officer was trying to dress a wound which the man had received in the lower part of the abdomen, but the man was too far gone.'

A turnstile operator recalled heading in to watch the game when the shooting began. 'I next saw a Black and Tan shoot at a man just outside the house in which the secretary of the Association lives. The man staggered through a door into the yard. I then went into the house and took one of the children into my arms when a Black and Tan came and, putting a revolver to my throat, threatened me.'

Eleven different people gave their accounts. Most of the evidence followed identical lines: No shots had come from the ground. The police began shooting from the bridge – and as soon as they entered the pitch. The evidence gathered by the Labour Party Commission supported the newspaper accounts and cast a shadow over the findings of both official inquiries. Taking aim at Hamar Greenwood's official statements in the Commons, the Commission's findings carefully prised apart his story.

The evidence accumulated by the Commission from actual eyewitnesses who were interviewed reveals certain important discrepancies between the official and unofficial accounts ... In the light of the mass of evi-

dence available this charge [of shots coming from Croke Park] would
appear to be quite untrue. Not one of the many witnesses examined
corroborated it. On the contrary, evidence was submitted to the effect
that the police commenced to fire almost immediately the lorries came
to a halt.

Rifle fire was directed down Russell Street whence the lorries came,
and also over the turnstile entrance to the football field at the specta-
tors inside. The consequence of this was that a man was mortally
wounded about halfway down Russell Street, a young woman was
shot dead at her fiancé's side near the centre line of the field, and a
small boy perched in a tree inside the turnstile entrance was brought
down wounded.

The Commission couldn't dismiss the suggestion that warning shots
were fired inside the ground as the police arrived but couldn't find any
evidence that suggested strongly it had happened, either. 'It is difficult
to understand,' said the report, 'why, if pickets and "gunmen" maintained a fire in the direction of the police, there were no casualties
among the police or among the militant civilians and no prisoners with
arms captured.'

The scheme in itself, was dangerous, its execution was a lamentable
failure, and there was no justification for what occurred. Not even
panic, itself a sufficiently serious reflection in the case of a disciplined
force, can excuse the action of the police amongst whom there appears
to have been a spirit of calculated brutality and lack of self-control
which, as has been officially admitted, resulted in twelve innocent
persons losing their lives, eleven being injured seriously enough to be
detained in hospital, and fifty others being more or less slightly hurt:
a grand total of 73 victims.

The central point of the Government's defence, namely, that the
police were fired on from two corners of the field, does not, in face
of the evidence submitted to the Commission, appear to be tenable.

Croke Park was a ghastly tragedy resulting from official errors of judgement and incompetence.

Official reaction to a report by a political party was predictably mixed. In Dublin, Nevil Macready was enraged by their depiction of the army. He wrote to Hamar Greenwood rejecting their allegations of indiscipline, reprisals and poor training, and concluded that the commission had been tugged and pulled by Sinn Féin like puppets on a string. 'The childlike belief of the Commission in statements made to them by persons,' he wrote in his memoir, 'including "town councillors", who were brought under their notice by Sinn Féin agency, was pathetically ludicrous to anyone acquainted with the natural genius of the Irish for the invention of fables which they think may please their audience, more especially if the relation should be to their own advantage.'

Once written and circulated, the hospital inquiry reports were buried and kept from the public for almost eighty years. The names of those who gave evidence were blacked out. When Greenwood was asked about the reports in March 1921, he restated the familiar explanation: 'All that I can say in this case is that the court, after a very exhaustive inquiry, formed the conclusion that the firing was started by certain civilians in the enclosure and that fire was opened by other civilians upon a detachment of the Royal Irish Constabulary who were approaching one of the entrance gates.'

The evidence said different. People in Dublin Castle and those in Croke Park said different. Major Mills and General Crozier knew different. So did George Dudley. The families of the dead were never heard from again.

On 5 March 1921, a couple of days before Greenwood said his last words on Bloody Sunday, a letter from a representative of the St Vincent de Paul

charity landed on the desk of the Deputy Adjutant General at the Irish command headquarters in the Phoenix Park. It told of a case among the poor of the district around Lower Mount Street. It was about a boy named Michael Feery who had lived with his aunt, Mrs Elston, since the death of his father at Croke Park the previous year.

'Mrs Elston tells us that the father was most anxious when school-leaving age should come – as it now has – that this only surviving child of his first marriage should be apprenticed to some trade and that any money coming to him from his trade Society should be devoted to this purpose.' The boy, continued the letter, had left school and found temporary employment. If the army could provide him with the necessary funds he could find a regular apprenticeship. 'We are told the deceased served in the Royal Dublin Fusiliers and subsequently the Marine Labour Corps in France,' concluded the letter. 'We understand that the military authorities are favourably disposed toward the end set forth and we shall be glad to co-operate in any way our services would be useful.'

A reply arrived eleven days later. 'No liability can be accepted by military authorities in respect of the shooting,' it said. 'Any application for compensation should be made through the civil court under the provisions of the criminal injuries in Ireland act.'

The frustration of reaching the truth of Bloody Sunday in Croke Park was captured in one short paragraph. The army weren't responsible for Croke Park. Neither was the government. Michael Feery's wish for something better for his son from his life in service came to nothing. The scars of Bloody Sunday stayed on them all. Decades passed. Their gravestones eventually disappeared. Their stories were lost.

CHAPTER 16

War Stories

JANUARY 1921–DECEMBER 1927

A final collection of stories: George Dudley runs to escape the truth. Frank Crozier is hunted from Dublin. Nevil Macready finally goes home. The Hogans find their place in history.

New Year's Eve 1927. George Dudley was thirsty. The dread stirring in the pit of his guts made him nauseous. The heat made his skin prickle and sweat. He had walked into a corner. Now he was trapped. For once, there was no escape hatch.

His debts were beyond his control. The Chinamen and the bars and the hotels wanted their money. His superiors in the police had tried to help by sending him inland away from the cattle thieves and the natives and the dust and grime to sober up, curb his habits and correct his finances, but it hadn't worked.

What had become of this life? Australia was meant to be a new start after Ireland, but he couldn't escape his weaknesses and demons. When he became the first Police Commissioner of the Northern Territory, many in Darwin saw him as a dashing, enterprising imperialist. 'He was a broker of dreams generating inspiration, hope and a sense of purpose and effectiveness in the organisation,' wrote historian Dr Bill Wilson. 'The missing ingredient was morality.'

Dudley had sold himself as a man with vision and the makings of a good leader. Although entirely sure of himself and his standing, he didn't discriminate with others. He carried himself with a certain regal air but was never aloof. He listened to people. He had ideas. He talked to everyone, from Aboriginal to lawmaker and everyone in between.

Northern Australia was a complicated, challenging place – barren and lifeless in so many ways, its towns spread across a vast red desert, separated by endless miles of empty land, but teeming with colliding cultures and different colours. The place needed someone to tie those different strands together and keep order.

In March 1924 Dudley had been appointed Commissioner covering an expanse of territory stretching out over half a million square miles. His salary was generous – £650 per year rising by yearly increments of £25 to £750, with that increment to be approved annually by the Minister of State for Home and Territories. He was given a rent-free house in Myilly Point, a smart area outside Darwin. His wife, Gladys, and the children came from Glasgow to join him.

His letter of application had depicted the perfect colonialist. He had served in three overseas police forces over twelve years and fought in the war. His war record mentioned he was wounded by enemy fire – once according to official files, twice according to Dudley. He was awarded the Military Cross and made a Companion of the Distinguished Service Order for 'distinguished service in connection with military operations in France and Flanders'. Ireland was a quickly forgotten footnote.

'I joined the Royal Irish Constabulary in June 1920,' Dudley wrote, 'and was promoted to Sergeant the following month and again to District Inspector in December 1920. I remained with the RIC until demobilisation in January 1922.'

They couldn't know the full truth. Not the horrors of Croke Park. Not the humiliations that followed. By December 1921, over a year after Bloody Sunday, Dudley had been transferred to Magherafelt, County Derry, to work as a district inspector. Over the space of a month he quietly gathered over £300 in expenses owed to the policemen stationed at the barracks before slipping away to Larne and taking the steamer to Scotland.

He went to his family in Glasgow. Arthur was only a year old. Angela was barely two. He lasted a few months before he saw an RIC man on the street coming towards him. By spring 1922 Dudley was in Derry jail, sitting in the cells with cattle rustlers and IRA men captured with explosives and ammunition.

His hearing took two days. A string of former colleagues took the stand to describe a litany of failed expenses payments and irregularities in the cash book. Precisely £303 18s, 4 ½ d was missing. Dudley didn't dispute any of it. He was charged with embezzlement. Bail was set at £300. His lawyer told the court he could afford whatever number they wished to strike. Once the RIC disbanded later in 1922, Dudley was due £1,000.

Dudley was ordered to appear for trial on 20 March and pleaded guilty. His counsel highlighted his distinguished war record, his plans to make good abroad in Australia and a commitment from a prominent Derry resident to cover Dudley's debts. Dudley returned to Glasgow and received notice to return in late July 1922 for sentencing.

But he never showed up and never paid his debt. A bench warrant was issued for his arrest but mistakenly made out in the name of Gerald Dudley, not George. While the courts bumbled with the paperwork, Dudley disappeared to Australia. His only hope of a new start lay in how the Australians saw him now – an upright, progressive, classically British officer, with the personality and temperament to inspire and lead a police force, not a fraudulent embezzler escaping a sentence on the other side of the world.

Shortly after taking over as Commissioner, Dudley took an Aboriginal man with him in a Ford car and headed out to inspect the countryside. Even then, people wondered what kind of man he was. Policemen never travelled into the bush, not in a motor car. He travelled almost two thousand miles, wearing out the original four tyres on his car and the spare wheel. He drove out through half-abandoned towns and villages and across deserts, past cattle men and Aboriginals wandering the bush. Some days the sun blistered him. Other times he saw rain like nowhere else in his life. Once, when travelling from Darwin to Borroloola near the Gulf of Carpentaria, so much rain fell he had to harness horses to the car and pull it for miles to the next town.

When they visited Katherine, a small town on the tip of the Northern Territory, with its yawning gorge and its rock paintings, his companion could tell him of how Katherine was the place where the traditional Aboriginal territories of the Jawoyn, Dagoman and Wardaman people met, melding together three different languages with over twenty-five different dialects. He could describe the Dreaming, the Aboriginal story of when all creation was born and the patterns of life for its different people were set.

By 1927, all those adventures were dust-coated, half-forgotten memories. The Northern Territory was split in two for policing purposes, requiring two new commmssioners. Dudley's position had already been under threat for a long time. When his salary increment was discussed in 1925, the Administrator's report touched a nerve. 'It is not that the Police work is not fairly well being carried out in the Terrritory,' he wrote, 'but I am dissatisfied with this officer's want of discretion in regard to visiting hotels and occasional indulgences in liquor which have given rise to remarks, and of course do not provide a good example for his men. I therefore do not recommend the granting of an increment this year.'

This time, he was out of friends and second chances. Dudley's position was terminated. He owed over £320 to bars and delinquents. He was drinking too much with his subordinates. Stories about him whipped up like a dust storm. Some of the hotels in Darwin were chasing him to settle his tab. If Dudley were to return to Darwin, wrote the Administrator in 1926, 'he would be sent to Fannie Bay Gaol'.

Dudley had seen too many things and heard too much fanciful talk and ideas cloak some of mankind's worst horrors. He had seen men die in a terrible war, a whole generation milled like grain into flour. He had stood on a football field in Ireland as the ground underneath his feet had been cut to shreds by bullets, and seen people pinned to walls and impaled on spikes.

These were the images that papered the walls of his memory. People outside hospitals in Dublin, saying prayers for the dying. An empty field covered in hats and umbrellas and bones and blood. What he saw in Ireland was underpinned by everything that had churned fields in France and men into mud. War had broken too many men down and rebuilt something harder. Maybe that was why he couldn't stop moving, because stopping meant thinking. This was his Dreaming, the endless journey of his soul.

The night after Bloody Sunday FP Crozier was in Galway investigating the death of a priest. Fr Michael Griffin's body had been found the previous Saturday night in a bog near Barna, buried in a shallow grave. Bullet holes were found in each temple. It looked like an execution. Crozier found evidence of Auxiliary involvement. He even reckoned he knew the culprit.

He also heard the military inquiry had made its final decision about the case before he had submitted the detail of his own investigation: a verdict of murder against person unknown. An official from Dublin Castle had already informed the inquiry in Galway of the outcome.

On 23 November Crozier received further evidence of a planned attack by the Auxiliaries on the Bishop of Killaloe, Dr Michael Fogarty, who was sympathetic to the Republican cause. As Crozier travelled back to Dublin with evidence of the cover-up in the Griffin case and the planned attack on the Bishop of Killaloe, his motor Tender crashed. He ended up in the Curragh Military hospital for a month. His attaché case had disappeared. The attack on Fogarty never occurred.

Instead of recuperating in France as planned, Crozier returned to Beggars Bush where the men were almost beyond his control. According to his own figures, the average consumption of liquor in the Auxiliary Division totalled £5 per head a week, totalling £30,000 a month in canteens alone.

On 9 February 1921, a group of Auxiliaries caused £325 worth of damage in a spirit grocer's shop in Trim, County Meath. Crozier decided to use the episode as a line in the sand. He dismissed twenty-one Auxiliary cadets and held five more to be tried for their part in the raid. Two prisoners had also been shot dead in Drumcondra – Crozier claimed the evidence was rigged in the favour of the Auxiliary commander and others involved in that situation. Five of the Trim cadets were convicted, but nineteen were reinstated. Crozier resigned in protest. In April three cadets in the Drumcondra case were acquitted due to a lack of evidence.

Shortly after his resignation Crozier returned to England and was married. While on honeymoon in Kent, his wife, looking out the window, pointed to a strange man watching the front door from the street. 'Shinners?' Crozier laughed. 'Black and Tans?'

She went to police station. 'It's all right, madam,' said the police inspector, 'I put him there. Your old friends Mr Asquith and other Members of Parliament said you were not to be murdered by your old friends the Black and Tans.'

Years later Crozier wrote a series of books depicting a dramatic life in service. *Ireland Forever* charted his time with the RIC. Crozier was a pacifist by then, repentant for all the cruel deeds of war and appalled by the forms of justice meted out in Ireland.

'A man connected with a church once asked me if I resigned from the RIC on moral grounds,' he wrote. '"I have no so-called morals that I know of," I said. "At least none to shout about or hold up as a standard of worthiness … although I hope I hold some soldierly qualities. I resigned because I am a soldier. You are a Bible-puncher. Remember the story of the centurion. What did that good soldier say? 'For I am a man under authority, having soldiers under me; and I say unto this man, Go and he goeth; and to another, Come and he cometh; and to my servant, Do thus, and he doeth'… and so he was trusted."'

Crozier recalled the last time he ever dined at the depot mess of the RIC. He enjoyed a hearty meal and drank the king's health with customary homage and regularity. Cigars were smoked and fine liquor held sway late into the night. He left for home long after curfew. As his car swept past the guard, turning sharply left towards the main gate of the Phoenix Park, a single shot rang out. The body of a man showed up in the glare of the headlights. A few yards further on, a Black and Tan patrol was walking along the footpath. They knew nothing. They heard nothing. 'The usual verdict was delivered,' wrote Crozier. 'An unknown man found shot dead, "murdered by some person or persons unknown". The scene was typical of the Ireland of that day – nobody heard, nobody knew – not even the name of the victim.'

Over five hundred IRA suspects were arrested in the forty-eight hours after Bloody Sunday. In the following six months over four thousand were eventually interned in camps at Ballykinlar, County Down, the Curragh in Kildare and Bere Island off the west coast of Cork. After the killings at Kilmichael in West Cork on 28 November 1920, full martial law was finally imposed to restrain certain parts of the country: Cork, Kerry, Tipperary and Limerick came under its yoke on 9 December. By January 1921 it extended to Clare, Kilkenny, Waterford and Wexford.

On 23 December 1920, the Government of Ireland Act was passed into law, preserving six northern counties – Derry, Tyrone, Antrim, Armagh, Fermanagh and Down – in the empire with a northern parliament, and establishing a parliament for the twenty-six-county south. It was out of step with the Dáil's demand for complete independence, and the Ulster Unionists' insistence that the entire province of Ulster, which also included counties Donegal, Monaghan and Cavan, should stay under British rule. Elections were set for May 1921 as the war continued throughout the south.

Between January and July 1921 alone, a thousand people spanning the RIC, army, IRA and civilians were killed. Nevil Macready occasionally issued orders to keep the troops in check. After soldiers were killed at Woodford, County Galway, and Bandon, County Cork, in February 1921, he wrote to every barracks pleading for restraint: 'The Commander-in-Chief looks to the troops, even in the face of provocation such as would not be indulged by the wildest savages in Central Africa, to maintain the discipline for which the British Army is, and always has been, justly renowned.'

The British government saw the war as being mired in stalemate, while the IRA was running low on weapons and ammunition. Both sides eventually agreed a truce, commencing at noon on 11 July 1921. Macready sat in his office that morning recording the final atrocities of a brutal conflict. On that morning alone, he noted, a constable was killed and a magistrate kidnapped; a Dublin bank was raided; Armagh Post Office was raided for RIC letters; two constables were wounded at Goolds Cross, Tipperary; an ambush occurred at Bailieboro, Cavan; an elderly soldier, Major GB O'Connor, was killed at Rochestown outside Cork city; a military patrol was attacked in Castleisland, Kerry – nine army and IRA men died; a woman died during a raid at Clonmel; the RIC barracks at Nobber, Meath, was attacked; the coastguards' station at Greencastle, County Donegal was attacked and a house near Trim was destroyed. Macready expected little to come of this fledgling Free State. 'I learned many things during the years I spent in the Emerald Isle,' he wrote in his memoirs, 'but confidence in its people was not one of them.'

In January 1922 the Anglo-Irish Treaty that established the Irish Free State was passed by the Dáil. Two weeks after the treaty had been rati-fied Michael Collins attended a ceremony in Dublin Castle to mark the handover of power from Britain to the new provisional government. Protestors outside on Dame Street held placards that crossed the spec-trum of opinion: 'Down with Small Nations', said one. 'We Belong to an Empire', proclaimed another, 'Heads Up! You Are Going into the British Empire'. 'The Republic Still Lives', read another.

The Castle had been busy all morning. At 11.30am the resident com-pany of Auxiliaries paraded out. Trucks laden with documents, bedding and furniture followed them out the gate. Ash flakes floated in the air overhead as papers were burned in the offices. Workmen were perched on the Castle walls, removing the barbed wire and canvas-covered look-out posts from the parapets.

A red baize carpet was laid along the hallway and down the staircase leading from the Chief Secretary's office to the Privy Council Chamber awaiting the arrival of the country's new leaders. Out in the court-yard Dan Hogan stood among a group of Free State soldiers hold-ing a tricolour about to be unfurled. Feeling the flag run through his hands and ascend the pole to flutter in the winter wind over Dublin Castle was a historic moment. It was also a day to remember Grange-mockler and his brother, Mick, and the sad sacrifices this moment had demanded of everyone.

On Sunday, 12 June 1922, six months after Dan Hogan unfurled the flag, the sun was burning Dublin to a crisp. The 1920 All-Ireland foot-ball final was scheduled for Croke Park, nearly two years since the vio-lent chaos of that summer had stopped everything. Although Dublin had already reached the All-Ireland final by October 1920, Tipperary didn't resume the 1920 Munster championship until 18 February 1922. They beat Waterford in the semi-finals on a wet, rotten day, 3-4 to 0-1, and Kerry in the final by two goals, 2-2 to 0-2, that April. Tipperary's victory was greeted with a few paragraphs in the newspapers and none of the surprise that heralded their win in 1918. That was the journey they had made in people's expectations.

Tipperary weren't troubled when they met Mayo in the All-Ireland semi-final, but didn't chase any lingering doubts away either about their ability to win the title. With the wind and sun behind them for the first half they pinned Mayo in for the first fifteen minutes, but only scored a point. Another from Mick Arrigan appeared to settle them down. Then Mayo broke out for a goal. A point from Vincent Vaughan settled Tip-perary's nerves before Tommy Powell bulldozed in for a goal, knocking out the Mayo keeper in the process.

Tipperary were 1-4 to 1-0 ahead at half-time and turned to face the wind. Mayo's forwards were having a horrendous day. They held onto the ball too long, attempting to work themselves closer to goal before shooting. They didn't kick long or regularly enough. Their passes were too timid and short. 'They not only missed chances,' said the *Irish Independent* reporter, 'but made the poorest use of frees, of which they had a fair number.' While Mayo fell over themselves, Tipperary fell over the line, 1-5 to 1-0.

The formlines were difficult to read. What few strands existed didn't bode well for Dublin. A year after Bloody Sunday, Dublin and Tipperary had convened again in Croke Park to play a match. That morning the Dublin Brigade of the IRA marched to the graves of the Bloody Sunday dead in Glasnevin. Crowds had turned out to see them. There were no orations, just a few wreaths.

Everything else had been arranged to mirror the year before. The game would throw-in at 2.45pm. Mick Sammon was again the referee. Both teams were given crêpe armlets to wear in memory of Mick Hogan. Dan Breen emerged from the crowd to throw the ball in and the game descended into a blur of hard tackling and ferocious running, played at a thrilling speed. Tipperary had brought a stronger team, but still their outstanding performance stunned everyone. 'The pace and vigour that Tipperary maintained from the very outset were remarkable,' reported the *Freeman's Journal*, 'considering that no matches have been played in that county for almost twelve months.'

By the end Tipperary had hit five goals, held Dublin scoreless and won by 18 points, 5-3 to 0-0. Although it appeared Dublin had been blown apart, they could spin a different story from the performance: they had fielded a weakened team but kept pace with Tipperary for long spells; most of Tipp's goals had come in clusters – two near the end, two heading towards half-time. The scoreline suggested a crushing defeat, but Dublin had played well in a good game, 'one of the most attractive and refreshing contests seen in Croke Park for a long time', said the *Journal*.

This final promised to be different. The hot weather made the ground so hard that plumes of dust rose as the players galloped onto the field. A reporter from the *Freeman's Journal* drifted among the crowds heading to Croke Park. He spotted a man sitting on a step eating a blood orange. 'Are you going to the match?' the reporter asked. 'No,' he replied. 'I came to count the people as they came in.' He squirted a shot of orange at the reporter. 'If you intend to ask any more damn fool questions, don't.' 'It was the heat,' wrote the reporter.

He noted people travelling from everywhere, ferried by trains and motor cars, charabancs and on asses' carts. 'To Lansdowne Road throng thousands drawn by desire to see and be seen,' he wrote. 'Curiosity and perhaps "divarshun" [diversion] will entice onlookers to sidle up to an election meeting; bookmakers and sideshows and fashions attract to race meetings. But at Croke Park, the game's the thing that counts.'

As the O'Tooles Pipers joined forces with the Kickham's Brass and Reed Band from Tipperary on the field, Dan Breen strode out to throw in the ball, no longer a wanted man. From the beginning, everything about the game was lifted a few levels out of the ordinary. The speed of play was bewildering. The hits were ferocious. Fouls were scarce. Bad wides and poor kicking even scarcer. 'It will rank among the best and most exciting championship [finals] in the history of the GAA,' said the *Freeman's Journal*.

Dublin hurtled at Tipperary like a train. Josie and Stephen Synnott quickly found their rhythm. Frank Burke, the scourge of Mick Hogan's dreams, was darting around. With the sun in Tipperary's eyes Dublin pressed them hard early on. When Tipp finally escaped after eight minutes, Tommy Powell popped a point to get them ahead.

The game had already assumed an unfamiliar look. Tipperary usually did the pressing when they met and Dublin the scoring. This time it was the other way around. Paddy McDonnell kicked two chances wide from fifty yards. Arthur Carroll was forced into a fine save for Tipperary. McDonnell finally got Dublin's first score after ten minutes, but Powell's second point had Tipperary ahead again two minutes later.

Dublin looked stronger but struggled to break Tipperary down, mainly because the outline of Ned O'Shea's greatest performance at full-back was taking shape. After beating out a thunderous shot from Stephen Synnott he shadowed Frank Burke as he took possession, like a lion stalking a zebra before pouncing. Burke was beaten, but Burke couldn't be held all day. After thirteen minutes the ball bounced into his chest near the sideline on the Jones's Road side of the pitch. He turned and headed for goal. He was still somewhere near thirty yards out when he struck his shot. It flew past Carroll to the net. A Dublin goal. The crowd gasped at first, almost unable to absorb the feat they had just witnessed.

Vincent Vaughan and Stephen Synnott swapped points before half-time. Dublin led, 1-2 to 0-3. Both teams left the field saturated in sweat and shattered. The crowd paused to draw breath. The half-time break went on longer than usual, but no one begrudged the players the extra rest. Dublin had played well but found Tipperary's defence hard to crack. Tipperary had played like a defensive fighter, ducking out of punches and hitting hard on the counter. To commemorate Mick Hogan's memory and chase away any final doubts about their supremacy over Dublin, they needed to deliver something greater. Something special.

They found their inspiration in Ned O'Shea. He had left Croke Park on Bloody Sunday lost in his thoughts, cloaked in a jacket he didn't own and carrying a cane he didn't want given to him by a policeman as a souvenir. This was the day for his team to reclaim Croke Park and football for Tipperary beyond the blood-stained sorrows of 1920; O'Shea rose again to gather a free kick from Paddy McDonnell and clear the first attack of the second half. When Dublin attacked again, he deftly dispossessed Frank Burke and got Tipperary moving again. Tipperary sallied downfield and won a free in front of goals to move within a point, 1-2 to 0-4.

The pace got hotter as the second half unfolded. Mick Arrigan kicked a point to bring Tipperary level. Then Tipperary had a goal disallowed. Dublin looked rattled. The first crack in either team had appeared. The Tipperary crowd roared again. Bill Grant, Tommy Ryan's old sidekick from Dungarvan, started a move and found Gus McCarthy. He spotted Tommy Powell on his own near goal. All his years of playmaking and guiding Tipperary funnelled down to one pass. The ball landed in Powell's chest. His shot to the net was immaculate. Tipperary were ahead. Dublin were almost broken.

'Tipperary were now pressing with surprising vigour,' said the *Journal*. 'Excitement was mounting – stirred by a marvellous burst of play that quite eclipsed all previous exhibitions.'

Tipperary were playing with unquenchable fire. After all the years hemmed in by their own poor shooting and misfortune, haunted by the death of close friends and the trauma of defeat, they were liberated for a glorious last ten minutes. Their final score came from Gus McCarthy, whose kick had drifted wide in 1918 and taken Tipperary's All-Ireland with it. This was his day. Tipperary's day.

As the crowds dispersed outside, the *Journal* reporter fell into conversation with a priest who captured the triumph of the country man over the genteel metropolitan. 'It was a victory of buttermilk over skimmed milk,' he said.

On the morning of 17 December 1922 Nevil Macready prepared to leave Dublin. The Free State troops were due at the Royal Hospital, Kilmainham, for nine o'clock. Sergeant Major Kennedy lowered the Union Jack and kept it as a souvenir. As Macready's car left through one gate he peered back through the rear window, catching sight of the Free State Guard marching in through another. He had no desire to witness their arrival.

He attended a parade outside the Royal Barracks near Arbour Hill, taking the salute from the Leicesters, Royal Welsh Fusiliers, Worcesters and Border Regiment as they marched off towards the port where boats waited to take them home. The Irish Legion of ex-servicemen presented him with a badge of their association. He noted people waving small Union Jacks and how the Free State soldiers saluted the regimental colours as they passed. Hats were even raised when the band on the last troop ship struck up 'God Save the King' as it moved away.

Once the last soldier left Ireland, Macready headed for Dun Laoghaire to board the HMS *Dragon*. A newspaper photographer asked him to pose on the deck. Another curse of this new age, he thought. His military career was now over.

He would begin work within a year on his memoirs, sifting through his own papers and his father's diaries that recorded his life as an actor, finding stories about how his grandfather hosted Admiral Nelson for dinner the night before he left for a journey that ended at the Battle of Trafalgar and his father's connection to John Wilkes Booth, Abraham Lincoln's assassin. He had written of Lucius Junius Booth, father of John. 'This man, Lucius Junius,' he wrote, 'was guilty of an act, shooting and wounding a pantomimist in Queen Square, Bristol, this being near murder. I think I heard of him in America as being occasionally deranged, but I gave little attention to the mention of his nature. His offspring is worthy of him.'

There was the story of the night Charles Dickens visited the Macreadys for dinner. As dessert was served, Nevil sat beside Dickens at the table. Dickens asked him what food he would like from the bowls in front of them. Macready nodded towards a bowl of olives. Dickens burst out laughing and told Nevil he could have one but if he took it, he must eat it even if he didn't like it. Macready took an olive and ate it. He didn't touch another till he landed in Palestine with the army in 1884.

Sifting through his life's work, he traced his finger back over the roads that brought him here. He recalled his father banning him from becoming an actor and guiding him towards a place of war and bloodshed, politics, strikes and years of atrocities in Ireland. When Macready finished writing his memoir, he burned every note and diary he ever kept. The past was a different world, but it had shaped everything about him. The boat pulled out of Dun Laoghaire at 3pm and anchored a mile out to sea, waiting for the *Venomous*, which had been guarding the embarkation of troops at Dublin dock. As darkness gathered overhead, this chapter was over. He left Ireland to its freedom.

The days had also shortened in Grangemockler. People returned to the familiar rituals of winter. Kate Browne drove her cows past the village church each morning in the darkness, peering over the wall at Mick Hogan's grave and her son's. Many times over the years Monsignor Browne insisted she give up farming and sell the house, leave her sad memories behind and come live with him.

'I can't,' she always replied. She would miss her neighbours and the village. She would miss the simple routine of the cows. The farm gave her purpose. The village was her family too.

She listened to her heart for the echo of better times, of Mick Hogan joking by the fireside and stories of John and football and the village. In time books would be written about her life, and Mick Hogan would be immortalised in Croke Park, but that was years away. Her heart was broken. This was her life now. Like Dudley and Macready, the IRA men and the other families of the Bloody Sunday dead, she would learn to live with all the good and bad in it.

CHAPTER 17

The Dead

JERVIS STREET HOSPITAL

JAMES BURKE

Annie Burke: The deceased is my husband. I have seen and recognised him. He left on Sunday morning to see the football match. It was 2 o'clock. He was employed in the Terenure Laundry. We lived at 293 Cottages, Windy Arbour, Co Dublin. My husband was 44 years of age.

DANIEL CARROLL

Martin Kennedy: I am Daniel Carroll's employer, he was employed by me as manager. I have been down to Jervis Street Hospital and recognise the deceased as Daniel Carroll. I have known him for years and would say he was about 30 years of age and unmarried. I saw him on Sunday Nov 21ˢᵗ 1920 at about 2.30pm and I believe he was going to Croke Park. He was a most inoffensive man I ever knew.

MICHAEL FEERY

Capt FG Power, RAMC: I have seen the body of the unidentified man. I believe he is about 40 years of age. He has light blue eyes. His height is about 5ft 6ins of slight build. His body is badly nourished. Dark brown hair turning grey. Sandy moustache falling over his mouth. Lean features and has a number of teeth missing in the front of his mouth in the upper jaw … he has a cardigan jacket, I believe of Army pattern. Dark grey coat somewhat faded. Navy blue trousers and a soiled grey cap and a pair of what appeared to be Army boots worn at the heels. In one of the pockets a leather tobacco pouch was found.

THOMAS RYAN

Mary Ryan: The deceased is my husband. I have seen him and recognised him. He was 27 years of age. He was a labourer employed by the Gas Company. The last time I saw him alive was Sunday about 2 o'clock.

JAMES TEEHAN

John Teehan: The deceased was my brother, he was about 26 years of age, he lived with me and had a licensed house. I last saw my brother about 2.30pm on Sunday at home. I have seen the body and I recognise it.

JOE TRAYNOR

Michael Traynor: I am the father of the deceased. I have seen his body and recognise him as my son. He lived in the house with me. I saw him about five mins after 12 o'clock on Sunday going out of the house. Word came about 5 o'clock that Joe Traynor was slightly wounded. I heard again about 9 o'clock he was dead.

MICHAEL HOGAN

Rev Patrick Browne: I am from St Patrick's College Maynooth. I am a relation of his, i.e 2nd cousin and the nearest relative who is able to get up here. I have identified the remains here of Michael Hogan. Age 24 years. His residence was in Grange Mockler in the County of Tipperary. He was a farmer.

MATER HOSPITAL

JANE BOYLE

James Boyle: I identified the deceased as my sister. Her age was 26, unmarried, and by occupation a charge hand to a pork butcher.

TOM HOGAN

Maggie Hogan: I identified the deceased as my brother. His age was 19. He was unmarried and was a mechanic by occupation. His address was 24, St James' Terrace, Dublin.

JAMES MATTHEWS

Kate Matthews, 32 North Cumberland Road: I identified one of the deceased as my husband, 32 North Cumberland Road. His age was 48, married, and a day labourer by occupation.

PATRICK O'DOWD

Mrs Julia O'Dowd: I identified one of the deceased as my husband. His age was 57, and by occupation a builder's labourer.

JEROME O'LEARY

Jerome O'Leary: I identified one of the deceased as my son. His age was 10 years and he was a schoolboy. He lived at 69 Blessington Street, Dublin.

JOHN WILLIAM SCOTT

John Frederick Scott: I identified one of the deceased as my eldest son, of 15 Fitzroy Avenue, Drumcondra. His age was 14 years old and he was a schoolboy.

DRUMCONDRA HOSPITAL

WILLIAM ROBINSON

Bridget Robinson: I identified the body of deceased as that of my son. He lived at 15, Little Britain Street. His age was 11 years and he was a schoolboy.

Postscript

- In total, thirty-two people were killed on Bloody Sunday. Fifteen people died as a result of the IRA's morning assault. Three men – Dick McKee, Peadar Clancy and Conor Clune – died in custody in Dublin Castle. Fourteen people were killed in Croke Park. Estimates for the wounded have ranged between fifty and a hundred.

- Over 3,400 people were killed during the Irish War of Independence between January 1919 and July 1921, including about two hundred civilians.

- After losing the 1920 All-Ireland final, Dublin returned to win two successive All-Ireland titles and establish themselves among Gaelic football's most dominant forces. Since winning the 1920 All-Ireland football title, the Tipperary footballers have never reached an All-Ireland final since.

- After being dismissed from his post in Australia as Chief Police Commissioner for the Northern Territory, George Vernon Dudley worked in a variety of jobs ranging from constable in the Victoria Police Force to sergeant in the Australian Tank Corps and uniformed attendant at the High Court of Australia and the New South Wales Supreme Court. He died in 1949, aged sixty-two, crushed to death by a tug at the dockside in Neutral Bay, Sydney.

- Nevil Macready's autobiography, *Annals of an Active Life*, was published in 1924 in two volumes. He died in 1946, aged eighty-three.

•   Frank Percy Crozier became a committed pacifist after leaving service in Ireland and published a string of books recounting his own military adventures in Africa, across Europe and Ireland. He died in August 1937.

•   The story of the Hogan family has endured into history. After being among the first party to officially unfurl the Free State tricolour over Dublin Castle, Dan Hogan became Chief of Staff of the Free State Defence Forces in 1927. Brother Tom Hogan's work in the GAA was marked in 1946 by the naming in his honour of the Hogan Cup, the All-Ireland trophy awarded in the premier Gaelic football competition for secondary schools. Of them all, Michael Hogan's name has lived longest. In 1926 the largest stand in Croke Park was named the Hogan Stand in his memory, and quickly entered the common language of the nation.

•   In 2007 a historic Six Nations rugby game between Ireland and England at Croke Park reignited interest in Bloody Sunday, but also served as a modern watershed in Anglo-Irish relations.

•   In 2011 Queen Elizabeth II visited Croke Park as part of her state visit to Ireland. That evening she spoke at a banquet in Dublin Castle:

So much of this visit reminds us of the complexity of our history, its many layers and traditions, but also the importance of forbearance and conciliation. Of being able to bow to the past, but not be bound by it. Of course, the relationship has not always been straightforward; nor has the record over the centuries been entirely benign. It is a sad and regrettable reality that through history our islands have experienced more than their fair share of heartache, turbulence and loss.

These events have touched us all, many of us personally, and are a painful legacy. We can never forget those who have died or been injured, and their families. To all those who have suffered as a consequence of our troubled past I extend my sincere thoughts and deep sympathy. With the benefit of historical hindsight we can all see things which we would wish had been done differently or not at all.

Selected Bibliography

BOOKS

A Brass Hat in No Man's Land, FP Crozier, Jonathan Cape, 1931

Ambushes and Armour, The Irish Rebellion 1919-21, WH Kautt, Irish Academic Press, 2010

Annals of an Active Life, Nevil Macready, Hutchinson and Co., 1924

Bloody Sunday, James Gleeson, Peter Davies Ltd, 1962

Bloody Sunday 1920-1995, A Commemorative Booklet, Miceál O'Meára (ed), CLCG Coiste Chontate Tiobraid Árann Theas, 1995

Courage and Conflict, Forgotten Stories of the Irish at War, Ian Kenneally, Collins Press, 2009

Croke Park, A History, Tim Carey, The Collins Press, 2005

Dan Breen and the IRA, Joe Ambrose, Mercier, 2006

Dublin's Fighting Story, Brian O Conchubhair (ed), Mercier, 1948

Dublin In Rebellion, A Directory 1913-23, Joseph EA O'Connell Jnr, Lilliput, 2006

Dublin Slums 1800-1925, A Study in Urban Geography, Jacinta Prunty, Irish Academic Press, 1998

Dublin Tenement Life, Kevin C. Kearns, Gill and Macmillan, 2006

Executed For Ireland, The Patrick Moran Story, May Moran, Mercier, 2010

Forging a Kingdom, the GAA in Kerry 1884-1934, Richard McElligott, The Collins Press, 2013

Impressions and Recollections, Brig Gen FP Crozier, T Werner Lawrie, 1930

Ireland Forever, Brig Gen FP Crozier, Jonathan Cape, 1932

Royal Irish Constabulary Officers, A Biographical Dictionary and Genealogical Guide 1816-1922, Jim Herlihy, Four Courts Press, 2005

Terence MacSwiney, The Hunger Strike that Rocked an Empire, Dave Hannigan, O'Brien Press, 2010

The Big Sycamore, Joseph Brady, MH Gill and Son, 1959

The Black and Tans, Richard Bennett, Pen and Sword Military (3rd ed), 1959

The GAA, A History, Marcus De Burca, Gill and MacMillan, 1999

The Gaelic Athletic Association in Dublin 1884-2000, Vol. 1: 1884-1959, William Nolan (ed), Geography Publications, 2005

The Glory and the Anguish, Padraig O'Toole, PS O'Toole, 1984

The Integrity of Ireland: Home Rule, Nationalism and Partition 1912-22, Stephen M Duffy, Associated University Press, 2009

The Northern Territory and Its Police Forces, WJ McLaren, 1988

The Republic, The Fight for Irish Independence, Charles Townshend, Allen Lane, 2013

The Royal Irish Constabulary, A Short History and Genealogical Guide, Jim Herlihy, Four Courts Press, 1997

The Squad, T Ryle Dwyer, Mercier Press, 2005

Their Friends at Court, James Comyn, Barry Rose, 1973

St Laurence O'Toole GAC 1901-2001, A Centenary History, Jim Wren, 2001

NEWSPAPERS (ARTICLES PRINCIPALLY COVERING THE PERIOD 1918-1922)

The Anglo-Celt

The Cork Examiner October 16-20, 1920

Daily Herald

Daily Mail

Daily Mirror

The Daily News

The Daily Telegraph

Dublin Evening Mail

Freeman's Journal

The Illustrated London News

Irish Independent

The Irish Times

The Manchester Guardian

The Nationalist (Clonmel)

The Nenagh Guardian

News of the World

Sport Newspaper

Sunday Pictorial

The Times

Tipperary Star

PAPERS, DOCUMENTS AND ARTICLES

'A Force Apart', PhD thesis on the Northern Territory Police Force (Australia), Bill Wilson, Northern Territory University, 2000

'A Sporting Challenge from Tipperary that Led to Death in the Afternoon', Denis Walsh, *Sunday Times*, February 18, 2007

'Before One Is Entitled to Have a Strong Opinion on Historical Matters, One Must At Least Learn Them', Kevin Myers, *Irish Independent*,

May 17 2011

'Born in a Castle – Killed in a Park', article on Joseph Traynor, Michael Nelson, 2010

'Bloody Sunday, A Reappraisal', Tom Bowden, European Studies Review, Vol 2, 1972

'Bloody Sunday 1920: New Evidence', Tim Carey and Marcus De Burca, *History Ireland*, Vol 11, no.2; summer 2003

'British Security Policy in Ireland, 1920-21, A Desperate Attempt by the Crown to Maintain Anglo-Irish Unity by Force', John Ainsworth, School of Humanities & Social Science, Queensland University of Technology, 2000

'Dan Breen Looks Back 50 Years from 1967', Jim Maher, *Tipperary Historical Journal*, 1998, County Tipperary Historical Society

'Death in the Afternoon and the Croke Park Massacre 21 Nov 1920'; David Leeson, *Canadian Journal of History*, Vol 38, no.1; April 2003

Eoin O'Duffy papers, NLI. MS 48,280/1, 48,280/2

File WO 35/88B, Public Records Office, Kew, London (Jervis Street and Mater Hospital Inquiries into the killings at Croke Park, maps, orders and other documents relating to the events)

'Hogan Got Three Bullets. My Father Always Said He Could Have Got Those Bullets'. Articles from the *Sunday Tribune*, February 18 2007, Ewan MacKenna

'Killing and Bloody Sunday', Anne Dolan, *Historical Journal*, Dept of History TCD, Vol 49 (3) 2006

'Life with a Flying Column', Tadhg Crowe, *Tipperary Historical Journal 2004*, County Tipperary Historical Society

'Life with the South Tipperary Volunteers 1914-21', Paul Merrigan, from the Bureau of Military History 1913-21, Marcus Bourke, *Tipperary Historical Journal 2005*, County Tipperary Historical Society

'Lions Led By Donkeys', Dr John Bourne, Centre for First World War Studies, University of Birmingham, 2008

Northern Territory Times articles and others from *The Argus* on George Dudley, July 24 1924 to May 10 1927

'One Man's Flying Column', Col. Thomas Ryan, taken from *Tipperary Historical Journal 1991*, Tipperary Historical Society

'Report of the Labour Party Commission to Ireland', The Labour Party, 1921

'The British Army's Effectiveness in the Irish Campaign 1919-21 and the Lessons for Modern Counterinsurgency Operations, with Special Reference to C3I Aspects', Gordon Pattison, UK Ministry of Defence, The Cornwallis Group XIV: Analysis of Societal Conflict and Counterinsurgency, 2009

'The Day that Croke Park Bled,' *Sunday Tribune* article, Denis Walsh, November 19, 1995

'The Operations of the South Tipperary IRA 1916-21', Joost Augusteijn, *Tipperary Historical Journal 1996*, County Tipperary Historical Society

'The Third Tipperary Brigade: Its Guerilla Campaign (1919-21)', Kate O'Dwyer (adapted from chapter in M.Phil thesis, UCG, 1995); *Tipperary Historical Journal 1997*, County Tipperary Historical Society

SELECTED WEB SOURCES, LECTURES AND MISCELLANEOUS

Hansard House of Commons debates on Ireland November 1920-March 1921

Interview with Bill Ryan, taken from the DVD 'Where Tipperary leads, Ireland Follows' – 3rd Tipperary Brigade Old IRA Commemoration Committee

Jim Herlihy talk – 'The Black and Tans and Auxiliaries; the RIC 1867-1922', Scoil Mhuire Gan Smal Secondary School, Blarney, Oct 6 2011

www.curragh.info/articles/mutiny

www.daverobinson.id.au/lautoka2.html

www.ntsearch.com.au/katherine/nitmiluk-national-park.asp

www.thecornwallisgroup.org/cornwallis_2009/6-Pattison-CXIV.pdf

www.thewildgeese.com/pages/forgten7.html

www.tipperarystar.ie/news/features/fethard-s-link-with-the-great-war-1914-1918-1-2259182

BUREAU OF MILITARY HISTORY WITNESS STATEMENTS

WS 316 Peter Folan, Head Constable RIC, Dublin 1913-21, Dublin Castle Easter Week 1916

WS 328 Garry Holohan, senior officer Fianna Eireann, 1914-21

WS 340 Oscar Traynor, Captain IV Dublin 1913-16, OC Dublin Brigade IRA, 1920-21

WS 353 James McGuill, Commandant IV, Dundalk 1916, IRB Louth 1919-20

WS 371 Rupert Holland, member IRB, Fianna Eireann and IV 1909-16, IRA Dublin, 1917-21

WS 380 David Neligan, IRA Intelligence Agent in British Police Service

WS 385 Maureen McGavock, member executive Cumann na mBan, 1920-21

WS 387 Patrick O'Daly, Lieutenant Fianna Eireann 1913-16, Lieutenant IV Dublin 1913-16, member ASU Dublin 1920-21

WS 397 Thomas Pugh, member IV, Dublin 1916

WS 398 Bridget Martin, member Cumann na mBan, Dublin 1913-21, courier to Cork, Easter 1916

WS 413 Patrick McCrea, IRB member and IV Dublin 1913-16, Officer Dublin IRA 1921, Squad member 1920-21

WS 423 Vincent Byrne, Squad member and ASU Dublin, 1919-21

WS 445 James Slattery, member IV Dublin 1914-16, Squad member 1919-21

WS 477 Edward J. Kelleher, member IRA Dublin, 1919-21

WS 481 Simon Donnelly, Captain IV and IRA, 1916-21, Chief of Republican Police

WS 486 Daniel McDonnell, Officer IRA, 1921

WS 499 Patrick Kennedy, Irish Citizen Army, 1916, Dublin IRA 1920-21

WS 502 Patrick Mannix, DMP Constable 1921, IRA Intelligence agent

WS 503 James Cahill, Member IRB and IV Cavan 1914-17, member ASU Dublin, 1921

WS 512 Sean McCluskey, Official, Dail Eireann, 1919

WS 519 Thomas Donnelly, Captain IRA, Monaghan 1921

WS 547 Joe Leonard, Squad member, IRA, Dublin, 1921

WS 548 Daithi O'Donoghue, Official Dept of Finance, Dail Eireann 1919-21

WS 581 Christopher Fitzsimons, member ASU IRA, Dublin 1921

WS 607 Joseph McGuinness, Member ASU, IRA, Dublin 1921

WS 615 Frank Thornton, Member IRB and IV Dublin, 1913-16, Deputy Assistant Director of Intelligence IRA, 1919-21

WS 621 Patrick J Mullen, member IV 1914-16, member ASU, Dublin IRA 1920-21

WS 624 Mary Flannery-Woods, Officer Cumann na mBan, 1916-21

WS 642 Christopher Byrne, Captain IV and IRA, Dublin 1921

WS 648 Catherine Rooney, member Cumann na mBan, 1916

WS 653 TM Sullivan, daughter of Tim Healy KC, Governor-General of Irish Free State, 1922-28

WS 657 Philip Marron, Commandant IRA, Monaghan 1921

WS 660 Thomas Leahy, Irish Citizen Army, 1916

WS 663 Joseph Dolan, Squad member, 1921

WS 667 Patrick Lawson, Squad member 1921

WS 679 John F. Shouldice, Lieutenant IV, Dublin, Captain IRA, Dublin 1921

WS 682 Vincent Ellis, rendered medical aid to IRA 1921, medical officer Garda Siochana 1923-57

WS 687 MJ Curran, Rector, Irish College Rome, 1921

WS 694 Frank Burke, member IV Dublin, 1916

WS 715 Frank Saurin, Member IV Dublin, 1916, IRA Intelligence attached to GHQ, 1921

WS 721 Nicholas Smyth, Vice Commandant IRA, South Tyrone, 1921

WS 723 Alice Barry, close friend of IRA leaders

WS 727 Michael J. Lawless, member IV and IRA, Dublin, 1915-21

WS 728 Joseph O'Carroll, member Irish Citizen Army, 1916

WS 742 Thomas Halpin, Captain IRA 1921

WS 747 Margaret O'Callaghan, member Cumann na mBan 1917

WS 755 Sean Prendergast, Member Fianna Eireann, 1911, Officer IV Dublin 1914-16, Capt IRA Dublin, 1921

WS 767 Patrick Moylett, Member IV 1914, Official Sinn Fein Court, Negotiator with British Cabinet pre-truce 1921

WS 779 Robert Brennan, Publicity Department, Dail Eireann, 1921

WS 783 Thomas Ryan, Commandant Tipperary IRA 1921

WS 813 Padraig O'Connor, Officer IRA, Dublin 1921

WS 820 Francis Tummon, Member IV and IRA Monaghan, 1916-22

WS 821 Frank Henderson, Captain IV, Dublin, 1916, Commandant IRA 1917-21

WS 822 William James Stapleton, member IV Dublin, 1913-19, Lieutenant IRA Dublin 1921, Squad Member 1921

WS 850 Patrick Colgan, Commandant IRA, Kildare 1921

WS 898 Sean Brunswick, Lieutenant, IRA, Dublin, 1921

WS 907 Laurence Nugent, Officer IV and IRA, Dublin 1913-21

WS 930 Jeremiah Frewen, Officer IRA, Tipperary 1921

WS 942 Patrick J Berry, prison warder Mountjoy, 1921, intelligence officer IRA

WS 956 George White, Officer IRA Dublin 1921, Quartermaster ASU Dublin, 1920-21

WS 1005 Liam Walsh, Member IRB, Portlaoise 1909, Officer IV and Waterford IRA 1918-21

WS 1028 James McKenna, OC North Monaghan Brigade, IRA 1921

WS 1127 Edward G. Glendon, Officer IRA, Tipperary 1921

WS 1187 Patrick Butler, Captain IRA, Cork, 1921

WS 1214 James J. O'Connor, Special Constable RIC Wexford, 1916, solicitor Dublin

WS 1223 Peter Tobin, Commandant IRA, Tipperary 1921

WS 1253 Liam Tobin, Director of Intelligence, IRA 1920-21

WS 1322 Art O'Donnell, Commandant IRA Clare, 1921, paymaster Clare County Council, Dail Eireann 1919-21

WS 1335 James Leahy, Commandant IRA, Kilkenny 1923

WS 1350 Jerome Davin, Commandant IRA, Tipperary 1921

WS 1361 MB Gerald Davis, Officer IRA, Westmeath, 1921

WS 1450 John C. Ryan, Officer IRA, Tipperary, 1921

WS 1553 Liam Hoolan, OC North Tipperary Brigade IRA, 1921

WS 1647 JJ O'Brien, Vice-Commandant IRA, Limerick 1921

WS 1687 Harry Colley, Officer IV 1915-19, Adjutant IRA Dublin Brigade, 1920-21

WS 1693 John Kenny, Officer 1 Battalion, Dublin Brigade 1921

WS 1721 Seumas Robinson, Office IV Dublin, senior officer IV and IRA, Tipperary 1917-21

WS 1739/1763 Daniel Breen, Quartermaster 3rd Tipperary Brigade IRA

WS 1760 Francis X. Coghlan, Officer IV and Dublin IRA, 1913-21

Also by
Michael Foley

KINGS OF
SEPTEMBER

THE DAY OFFALY DENIED KERRY
FIVE IN A ROW

A heartfelt account of the most famous All-Ireland final in Gaelic
football history. The year and the game from both sides.

MICHAEL FOLEY
KINGS OF SEPTEMBER

'An extraordinary book recalling
an extraordinary game.'
TOM HUMPHRIES

THE DAY OFFALY DENIED
KERRY FIVE IN A ROW

O'BRIEN